Gender, Migration, and the Work
of Care

Sonya Michel • Ito Peng
Editors

Gender, Migration, and the Work of Care

A Multi-Scalar Approach to the Pacific Rim

Editors
Sonya Michel
Department of History
University of Maryland
College Park, Maryland, USA

Ito Peng
Department of Sociology
University of Toronto
Toronto, Ontario, Canada

ISBN 978-3-319-55085-5   ISBN 978-3-319-55086-2 (eBook)
DOI 10.1007/978-3-319-55086-2

Library of Congress Control Number: 2017946491

Cover illustration © DCPhoto / Alamy Stock Photo

Printed on acid-free paper

This Palgrave Macmillan imprint is published by Springer Nature
The registered company is Springer International Publishing AG
The registered company address is: Gewerbestrasse 11, 6330 Cham, Switzerland

ACKNOWLEDGEMENTS

We would like to thank the Social Science and Humanities Research Council of Canada (SSHRC) for their generous grant in support of the research that has made this volume possible. The project has been funded by the SSHRC Partnership Grant on *Gender, Migration, and the Work of Care* ((File No: 895-2012-1021), Ito Peng, Principal Investigator.

We also thank the institutional partners who have contributed to our research: Immigration Refugees and Citizenship Canada; the Asia Pacific Foundation; Asian Research Center for the Intimate and Public Spheres at Kyoto University; Asian Immigrant Advocates; Asia Research Institute at National University of Singapore; Asian Women at Work; Centre for International Research on Care, Labour & Equalities (CIRCLE) at the University of Sheffield; the Centre for Sustainable Organization and Work Employment and Social Development Canada; Human Rights Research and Education Centre at University of Ottawa; Kookmin University; the International Labor Office (ILO); the Migration Policy Institute (MPI), Washington, DC; Service Employees International Union (SEIU); the Sociology Department at the University of Toronto; United Nations Research Institute for Social Development (UNRISD); United Nations Entity for Gender Equality and the Empowerment of Women (UN Women); and United Voice.

We are grateful to the authors whose chapters appear here, as well as to two other scholars who participated in the book workshop but did not become authors: Rachel Silvey and Rhacel Parreñas. Pat Armstrong (York University, Toronto) provided significant insights as a workshop discussant, as did Shahra Razavi and Fiona Williams, who also contributed to the volume. We also thank the many students and student research assistants who participated at different stages of our research project and the production of this edited volume. Elizabeth Thompson compiled an excellent index, Kyra Saniewski of Palgrave ably shepherded the book through the publication process and Ayswaraya Nagarajan of Springer Nature oversaw its production with great care and patience.

Finally, we wish to thank, first, Marianne Noh and then Deanna Pikkov, who have provided key administrative support to the entire research project.

CONTENTS

Part V Going Global?

LIST OF FIGURES

LIST OF TABLES

PART I

Caring Around the Pacific Rim

CHAPTER 1

Introduction

Sonya Michel and Ito Peng

Over the past several decades, as a result of broadscale economic and social developments, more and more women have left traditional roles as primary family caregivers to enter the paid labor force, and the gender division of labor in households around the globe has been reordered. Today, in almost every country, including China, the service sector of the economy far outweighs manufacturing in nearly all dimensions—economic activity, output, and the number of people employed. And women are increasingly being drawn into this new economy. Although global in scope, this trend affects different regions differently depending on their cultures, economies, and politics; the nature and scale of their welfare states; and the range of employment opportunities offered to women. While professional/managerial and service positions have opened up for women in wealthier countries, those in "emerging economies" have been restricted to low-paying or rapidly disappearing agricultural and industrial work, pushing many, regardless of their educational levels and professional training, to seek service-sector jobs in wealthier parts of the

S. Michel (✉)
Department of History, University of Maryland, College Park, USA

I. Peng
Department of Sociology, University of Toronto, Toronto, Canada

© The Author(s) 2017
S. Michel, I. Peng (eds.), *Gender, Migration, and the Work of Care*,
DOI 10.1007/978-3-319-55086-2_1

3

country and abroad. Increasingly, this latter group has found employment as domestic workers and caregivers in rapidly growing cities and rich countries, where the rise in local or native-born mothers' entry into the labor force, coupled with aging populations, limited welfare-state support, and the low market valuation of care work, has created a growing demand for non-family caregivers. This demand is being filled by migrant care workers who have little choice but to work for substandard wages. With migrant women from poorer regions and emerging economies now working in private households in wealthier cities and countries, we can see global and multiple forms of inequalities—gender, class, race, immigration status—playing out in the most intimate of spaces.

The globalization of care work affects every corner of the world today. This book focuses on changing patterns of family and gender relations, migration, and care work in one region: the countries of the Pacific Rim, broadly defined. We have chosen this focus for several reasons. First, the Pacific Rim combines two major global epicenters of transnational migration today—Asia and North America. With 75 million international migrants living and working in the region, Asia now has the world's second largest international migrant population after Europe (76 million before the current refugee crisis), while North America is home to another 54 million, 47 million of them in the United States alone. Until this past year, these two continents' migrant populations were also growing at rates faster than in any other parts of the world. Between 2000 and 2015, the number of international migrants swelled by 26 million in Asia, the largest absolute increase of all regions in the world. During the same period, North America added another 14 million (UN-DESA 2016). But this does not even take into account the 253 million "floating people" within China, most of whom are rural-to-urban migrants (China-NBS 2015). True, these are not "international migrants," but, given the size of the country and the huge social, economic, cultural, and policy disparities between the urban and the rural, migration dynamics in China closely mirror what we see at the global scale. In China as in other parts of the world, a large proportion of new migrants work as domestics, nurses, caregivers, and other personal service workers.

Second, despite similarities with the broader global trend in care migration, significant social, cultural, and institutional diversities exist among receiving and sending countries within the Pacific Rim. These in turn provide a rich ground for comparative, interdisciplinary, and multi-scalar analyses of transnational care migration processes. The region comprises some of the world's richest countries (the United States, Japan, Canada, Australia, and Singapore) and some of its poorest (Vietnam, Cambodia, Indonesia, and the Philippines); the country with the largest population (China) and one of the smallest (Singapore); and some of the longest-established democracies (the United States, Canada, Australia, and Japan) as well as communist and post-communist capitalist economies (China and Vietnam). These countries also vary widely in terms of culture, ranging from markedly Confucian, such as China, Japan, South Korea, Taiwan, and Singapore, to Catholic (Mexico and the Philippines) to Anglo-Protestant (Australia, the United States, and Canada), though immigration, whether historic or recent, has produced increasing cultural heterogeneity almost everywhere. Thus the region contains a wide spectrum of economic development stages, political regimes, and cultural and religious backgrounds, and this diversity offers an invaluable terrain for research aimed at understanding different modalities and dynamics associated with care and migration, as well as the growing interdependencies between richer and poorer countries through care relationships.

A third reason for our choice of focus is the fact that, despite the burgeoning of research on care and migration and the growing importance of the Pacific Rim for care migration (Oishi 2005; Parreñas and Siu 2007), very little in-depth research has explored the intersections between care, migration, and policy regimes or analyzed their articulations and alignments from local to global scales in this region. The dearth of such research is understandable. The region's size, complexity, and diversity means that any meaningful research at the regional level will invariably require extensive collaboration and significant commitments of time and resources. The lack of an established regional economic and governing body (such as the European Union or North American Free Trade Agreement) or a global-level policy institution (e.g. the Organisation for Economic Co-operation and Development [OECD]) focusing solely on the Pacific Rim means that there is no coherent and comparable regional data to help researchers gain an initial research foothold. As well, until very recently, very few scholars working in Pacific Rim cross-national or cross-regional research addressed care and migration, and the intra-regional research network was relatively weak. Some of these challenges are, however, being mitigated by heightened research and policy interest in the Pacific Rim care migration in recent years.[1] This book begins to address this crucial void by highlighting the work of a growing number of students and new scholars engaged in this area.

The book draws on research conducted under the aegis of the Social Sciences and Humanities Research Council of Canada (SSHRC)-funded partnership research project (#895–2012–1021), "Gender, Migration and the Work of Care: Comparative Perspectives" (see www.cgsp.ca). This international multidisciplinary project examines three interlocking "domains": care provisioning, the supply of and demand for care work, and the shaping and framing of care. It assumes that these three domains, roughly corresponding to, respectively, local, national, and global social-spatial scales, consist of forces and actors that are constantly operating within and across domains to shape understandings of care, work, and migration, and the "policy regimes" that govern labor, migration, and care work. In turn, these domains are also shaped by various policy regimes through feedback mechanisms (see Fig.1.1). We emphasize the fluid and iterative nature of these domains as actors, ideas, and institutions in each of the domains influence one another and across the domains to affect behavioral and policy changes.

How We Started

This research comes out of an ongoing collaboration among a group of academics, researchers, and policy experts in different disciplines and continents over the last fifteen years. For many of us, it began with a flagship project by the United Nation's Research Institute for Social Development (UNRISD) on gender and development launched in 2006, called *The Social and Political Economy of Care* (http://www.unrisd.org/research/gd/care). That project brought together researchers from across the globe to investigate multiple and changing institutions, policies, economies, and modalities of care in eight selected countries on four continents. The project generated a rich country-specific and cross-national body of comparative work that analyzed the changing nature and contexts of care in different localities.

Coming out of the UNRISD project in 2010, participants were clear that the next crucial research agenda was care migration. Despite their strong interdisciplinary bases, research on care and on migration has hitherto operated, and in some cases continues to operate, in parallel spheres that rarely intersect with each other. Our earlier analyses confirmed that care and migration were becoming increasingly enmeshed and indicated that further investigation of this global phenomenon was

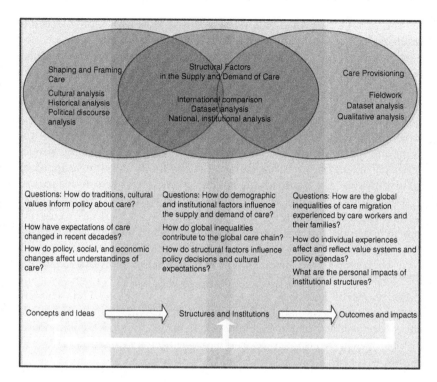

Fig. 1.1 Conceptual framework

necessary. Rapid demographic aging, increased women's paid employment, the shift from a male-breadwinner to an adult-worker household norm, and the increased family and intergenerational distanciation resulting from widespread adoption of nuclear family norms and the migration of young people from rural to urban centers and out of countries have all contributed to a huge increase in the demand for care. At the same time, the shrinking supply of educated and middle-class women willing to work for low wages and the low status and precarious conditions associated with care work have intensified labor shortages in the care sector, creating a powerful magnet for women from poorer regions and countries to migrate to perform the work of care. Globally, but particularly in the Pacific Rim, the number of migrant care workers has exploded since the 1990s, as have the number of people and families dependent on migrant care workers.

The project on which this book is based thus draws on the earlier international research effort. Pooling individual research networks and existing research collaborations, we created a strong base for global research and policy network, so in 2012, when the SSHRC announced a new Partnership Research Grant program that called for knowledge production and dissemination through research collaborations, we were among the first to apply. Our application received strong endorsement from the SSHRC review committee not simply for the relevance of the topic and the accomplishments of the research team members, but also for its specific focus on the Pacific Rim region and for our innovative approach to investigating the transnational migration of care workers in this region.

Our project contains eight interlinking sub-projects that are nested within the three domains. Since it began in 2013, over twenty-five research co-investigators and collaborators, twenty institutional partners (ranging from local to global), and nearly fifty students in ten countries have been engaged in this research by undertaking fieldwork, collecting and analyzing data, and participating in policy debates and analyses and other forms of knowledge creation and dissemination. Thus far, this wonderful, if at times chaotic, confluence of activities driven by diverse ideas, perspectives, and voices, all seeking to understand a common yet complex phenomenon, has led to the publication of three single-authored books, two special journal issues and several more in progress, as well as the completion of several PhD and MA theses and two edited books (including this one). The present collection brings together some of the research highlights from this intensive and interactive engagement.

Intersecting Care and Migration Research

We ground our research on care migration by conjoining two sets of feminist literature—one on comparative welfare states and care, and the other on gender and migration—paying particular attention to the Pacific Rim context. By embedding care as a constitutive part of welfare regime analysis, early feminist welfare state scholars pinpointed the relationships between paid work, unpaid work (including care), and welfare in their reconceptualization and analyses of welfare states and social policy (Lewis 1992; Daly and Lewis 2000; Jenson and Sineau 2001). Building on this, scholars devised the widely used conceptual framework of the "care mix" or "care diamond," which frames care as the product of a political-economic accord among four key socioeconomic institutions—family/

household, state, market, and the voluntary sector or community. These institutions not only encapsulate both the unpaid and paid forms of care that are provided via different relational and market mechanisms but also constantly interact with each other to determine modes of welfare and care provision, more specifically who receives and who provides care, how care is provided, where, and in what forms (Jenson and St. Martin 2006; Razavi 2007).

Studies using the care diamond have shown that care regimes vary significantly not only across countries and regions and among care sectors (e.g., child care versus elder care versus care of the disabled) (Bettio and Plantenga 2004; Knijn and Komter 2004; Brennan et al. 2012), but also over time (van Hooren and Becker 2012; Mahon and Michel 2002; Mahon 2006b). Traditionally, in familialistic East Asian countries, neither the state nor the market played much role in financing or providing care for either children or elders, obliging families to take most of the responsibility. However, as in Europe and North America, a significant reconfiguration of the care diamond has been taking place in East Asia since the 1990s. The increased outsourcing and subcontracting of familial care to paid caregivers have served to enlarge the roles of both the market and the voluntary sector/community in care provision (Peng 2009; Ochiai et al. 2012). At the same time, many East Asian states, motivated by economic growth and pronatalist imperatives, are also expanding public care provisions or offering financial support to families to facilitate female employment and ensure better work-family harmonization. Some of the latter policies in turn spur the growth of the market and voluntary/community roles in care.

The expansion of state and market roles in the care diamond in East Asia, as in Europe and North America, is both a response to and a further cause of increased commodification of care. In the context of increasing global and regional inequality, this also promotes migration of care workers. Whereas in Europe, the free movement of labor for citizens of the EU states alerted feminist welfare state researchers early on to the importance of intersecting care and migration as changing care policy in wealthier EU states drew female care workers from poorer EU nations (Lutz 2008, 2011), in the Pacific Rim, research on care and on migration remained separate until very recently. Feminist migration scholars in the Pacific Rim have made a substantial advance in conceptualizing gender and transnational migration since the 1990s, much of this through the concept of global care chains. Building on the notion of global supply chains, the global care chain emphasizes the global production and supply system involving reproductive labor that links women in the global North and South, thus creating social, economic, and emotional interdependencies through care (Hochschild 2000; Parreñas 2000; Ehrenreich and Hochschild 2004). What this also suggests is the way in which the system of production is upheld by a parallel system of reproduction. Most global care chain research in the Pacific Rim focuses on "traditional" intimate care work, such as live-in caregivers and domestic work, but some of it pushes for a broader conceptualization, including health, education, and other service-sector workers (Bakker and Silvey 2008; Yeates 2008; Anderson 2000). Although recent research on the migration of care workers in the Pacific Rim is beginning to pay more attention to the roles played by the state and policies in structuring and transnationalizing care work (Asis and Piper 2008; Huang, Thang and Toyota 2012; Isaksen, Devi and Hochschild 2008; Kofman and Raghuram 2012; Oishi 2005; Raghuram 2012), most studies remain focused on the roles of the state and intermediary institutions in managing/facilitating the flows of foreign migrant care workers (Yeoh and Huang 2010; Lopez 2012; Cortés and Pan 2013). Attention to the intersection of care and migration policies in this region remains relatively weak.

The literatures on welfare states and transnational care migration are, however, beginning to dovetail (Anderson and Shutes 2014; Williams 2010, 2014), and in this book we try to advance that project. Both literatures point to the fact that the combination of broader socioeconomic changes and neoliberal social policy reforms in sending and receiving countries have altered the ways in which care is understood, provided, and regulated, and furthermore, that these changes have in turn directly contributed to the transnational migration of care workers. More specifically, the combination of welfare cuts and the increased privatization and marketization of care has forced families in the receiving regions/countries to rely more on the market and community/voluntary sectors to meet their care needs, while in the sending regions/countries, economic and policy changes have pushed up unemployment and underemployment, intensifying financial insecurity and making care migration an increasingly compelling and necessary alternative for those hoping to escape poverty (Ehrenreich and Hochschild 2004; Fudge 2012; Lutz 2008; Yeates 2008; Michel and Peng 2012; Page and Plaza 2006). The rebalancing of care diamonds in wealthy cities, countries, and regions therefore has direct repercussions on migration in poorer locales.

The Organization of the Book

The chapters here analyze the three domains that roughly correspond to micro, meso, and macro socio-spatial scales (Mahon 2006a). This multiscalar approach allows us to see interconnections among the domains and policy regimes—how, for example, local, subnational, and national laws and regulations governing care, domestic labor and immigration (meso) affect caregivers' working conditions and shape caring relationships and both care receivers' and caregivers' experiences of care (micro); how national laws (meso) toward migrant care workers are influenced by, on the one hand, international labor standards and economic agreements (macro), and on the other, local responses such as civil society mobilization and electoral politics (meso and micro). Our comparative and multiscalar lens thus helps us understand the multiple and competing forces that shape the way people think about and deal with care needs, the supply of and demands for migrant caregivers (whether foreign or internal), and the types of national and subnational policies required to address the specific issues arising from this unique and intimate form of employment. Chapters in this book aim to capture the fluidity of people, ideas, and policies as they move across institutions, cultures, and scales, and in the process reorganize and reshape care.

While the interconnections have become increasingly apparent to us as our research project has moved forward, to policymakers and care worker advocates, they continue to appear especially difficult to regulate and *change*. Inequalities in caring relationships and the "tilt" of caring resources from the global South to the global North create a set of problems that can best be assessed and addressed at the transnational level, yet because most nations insist on their sovereignty and thus oppose "intervention" in their "domestic" affairs on the part of international governing bodies, current inequities remain deeply entrenched. Similarly, at the national level, even if governments resolve to alter policies to better address care needs, cultural and institutional factors often impede reform. At the subnational or local level, the location of much care work within private households also tends to obscure what transpires in employer-employee or caregiver/care receiver relationships, making it difficult to root out and address instances of abuse and exploitation.

Yet the situation is not static. Domestic and care workers are increasingly organizing at all levels, and national and local laws and regulations are in flux. These mobilizations have also begun to shape discussions within international organizations, leading, most significantly, to adoption of Convention 189, "Decent Work for Domestic Workers," at the International Labour Organization in Geneva in 2011. The impacts of this resolution at the national level are just beginning to be seen. At the same time, transnational flows of knowledge and culture—"cultural remittances"—are changing relationships and expectations among family members and policy practices, leading to new social patterns at the micro and meso levels, especially in sending countries.

This book begins with a theoretical overview by social policy scholar Fiona Williams, a longtime student of gender and welfare states. In addition to providing an insightful synthesis of all the chapters, Williams situates the issue of care migration within the broader context of current geopolitical events and argues, quite provocatively, that "[t]he phenomenon of the movement of female migrants into care and domestic work in richer countries encapsulates many of the world's inequalities." This theme is clearly borne out by the chapters that follow.

Opening Part II, "Everyday Realities and Cultures of Care," sociologists Cynthia Cranford and Jennifer Jihye Chun examine the situations of middle-aged Chinese immigrant women workers in Oakland, California, who are switching from informal low-wage manufacturing and service work to jobs as personal home-based care workers within their ethnic community—jobs that, under California law, may provide a pathway to unionized state-subsidized employment. The authors highlight the growing importance of home care as a new form of informal ethnic economy and, drawing on their extensive interviews, show how these immigrant women workers navigate the transition from informal to more formal employment under new social, political, and economic conditions. In particular, they note that union membership, while empowering with regard to issues like hours and pay, is ineffective when it comes to addressing interpersonal difficulties in this intimate form of employment. For the latter, community organizations prove to be more helpful.

The next chapter, by social policy and social work scholar Liu Hong, offers a striking insight into care provision in mainland China, specifically Shanghai. Despite growing care needs produced by major shifts in demography and family structure over the past three decades, China, unlike other Pacific Rim societies, has not turned to foreign migrant care workers. This is because of its reserve of some 270 million *internal* migrants, who move from poorer rural to more prosperous urban regions in search of better work opportunities. Hong shows that most female migrants find employment in care work, an occupation that in China, as elsewhere, is highly gendered, low-status, and unregulated. A new publicly funded home-care program intended to formalize care work has succeeded in raising societal recognition in the form of decent wages and guaranteed social protection eligibility, but it fails to overcome institutional and cultural discrimination against migrant workers. The result is what Hong calls "a dual world of care," one that casts paid care *below* traditional family practices.

In addition to delineating ways in which immigrant women negotiate the changing policy contours in relations of care and care work to find better occupational paths, this chapter, along with that by Cranford and Chun, also addresses the tensions produced by the shift from the Confucian ethic of filial care to care as a form of paid work. Their analyses reveal subtle and not so subtle ways in which Confucian tradition is being de-centered, re-cultured, and appropriated by both caregivers and care-receivers in the contexts where care is also becoming commodified.

The challenge to traditions of care posed by commodified care work is also a theme in the final chapter in this section, in which anthropologist and education scholar Gabrielle Oliveira explores the interface between Mexican migrant nannies and their native-born American employers. Drawing on extensive ethnographic research, Oliveira explains how these nannies, who work in New York City, reconcile their experience of child-rearing at home with the practices and standards they encounter as care workers for middle- and upper-class US families. Especially interesting are Oliveira's insights into the emotional dimensions of the complex relationships between caregivers, their charges, and their own children, both those in the United States and those "left behind"—insights gleaned from her fieldwork both in New York City and in migrants' hometowns across the border.[2] While cell phones, Skype, and other communication technologies help reduce time and space, giving the immigrant mother a sense of immediate connection with her children thousands of miles distant, they do little to lessen her sense of guilt or help her combat the pervasive cultural construction of motherhood in Mexico that naturalizes and moralizes the physical bonding between mother and child.

With its focus on several different groups of care workers—Chinese women in mainland China and abroad and a Latina group in the United States—this section allows for a number of comparisons of care practices and working conditions while also taking us inside workers' experience. The chapters by Cranford and Chun and Hong show in rich detail how

Confucian norms of family care play out both within China and in a Chinese émigré community. At the same time, they demonstrate how roughly similar types of governmental policy in Shanghai and Oakland affect Chinese care workers' status differently, how workers from different backgrounds seek to shape the conditions under which they provide care, and how becoming care *workers* (as opposed to being family care*givers*) may challenge their values and identities. Across all three cases in this section, the social and cultural distance between care workers and their employers varies considerably. That between the Mexican nanny and the family she works for in New York City is perhaps the most striking, but the other two chapters reveal that the commodification of care creates a divide between care workers and employer families even when they share a commitment to similar values—in this case, Confucian.

Part III, "All (Global) Politics Are Local," continues the comparison of care work in various settings, emphasizing the impact of different types of public policy on care and migration. Political scientist André Laliberté offers a multi-scalar comparison of responses on the part of both governments and the private sector (civil society) to the abuse of migrant domestic and care workers in Taiwan, Hong Kong, and Shanghai. His aim is to identify the optimal level of government intervention to efficiently prevent abuse against these workers. Although the three locations have similar demographic, socioeconomic, and cultural (again, Confucian-influenced) characteristics, the authorities he examines represent three different levels of government: national, semi-autonomous, and municipal. Drawing on fieldwork in all three locations, Laliberté presents the actors in government, domestic/care worker recruitment/placement agencies, and domestic/care workers' rights advocacy organizations, and assesses their relative influence and resources and their ability and interest in promoting/guaranteeing and/or respecting the rights of domestic and care workers.

Looking at Australia in the next chapter, Deborah Brennan, Sara Charlesworth, Liz Adamson, and Natasha Cortis, a team consisting of social policy, industrial relations, and legal studies scholars, also focus on policy, but here the issue of immigration becomes key. The authors show that care migration is increasingly being promoted as a way to meet predicted labor shortages in aged care and child care in Australia. Under current migration policy settings, it is virtually impossible for low-skilled workers (a category that comprises care workers) to enter the country in their own right, but this may be changing. Brennan and her co-authors examine current debates about care migration, drawing on submissions made to public inquiries into aged care, child care and care for people with disabilities in the last five years. They analyze the sources of support for, and opposition to, care migration and the policy context that frames these debates, situating Australia within an international context. These debates suggest a growing tension between the state's instrumentalist impulse to use immigration policy to address labor, care, and the demographic agenda, and civil society's concerns for human rights and equality in the context of Australia's immigration policy reform. Will social needs overcome the country's historical preference for a "White Australia"?

Shifting the focus to Canada in the next chapter, sociologist Monica Boyd similarly zeroes in on how immigration affects the nature of care work. Canada is notable for its pioneering "Live-in Care Program," which, starting in 1992, permitted workers to enter the country legally to take up jobs in care work and gain permanent residency status following a required length of employment. In 2014, however, under the Conservative government of Stephen Harper, Canada terminated the official Live-in Care Program by decoupling the entitlement to permanent residency status from live-in care work and changing it into a two-stream program, thus barring a pathway for foreign care workers to gain Canadian citizenship. Boyd reviews past policies and then assesses the likely consequences of the policy shift and the prospects for care work under the newly elected Liberal Prime Minister Justin Trudeau.

In their heavy reliance on immigrants to meet demands for care labor, Canada and Australia are similar to many post-industrial societies in Europe as well as around the Pacific Rim. However, two other Pacific-Rim countries, Japan and South Korea, stand out against this global trend by continuing to resist taking in foreigners for this purpose. In her chapter, sociologist and public policy scholar Ito Peng explains why, despite serious shortages of care workers, these two countries have maintained highly restricted immigration policies toward foreign migrant care workers. She argues that their resistance can be explained by a combination of social, cultural, and institutional factors that are shaping the two countries' care, migration, and employment regimes. The resistance to immigration in these countries is partially a result of powerful collective imaginaries about their racially and ethnically homogeneous national identity. But equally important in relation to care and care work are the countries' path-dependent policy patterns, which steer them toward social care systems in the forms of public child care and elder care. In turn, regulated social care systems create institutional entry barriers to unlicensed and/or foreign care workers. Nevertheless, the two countries are not identical. For example the use of co-ethnic migrant workers in the elder care sector is more extensive in Korea than in Japan, as is the role of the private market in the delivery of care. These factors underscore the importance of national cultural and institutional diversities and raise questions about the long-term sustainability of Japanese and Korean efforts to avoid employing foreign workers for social care.

One theme that resonates through these four chapters is the tensions between insatiable demands for care workers and the relative unwillingness of national governments to recognize the value of their work and to accept foreign care workers as citizens. This tension in many ways strikes at the heart of care migration debate and underscores the disjuncture and unequal relationship between productive and reproductive economies. Despite its crucial role in upholding economic production and growth, care as a form of reproductive work is constantly devalued in terms of its economic contribution and hence considered "low-skilled." This in turn renders care workers undesirable or unsuitable for immigration policies that are driven by the priorities of a human-capital-and-"productive-sector" economy. In all cases—whether there is an outright resistance to accepting foreign care workers, as in Japan and South Korea, or a willingness to accept them only under highly restrictive conditions, as in Canada and Australia (what Michel and Peng [2012] refer to as "demand and denial" policy)—the cultural failure to see the real contribution of care to the national economy, and the insistence on care work as "low-skilled" rather than "high-value," makes it difficult to reconcile care and immigration policies. Both researchers and policymakers thus need to pay attention to the ways in which the association of care with women naturalizes it and renders it invisible as a form of work—and thus widely undervalued (Anderson 2000).

Part IV, "From the Global to the Local, and Back Again," takes up the issue of global governance and its potential for regulating—and bringing greater equality to—the realm of care work, a project that is complicated by individual nations' resistance to intervention by international organizations as well as by the privatized work settings and predominance by migrant workers that characterize this occupational sector. Global governance may, in theory, be able to bridge inequalities between sending and receiving countries by articulating international norms, but, as two of the chapters in this part emphasize, it is a two-way street. Local mobilizations can both serve as an impetus for global norm-setting and then draw on those enunciations (which carry great prestige) to bolster local claims.

This point is made well by sociologists Jennifer Fish and Moriah Shumpert, who open the section by exploring how local and national organizations of domestic workers have shaped policy in and through international organizations. Using examples drawn from their work with organizers in Hong Kong, the authors demonstrate that the campaign for ILO Convention 189, "Decent Work for Domestic Workers," in 2011 provided a venue for the alignment of domestic worker organizations from around the world and put them in touch with NGOs and trade unions who became their allies and helped strengthen them. Once adopted, C189 has served as a powerful lever for continuing mobilization as domestic workers drive national ratification campaigns and seek to make the ideals expressed in its lofty text a reality on the ground.

In the next chapter, historians Eileen Boris and Megan Undén expand on the theme of circularity by interrogating the interaction between the local and the global in domestic workers' efforts to pass some form of a Domestic Worker's Bill of Rights in several American states. Crafted with reference to C 189, these laws give evidence of policy feedback and policy transference between the two levels. Boris and Undén consider what roles the National Domestic Workers Alliance and US delegates played in the making of the ILO convention and then show how domestic workers in the United States subsequently deployed that convention in state-level campaigns. Juxtaposing the proposed US laws to the ILO convention and its accompanying recommendation, R201 (ILO 2011), they note the differences among the international (ILO), nation-states (country) and state (subnational) legislatures as interactive spheres of political power in shaping law, policy, and enforcement. They also point to the irony that C189 can serve as an organizing and mobilizing device on the ground in the United States, even though the country has not (yet) ratified it. In their analysis, the transnational emerges as a space for struggle, as national, subnational and local actors mobilize global-level law and enforcement to enact changes at the national, subnational, and local levels.

The final chapter casts light on the inner workings of two international organizations that are in a position to play a key role in regulating migrant care work but, puzzlingly, do not. Political scientist Rianne Mahon and historian Sonya Michel ask why the ILO and OECD have failed to address the needs of migrant women care workers in a comprehensive fashion. They argue that, through the ways these two organizations have understood and framed issues pertaining to the needs of women workers and their families, to care work and to migration, they have created a situation of "siloization" that prevents them from "seeing" these issues as interrelated and formulating policies to address them in a holistic, transnational manner. Further, the chapter points out that, to a great extent, both organizations tend to view migrant women care workers from the perspective of the care needs of women from wealthier countries, thereby ignoring the plight of the care workers themselves, most of whom come from emerging economies, and of their family members, many of whom have been left behind.

The chapters in this section highlight the fluidity of discursive and policy iterations across the scales. The first two chapters illustrate ways in which grassroots social mobilizations, seeking to circumvent the lack of, or sometimes negative, national policy responses, "scale-jump" to global-level governance bodies to voice their demands, and then use the global-level instruments they have achieved (such as C189) to effect national and subnational-level changes. While the final chapter emphasizes the limits of global governance power in developing comprehensive multilateral policies and imposing transnational legal conventions upon national governments, the previous two show how local and national mobilizations of domestic and care workers can sometimes make up for these inadequacies through the ways in which they invoke and seek to implement international instruments that first appear to be too blunt to protect them and ensure their rights on the ground. A case in point is the International Domestic Workers Federation's insistence, in discussions of C189, that the ILO take into account domestic workers' migration status as well as their working conditions. Here careful fieldwork on the part of Fish and Shumpert reveals a key moment in the policymaking process that did not show up in the ILO documents analyzed by Mahon and Michel, emphasizing the need for a variety of methodologies as well as multi-scalar perspectives in this complex research.

Finally, in her afterword, Shahra Razavi, chief of the Research and Data Section at UN Women and a gender and development scholar, highlights three overarching themes emerging from this book. First is the multiple intersecting inequalities that are evident across localities and through all scales. Here she echoes the point made earlier by Fiona Williams: that global care migration "encapsulates many of the world's inequalities." Second, Razavi emphasizes the relevance of policy and governance in shaping both care and transnationalization, noting that it is thus important for activists, academics, and international organizations to engage in policy/governance processes at all levels, from local to global. Finally, she points to the need for devising a different model of development that is capable of addressing its unevenness and inequalities, since both serve as causal underpinnings for transnational care migration.

Razavi's astute and thoughtful reflection points to a new research and policy agenda. Fittingly, she reminds us that while this book marks the culmination of a long and fruitful project, our work is not done. We trust, however, that even in its present state, it will provide a sturdy platform not just for the scholarship that follows, but for the many care workers and their advocates who are seeking decent work and well-being for themselves and those they care for—both their own families and clients—throughout the Pacific Rim and around the world.

NOTES

1. Consider, for example, the research cluster on Asian Migration at the Asia Research Institute, National University of Singapore, led by Brenda Yeoh; and CHAMPSEA, the project for the Study of Transnational Migration in South-East Asia and the Health of Children Left Behind, also at the Asia Research Institute, NUS.
2. Such double-sited fieldwork, which allowed Oliveira to match migrants with family members in Mexico, is unusual. Ironically, while the migration status of her New York City subjects often prevented them from crossing back across the border to visit loved ones in Mexico, Oliveira could travel freely between the two sites and even served as a courier for gifts, messages and photographs between family members kept apart by immigration restrictions.

REFERENCES

Anderson, Bridget. 2000. *Doing the Dirty Work: The Global Politics of Domestic Labour*. London and New York: Zed.

Anderson, Bridget and Isabel Shutes, eds. 2014. *Migration and Care Labour: Theory, Policy and Politics*. New York: Palgrave.

Asis, Maruja M.B. and Nicola Piper. 2008. "Researching International Labor Migration in Asia." *Sociological Quarterly* 49: 423–44.

Bakker, Isabella and Rachel Silvey, eds. 2008. *Beyond States and Markets: The Challenge of Social Reproduction*. New York: Routledge.

Bettio, Francesca and Janneke Plantenga. 2004. "Comparing Care Regimes in Europe." *Feminist Economics* 10: 85–113.

Brennan, Deborah et al. 2012. "The Marketization of Care: Rationales and Consequences in Nordic and Liberal Care Regimes." *Journal of European Social Policy* 22: 377–91.

China National Bureau of Statistics (China-NBS). *China Statistical Yearbook 2015*, http://www.stats.gov.cn/tjsj/ndsj/2015/indexeh.htm (accessed 28/03/2016).

Cortés, Patricia and Jessica Pan. 2013. "Outsourcing Household Production: Foreign Domestic Workers and Native Labor Supply in Hong Kong." *Journal of Labor Economics* 31: 329–371.

Daly, Mary and Jane Lewis. 2000. "The Concept of Social Care and the Analysis of Contemporary Welfare State." *British Journal of Sociology*, 51: 281–298.

Ehrenreich, Barbara and Arlie Hochschild, eds. 2004. *Global Woman: Nannies, Maids and Sex Workers in the New Economy*. New York: Metropolitan Books.

Fudge, Judy. 2012. "Precarious Migrant Status and Precarious Employment: The Paradox of International Rights for Migrant Workers." *Comparative Labor Law and Policy Journal* 34: 95–132.

Huang, Shirlena, Leng Leng Thang and Mika Toyota. 2012. "Transnational Mobilities for Care: Rethinking the Dynamics of Care in Asia." *Global Networks* 12, 2: 129–34.

Hochschild, Arlie. 2000. "The Nanny Chain." *The American Prospect* 3:32–36.

International Labour Organization (ILO). 2011. Domestic Workers Recommendation, 2011 (No. 201). http://www.ilo.org/dyn/normlex/en/f?p=NORMLEXPUB:12100:0::NO::P12100_ILO_CODE:R201.

Isaksen, Lise, Sambasivan Devi and Arlie Hochschild. 2008. "Global Care Crisis." *American Behavioral Scientist* 52: 405–25.

Jenson, Jane and Denis St. Martin. 2006. "Building Blocks for a New Social Architecture: The LEGO™ Paradigm of an Active Society." *Policy and Politics* 34: 429–51.

Jenson, Jane and Mariette Sineau, eds. 2001. *Who Cares?: Women's Work, Childcare and Welfare State Design*. Toronto: University of Toronto Press.

Knijn, Trudie and Aafke Komter. 2004. *Solidarity between the Sexes and the Generations: Transformations in Europe*. Cheltenham, UK and Northampton, MA: Edward Elgar.

Kofman, Eleonore and Parvati Raghuram. 2012. "Women, Migration and Care: Explorations of Diversity in the Global South." *Social Politics* 19: 408–32.

Lewis, Jane. 1992. *Women in Britain since 1945: Women, Family, Work and the State in the Postwar Years*. Oxford, UK and Cambridge, MA: Blackwell.

Lopez, Mario. 2012. "Reconstructing the Affective Labour of Filipinos as Care Workers in Japan." *Global Networks* 12, 2: 252–268.

Lutz, Helma, ed. 2008. *Migration and Domestic Work: A European Perspective on a Global Theme*. Aldershot, UK and Burlington, VT: Ashgate.

Lutz, Helma. 2011. *The New Maids: Transnational Women and the Care Economy.* New York and London: Zed.

Mahon, Rianne. 2006a. "Introduction: Gender and the Politics of Scale. *Social Politics* 13: 457–461.

Mahon, Rianne. 2006b. "Of Scalar Hierarchies and Welfare Redesign: Child Care in Three Canadian Cities." *Transactions of the Institute of British Geographers* 31: 452–466.

Mahon, Rianne. and Sonya Michel, eds. 2002. *Child Care Policy at the Crossroads: Gender and Welfare State Restructuring.* New York: Routledge.

Michel, Sonya and Ito Peng. 2012. "All in the Family? Migrants, Nationhood and Care Regimes in Asia and North America." *Journal of European Social Policy* 22: 406–18.

Ochiai, Emiko et al. 2012. "The Struggle Against Familialism: Reconfiguring the Care Diamond in Japan." In *Global Variations in the Political and Social Economy of Care: Worlds Apart*, edited by Shahra Razavi and Silke Staab, 61–79. United Kingdom: Routledge.

Oishi, Nana. 2005. *Women in Motion: Globalization, State Policies and Labor Migration in Asia.* Stanford, CA: Stanford University Press.

Page, John and Sonia Plaza. 2006. "Migration Remittances and Development: A Review of Global Evidence." *Journal of African Economies* 15, issue suppl. 2: 245–336.

Parreñas, Rhacel Salazar. 2000. "Migrant Filipina Domestic Workers and the International Division of Reproductive Labor." *Gender and Society* 14: 560–80.

Parreñas, Rhacel Salazar. and Lok C. D. Siu, eds. 2007. *Asian Diasporas: New Formations, New Conceptions.* Stanford, CA: Stanford University Press.

Peng, Ito. 2009. "The Political and Social Economy of Care in the Republic of Korea." UNRISD Gender and Development Program, Published Paper #6, PP-GD-6 http://www.unrisd.org/unrisd/website/document.nsf/(httpPublications)/ 2B5879FBCD1DBD3FC12576A200470FA3?OpenDocument https://www. hrw.org/report/2014/10/22/i-already-bought-you/abuse-and-exploitation-female-migrant-domestic-workers-united

Raghuram, Parvati. 2012. "Global Care, Local Configurations: Challenges to the Conceptualization of Care." *Global Networks* 12: 155–74.

Razavi, Shahra. 2007. "The Political and Social Economy of Care in a Development Context Conceptual Issues, Research Questions and Policy Options." UNRISD Gender and Development Programme Paper Number 3. June.

UN Department of Economic and Social Affairs, Population Division (UN-DESA). 2016. *International Migration Report 2015: Highlights* (ST/ESA/ SER.A/375).

van Hooren, Franca and Uwe Becker. 2012. "One Welfare State, Two Care Regimes: Understanding Developments in Child and Elderly Care in the Netherlands." *Social Policy and Administration* 46: 83–107.

Yeates, Nicola. 2008. *Globalizing Care Economies and Migrant Workers: Explorations in Global Care Chains*. New York: Palgrave Macmillan.

Yeoh, Brenda S. A. and Shirlena Huang. 2010. "Foreign Domestic Workers and Home-Based Care for Elders in Singapore." *Journal of Aging & Social Policy* 22: 69–88.

Williams, J. Fiona. 2010. "Themes and Concepts in Migration, Gender and Care." *Social Policy and Society* 9: 385–396

Williams, J. Fiona 2014. "Making Connections across the Transnational Political Economy of Care." In *Migration and Care Labour: Theory, Policy and Politics*, edited by Bridget Anderson and Isabel Shutes, 11–30. London: Palgrave.

Sonya Michel is professor emerita of history, American studies, and women's and gender studies at the University of Maryland, College Park, USA, and a senior scholar at the Woodrow Wilson International Center for Scholars, Washington, DC. She is a founding editor of the journal *Social Politics: International Studies in Gender, State and Society* and the author/editor of many books and articles on gender and social policy in the United States and comparatively, past and present.

Ito Peng is a professor of sociology and public policy, and the Canada Research Chair in Global Social Policy, at the Department of Sociology, and the School of Public Policy and Governance, University of Toronto. She has written extensively on family, gender, and social policies in East Asia. She is currently leading a large international partnership research project entitled *Gender, Migration, and the Work of Care*, funded by a major Partnership Grant from the Social Sciences and Humanities Research Council of Canada.

CHAPTER 2

Intersections of Migrant Care Work: An Overview

Fiona Williams

The phenomenon of the movement of female migrants from developing countries into care and domestic work in richer countries encapsulates many of the world's inequalities. It provides a lens through which to see connections between the most significant social, cultural, political, demographic and economic changes in the twenty-first century. First is the global increase of women's involvement in the labour market and the greater reliance in both the Global North and South on a woman's wage. Figures for OECD countries show an average rate of 63 percent for female labour force participation (OECD 2015). In developing countries, too, female participation in formal work (often as breadwinners) has risen, ranging, by 2008, from 24.7 percent in the Middle East to 62.9 percent in sub-Saharan Africa for women over 25, both increases from the previous ten years (ILO 2009, 9).[1] In developed welfare states, this has been characterized by the move from a "male-breadwinner" to an "adult-worker" society in which "hard-working" men and women support themselves and their families through employment.

This affects the second change: the growing need for care for older people, disabled people and young children, which has been described as a "new social risk" in the context of aging societies, declining fertility and political imperatives towards social expenditure cuts. Such care risks are no

F. Williams (✉)
School of Sociology and Social Policy, University of Leeds, Leeds, UK

© The Author(s) 2017
S. Michel, I. Peng (eds.), *Gender, Migration, and the Work of Care*,
DOI 10.1007/978-3-319-55086-2_2

23

less insistent in poorer regions, where unemployment, wars, ethnic conflict, natural disasters and chronic illnesses place enormous responsibilities on women to maintain their families with little infrastructural support. It is this that intensifies the reason for women to migrate: in order to provide support while simultaneously intensifying the caring responsibilities of those left behind.

Third, migration patterns too have changed. Half of the world's 232 million international migrants are now women: 52 percent of those in the global North and 43 percent in the global South (OECD-UNDESA 2013, 1). Many find work in low-paid care and domestic work in private homes or institutions. In some countries, such as Indonesia and the Philippines, the export of qualified nurses is part of national policy and bilateral agreements (Guevarra 2010, and see Peng, this volume). Fourth, care provision in many destination countries has also changed, where care policies have shifted over the past two decades from providing public services (or in some places, no services) to giving people cash payments or tax credits to buy in care or domestic help in their private homes. The reliance on voluntary but especially for-profit provision has led to care being treated as a commodity that is bought and sold in the care market.

It is in the juxtaposition of these four changes that migrant women workers, already often disadvantaged by their migrant and racialized status, are susceptible to the poor conditions that beset the low-wage economy of care and domestic work. Their precariousness is exacerbated by migration policies in countries of destination which have become more restrictive in order to favour skilled workers, as analysed in the chapter by Boyd in this book. This has been accompanied by the contradictory dependence of richer countries on migrant care workers, combined with populist and political nationalist and anti-immigration sentiment.

However, the factors that deliver these connections between changes in migration and care are complex. To begin with, they are superimposed upon older, continuing and sometimes revived inequalities: gendered divisions where women carry the responsibilities for care; the devaluation of care as paid and unpaid work; imperialist, post-colonial and geo-political hierarchies and inequalities; and the racialization of servitude. In addition, the picture I have described above, while global in its reach, contains significant variations and multiple layerings across countries and regions. Pursuing a "multi-scalar" approach, as this book does, involves unravelling these complexities in the relatively less researched regions of the Pacific Rim. It is what makes this collection a major and original contribution to work on care migration. In the light of this contribution, I outline below some key points and frames that can enable researchers and activists to think through the multiple connections and directions of travel that these complexities take.

THE BIG PICTURE

One characteristic of the study of migrant care work is its huge span, from the economic, social and political dimensions of globalization to the most intimate practices of care carried out in private homes. This span moves horizontally through transnational connections and vertically through different contextual layers: macro, meso and micro, not unidirectionally but traversing this way and that, up and down. Two concepts that attempt to grasp the circumference of the broader picture are, first, "the international division of reproductive labor" (Parreñas 2001) and, second, "the transnational political economy of care" (Williams 2011; Mahon and Robinson 2011; Razavi and Staab 2012).[2]

In the first, Rhacel Parreñas builds on Evelyn Nakano Glenn's (1992) work on "the racial division of reproductive labor" in order to highlight the historical and continuing role in care work and domestic service played by black and minority ethnic women. It references the way women from poorer regions have been pulled into a new international division of labour where corporations in global cities now employ highly professionalized male and female workers whose catering, cleaning and care needs are serviced at low cost by migrant workers (Sassen 1984; Carbonnier and Morel 2015). In this context, migrant women express their individual and collective agency through transnational institutions and networks which they create to sustain and maintain their cultural, financial and care commitments across the diasporic space between home and work, as well as their dignity as workers (Parreñas 2005).

The concept of "the transnational political economy of care" identifies five key dynamics that attend migrant care work (Williams 2011, 2012). The first is the *transnational movement of care labour*, which is seen as not only specifically meeting reproductive care needs but also operating in parallel with the movement of skilled health workers from poorer regions into public and private institutions in richer countries.[3] While the latter includes highly qualified workers such as doctors and nurses, the overall effect is as similar and cumulative as that of migrant care work: draining poorer countries of their trained professional infrastructure while saving the social expenditure costs of richer countries. It reproduces the very geo-political inequalities which are at its root. Second are the *transnational dynamics of care commitments* as people migrate and leave family behind. In her chapter, Gabrielle Oliveira calls these "transnational care constellations." She describes in detail how Sara, an undocumented mother of two from Mexico, simultaneously cares for the child of her employer, one of her own children, whom she has with her in New York, as well as her other child, who has remained in Mexico but with whom she keeps in constant touch by phone. The chapter points to the emotional plasticity required to hold these the complex layers in place.

The third dynamic is the *transnational movement of care capital*, in which international corporations now dominate much care provision, driving out the smaller, more co-operatively run care homes and agencies. In many ways this apex of the marketization and commodification of care reveals some of its most incompatible features (Sandel 2012). The labour-intensive nature of care means that profits are made through economies of scale, forcing the smaller specialist providers out of the market. Efficiency strategies pursued by multinationals which seek to lower the costs of care labour in the private sector often influence labour strategies in the public sector, adding to the general devaluation of care work (Holden 2002). Market principles, such as risk, expansion and profit, can undermine the principles of individual needs, continuity and quality of services. In addition, in many places brokers and placement agencies run highly competitive businesses finding employment for migrant workers. André Laliberté in this book describes the highly exploitative tendencies of such companies in Taiwan, Hong Kong and Shanghai. Profits from care labour also flow in different directions: for the Philippines, one of the main countries of origin of domestic, care and health workers, such labour provides, through remittances that workers send home, its largest source of foreign currency (Parreñas 2005; Guevarra 2010).

The transnational and international political actors involved in improving the rights and conditions of migrant care workers constitute the fourth and fifth elements in the transnational political care economy. On the one side is *transnational governance,* represented by the policies, agreements and conventions in which international organizations such as the ILO and OECD have played an important recent role, as well as the WHO in health care. On the other side are the struggles by local and *transnational networks of care and domestic work activists* that have been the force behind such developments. Bearing in mind that care workers may be providing care for frail or disabled people, the development of claims from transnational disability and informal carer movements for the recognition of care recipients' rights and dignity has also been important.

The three chapters in Part III of this book provide very clear examples of these different political actors. One of the most significant markers of progress was the ILO Convention passed in 2011 on "Decent Work for Domestic Workers," which set standards—to be ratified and implemented by its member states—for rights to decent working conditions and collective organization. In many ways the processes involved in determining this policy were as significant as the policy itself. Grassroots domestic worker organizations across the world were brought together in an International Domestic Workers Network. Jennifer Fish and Moriah Shumpert describe how the inclusion of this network in the negotiation of the convention to give workers greater visibility, recognition and dignity was a new departure in a number of ways for the ILO. It went beyond the usual tripartite social dialogue of states, unions and employers by having "real" domestic workers who could testify to their own experiences; and it was forced to consider the hitherto "invisible" informal economy—"the work that makes all other work possible."[4]

In addition, as Eileen Boris and Megan Undén observe in the case of passing the Domestic Worker Bill of Rights in New York State and California, the pressuring and mobilizing constituted a circular process that generated demands from local organizations to national NGOs and policymakers and on to international protocols whose ordinance then became the basis for further pressure for implementation at both national and local levels.

At the same time, the convention also reflected limitations in the thinking of international organizations being able to "bring both ends of the global care chain together" (Mahon and Michel, this book). In other words, the problems that attend contemporary domestic and care work belong not only to the conditions of workers in richer countries but to migration regimes, global geo-political inequalities and the devaluation of care in both countries of origin and of destination. This is precisely why conceptual frames such as the international division of reproductive labour and the transnational political economy of care are important in being able to hold together the elements that contribute to the bigger picture. Being able to do that also helps think through political strategies, which I return to later. However, bigger pictures only go so far. They are less able to tell us about the complexities in each layer of micro, meso and macro and how the relation among these makes for different pictures, especially with regard to different countries or regions.

Micro-Layers and Intersections

At the microlevel of migrant care work are the complex interpersonal encounters between migrant care workers and the people for whom they provide care or support, who may or may not be their employers. These encounters are saturated with social and cultural power attached not only to their class, gender, age, sexuality and dis/ability relations but also to the employment and migrant status of the worker, and, not least, the relations of nationality, ethnicity and religion and the extent to which these are racialized. Criss-crossing these are the social relations of care, and these may construct multiple vulnerable dependencies (of frailty in old age on the part of the recipient and of insecurity of employment and the indignities of racism and sexism on the part of the worker), especially where care has little social or economic value. Intersectionality analysis is particularly helpful to unpack this complexity. This approach emerged originally from Black Feminist movements in the USA to challenge the separation of analytic and activist categories of race and gender and to highlight how, for women of colour, the axes of gender and race intersect and, in doing so, reconstitute the experiences of subordination/domination for women of colour (Crenshaw 1989). Over time this principle has embraced multiple social relations to become a method for analysing different manifestations of social relations of power at any given time or place, "conceiving of categories not as distinct but always permeated by other categories, fluid and changing, always in the process of creating and being created by dynamics of power" (Cho, Crenshaw and McCall 2013, 795).

In this book, the chapter by Cynthia Cranford and Jennifer Jihye Chun provides a good example of this complexity in a case study in which the care relations do not follow the assumed patterns of social or economic power where the employer is of a wealthier dominant ethnic group and the worker is poor female, of minority ethnicity and a migrant. Both care workers and care recipients in their study are from the minority ethnic and racialized urban community of Oakland Chinatown in California. By virtue of California's In-Home Supportive Services, the recipients are older and disabled people, and many, like their workers, are poor. Recipients are allowed to employ family, friends or agency staff as care workers, and they share employment responsibilities with the state, which pays the employees directly as well as recognizing the union that represents care workers. The question here is whether these different features shift care away from traditional relations of coercive servitude towards a potentially more reciprocal model in which the dignity and conditions of both worker and recipient are recognized and respected. The researchers find elements of both continuity with the old model and changes to the new (as well as care recipients who can be kind or callous). However, what made for the continuities was insufficient state funding that gave rise to precarious, low-paid work, as well as difficulties in regulating home-based employment. And what made for a better model of care had less to do with shared ethnic and racialized positioning of workers and recipients, and more with workers' capacity for collective agency through both the unions and an advocacy organization for women immigrants. Importantly, too, alliances with disability movements ensured representation of the experiences of recipients. In a sense, these alliances represent a form of "intersectionality in action."

Institutional Intersections at the Meso Level

Such interpersonal care relations are shaped by different institutional, political and cultural processes at the meso level. Here, too, it is useful to look at the ways these processes intersect, for this can provide an understanding of the diverse ways the migration-care nexus operates in different countries, even where those countries are faced with similar pressures. This cross-national diversity has been termed one of "converging variations" which has been shaped by the way a destination country's *care regime* intersects with its *migration regime* and its *employment regime* (Williams 2012). These three regimes are, arguably, the most significant to shape a country's response to its care crisis. They refer not only to clusters of state policies around care, migration and employment but, importantly, to cultures and practices—legacies—to major forms of social relations of power and inequality inherent in each domain and to the forms of mobilization and contestation that each regime in each country provokes (Williams 2012; see also Shutes and Chiatti 2012).

The chapters in Part II of this book provide enlightening explanations of how this diversity works. For example, Deborah Brennan and her colleagues show that while Australia's care regime has been marketized, stronger standards for work in the child care sector mean that it attracts fewer low-paid migrant workers than in care work with older people. At the same time, Australia's highly regulated migration regime, which traditionally has focussed on skilled workers, results in turning a blind eye to the growing numbers of temporary migrant workers in low-paid work, including care work. Ito Peng's chapter highlights the exceptionality of South Korea and Japan in dealing with common social and demographic problems faced by many OECD countries: increasing elder care, child care and care labour shortages. While many other countries have followed a market model with cash subsidies for home-based and/or live-in care often provided by migrant workers, Japan and South Korea have increased their publicly funded services and subsidies (such as long-term care insurance) to meet their elder care and child care needs and have resisted the employment of migrant home-based workers. A highly selective migration regime allows (often co-ethnic) migrants only into institutional care work. What marks the care and migration regimes of Japan and Korea is a high degree of institutional regulation combined with a cultural aversion towards "foreigners" (especially in the private home) and a historical legacy of socialized care. Both these emerged from the development of those countries' welfare states as a form of nation-building constructed through the ideas and practices of an imagined cultural/racial/ethnic homogeneity (a process also present in earlier twentieth-century welfare state foundations of Europe and North America; see Kettunen et al. 2015). It is this that persists in the face of global trends towards multiculturalism.

In contrast, as André Laliberté's chapter shows, these aspects are not reproduced in other East Asian countries. Taiwan, Hong Kong and China have pursued a market model that depends on low-paid home-based care carried out by migrant workers. Here, Confucian values of filial piety are used to defend quasi-family care in the home by migrants, even though in modern China religious values have long been repudiated. Furthermore, in China, Liu Hong's chapter notes, it is the administrative boundaries between provinces rather than between countries that construct the *rural* migrant as a low-paid, insecure and racialized care worker.

In some ways the Korean and Japanese commitments to socialized care appear to have more in common, as Peng concludes, with some of the European welfare states of Austria, Germany and the Nordic countries than with other Pacific Rim countries. At the same time, another recent development in many of these European care-friendly societies marks a departure from socialized care. This is the policy of offering tax credits to households to assist in buying home-based domestic services. Austria,

Germany, Belgium, France, Finland, Denmark and Sweden have all actively promoted domestic work in this way (Carbonnier and Morel 2015). This has been justified in two ways: as a form of job creation and social inclusion for marginalized workers (many of whom are minority ethnic women), and as a "productivity boost" that enables professional women in the labour market to maintain their productivity as highly skilled workers in the knowledge economy. However, it also reproduces a growing dualization between the highly qualified and well-paid and those without qualifications in precarious low-paid work, as well as a trend towards the fiscalization of welfare, which tend to favour better-off households. Thus, a form of social policy that can be presented as supporting gender equality in access to paid work and reconciling work and care responsibilities can also intensify gendered class and race inequalities.

INTERSECTING CRISES IN THE MACRO

I described earlier the dynamics of the bigger, global picture which wrap around the micro and meso processes. Over the past decade, there has been an escalation of global crises that have relevance for the migrant care phenomenon. Here, too, understanding the intersections across crises is important in order to think about the implications for strategies towards global justice that improve both care and migration in the global North and South.

When the global financial crisis occurred in 2008, most analysts focussed on its economic causes and consequences. However, philosopher Nancy Fraser framed it in different terms (Fraser 2013). Recalling Karl Polanyi's work on the self-destructive impulse behind capitalism being its capacity to devalue land, labour and money by turning them into "fictitious commodities" (Polanyi 1944/57), she argues that the same impulse is seen today in the global crises of finance, the environment and care. Thus, speculation led to the global financial crisis in which investment was destabilized and devalued with the subsequent intensification of austerity policies. Similarly, the exploitation of the world's natural resources has devalued the planet and contributed to an environmental crisis, while the commodification of care has also led to its devaluation across the globe. These crises are linked by the ways in which each jeopardizes security, human solidarity and sustainability. They are also interconnected in their knock-on effects; for example, austerity has given rise to public expenditure cuts; climate change and collapsing economies propel migration; care migration solves some countries' care crisis at others' expense.

To these three I would add a fourth crisis—the crisis of migration (see UNHCR 2013).[5] Increases in migration caused by wars, fragile states, ethnic conflicts, environmental disasters and intensified geo-political inequalities have created a political discourse in which the economic costs and benefits of migration predominate over the ethics of solidarity, interdependence and hospitality. In this way it is possible to see the discourses of welfare, sustainability, social protection and human rights being jeopardized. Although migrants seeking asylum are not usually the same ones who end up in care and domestic work (although they may be), there are two aspects of this crisis that warrant further reflection in migrant care work research.

First, many in both groups are, one way or another, *survival* migrants. In other words, the distinction between economic migrants and refugees holds only to a certain degree. Second, the political debates about the refugee crisis, especially in Europe and the USA, are shaping changes in immigration policies which affect migrant care workers. These are becoming more restrictive not only towards "unskilled" workers (into which category care workers fall), but also in limiting migrant eligibility to basic welfare provision as well as requiring greater cultural assimilation.[6] Many of the political debates concerned with these issues set state sovereignty against human rights and humanitarianism. This was very clear in the 2016 referendum in the UK on leaving the European Union. The choice to leave ("Brexit") was popularly framed as an anti-immigration vote that would lead to a better-funded national health service and jobs for British workers. The victory was followed by a 57 percent increase in race-hate crimes, according to the National Police Chiefs Council (Independent Newspaper 2016). A subsequent report from the UK NGO *Independent Age* warned of the serious consequences to the social care infrastructure if exit from the European Union affected the migrant status of the 78,000 European Economic Area migrants who work with older people who do not have British citizenship (Independent Age 2016).

Strategic Considerations

One of the important aspects of this book is that it documents and assesses the role of political actors in reforms for migrant care and domestic work. The complexity of different issues can be overwhelming, but it is possible to conceive of strategies for reform as operating in three ways. First the temporality of strategies involves both short-term and longer-term goals.

Second they need to operate in countries of migrants' origin as well as in the destination countries. Third, pressure has to be brought to bear at local, national, bi-lateral, international and global levels of policymaking. Thus, for example, short-term goals would include many of those mentioned by Cranford and Chun, Fish and Shumpert, and Boris and Undén in this book: the regularization of care and domestic work, union and community representation for workers, improving migrants' right of citizenship including family reunion, rights to contracts, social protection, training, guidance on cultural norms, language acquisition, freedom from discrimination. This involves different levels of policymaking, as mentioned earlier, since the positive effects of activism travel along local, national and global circuits. Cutting across these are links that require co-ordination across different sectors. One conclusion to be drawn from many of the studies in this book is that care migration and employment policy areas are often operating without reference to each other, especially where the care sector depends on "unskilled" migrant workers while migration policies are restricting migration to "skilled" workers (see the chapters by Boyd and Brennan et al.). At the same time, another connection has to be made given that, as Mahon and Michel comment in their chapter on global policymaking, the focus has tended to be on improving rights in countries of destination rather than also focusing on countries of origin. Parallel strategies at local and national level in countries of migrants' origin also involve opportunities for representation for potential migrants, for social dialogue, for co-ordinated development of ethical emigration policies, as well as countering the understaffing and underfunding of public health and care infrastructure (see Pillinger 2011).

In certain ways some of the developments in global health care strategy may be instructive. The World Health Organization's "WHO's 2010 Global Code of Practice" (WHO 2010) recommended a more extensive application of bilateral ethical recruitment codes in health care which have been implemented in a number of countries to prevent "poaching" health care workers from poorer countries, combined with the guarantee to provide free training and support for returning doctors and nurses. This was important in building on a human rights approach as well as prioritizing measures to counter global inequalities in health (Connell and Buchan 2011). Although this represents soft rather than hard law and raises as many new complexities as those it seeks answer (e.g. do ethical recruitment policies interfere with the right of workers to mobility? How far would the costs associated with ethical recruitment make migrant workers less attractive to employers, and if so, would this drive them underground?), it provides a way of thinking about the geopolitical inequalities generated by migrant care work. It encompasses some important guidelines in moving towards global social justice, including the right to health, individual autonomy, accountability, transnational reciprocity and mutualism and fair workplace practices (Connell and Buchan 2011, 14–15), which could also be applied to care work.

Care and migration are both human rights issues. Migration has long been considered in this way. For care this entails the recognition that there is a fundamental human right to be able to receive and to provide care. Free movement and asylum for those fleeing violence are important rights, but the issue of migrant care work needs to go beyond this to consider the inequalities that result in wealthier countries offloading their work/life balance problems and care deficits onto the labour of those who migrate, and the knock-on effect on families left behind. Underlying this are the limited advances of gender equality in both countries of origin and destination combined with the marketization of care provision and the legacies of racialized domestic servitude.

One part of putting this into a longer-term perspective requires that care is seen as central to global social justice, that is to say, that the everyday relations of care carried out within unequal socio-economic, gendered and racialized relations are embedded conceptually and strategically in global social justice. In the political discourses of national and global social policy actors, care work is often hidden, subsumed under the requirements and duty of paid work for individuals and economic competitiveness for nation states. Care is a practice, a responsibility and an ethic in people's everyday lives, and it is part of what it means to be a citizen. People not only are holders of individual rights but also have care needs and care responsibilities which shape their actions and decisions. In policy terms, this necessitates the recognition of care, the representation of its providers and receivers, and the rights and redistribution of care needs and responsibilities as central tenets in global justice. Ethically, politically and practically, care constitutes the social reproduction activities that sustain society, as much as labour, local, national and migrant, sustains the economy, and ecological justice sustains the planet. It is within this framing of justice, sustainability, interdependence, humanitarianism and hospitality that we might understand the complexities of the politics of migrant care work and the struggles around it. This book contributes greatly to this understanding.

NOTES

1. More recent figures show a differential impact of the global financial and economic crisis and project the trend towards closing the gap between male and female employment levelling off and increasing in some regions. The gap increased in South Asia, East Asia, Central and Southeastern Europe and the Russian Commonwealth (ILO 2012, Table 4:17)
2. Razavi and Staab (2012) call this "the political *and social* economy of care" (my emphasis).
3. Reliance on doctor and nurse migration is commonplace across many welfare states (Yeates 2009). For example in 2009 in the UK, 23 percent of nurses were foreign-born (Cangiano et al. 2009). The highest employment rates for foreign-born people in health and community services in 2004–2005 was 18.6 percent in Sweden and 24.2 percent in Norway (OECD 2006, 57).
4. This is the slogan of the National Domestic Workers Network, a US organization.
5. While general international migration started to slow down a little after 2007 (OECD-UNDESA 2013), at the same time refugee migration began to accelerate. There were 11.7 million refugees under the UNHCR's mandate in 2013, 1.2 million more than the previous year (UNHCR 2013).
6. In the UK, for example, rules introduced in 2014 prevented migrant workers from claiming the housing benefit or job seekers' allowance (a benefit for people who are out of work) for six months after entry and then only on proof of a habitual residence test. By 2016, France, Belgium and the Netherlands had banned the full-face veil worn by Muslim women and some cities in Switzerland, Spain and Italy followed suit.

REFERENCES

Cangiano, Alessio, Isabel Shutes, Sarah Spencer and George Leeson. 2009. *Migrant Care Workers in Ageing Societies: Research Findings in the UK.* Oxford University: COMPAS.

Carbonnier, Clément and Nathalie Morel, eds. 2015 *The Political Economy of Household Services in Europe.* Basingstoke: Palgrave Macmillan.

Cho, Sumi, Kimberlé Williams Crenshaw, and Leslie McCall. 2013. "Toward a Field of Intersectionality Studies: Theory, Application and Praxis." *Signs* 38: 785–810.

Connell, John and James Buchan. 2011 "The Impossible Dream? Codes of Practice and International Migration of Skilled Health Workers." *World Medical and Health Policy* 3, 3: 1–17.

Crenshaw, Kimberlé. 1989. "Demarginalizing the Intersection of Race and Sex: A Black Feminist Critique of Anti-Discrimination Doctrine, Feminist Theory and Antiracist Politics." *University of Chicago Legal Forum* 1989: 1241–99.

Fraser, Nancy. 2013. "A Triple Movement? Parsing the Politics of Crisis after Polanyi." *New Left Review* 81: 119–132

Glenn, Evelyn Nakano. 1992. "From Servitude to Service Work: The Historical Continuities of Women's Paid and Unpaid Reproductive Labor." *Signs* 18: 1–44.

Guevarra, Anna Romina. 2010. *Marketing Dreams, Manufacturing Heroes: The Transnational Labor Brokering of Filipino Workers.* New Brunswick, NJ: Rutgers University Press.

Holden, Chris. 2002. "The Internationalization of Long Term Care Provision: Economics and Strategy." *Global Social Policy* 2: 47–67.

International Labour Organization (ILO). 2009. *Global Employment Trends for Women.* Geneva: ILO.

ILO. 2012. *Global Employment Trends for Women.* Geneva: ILO.

Independent Age. 2016. *Brexit and the Future of Migrants in the Social Care Workforce.* London: Independent Longevity Centre-UK.

Independent Newspaper. 2016. "EU Referendum: reports of hate crime increase of 57% after Brexit vote." http://www.independent.co.uk/news/uk/home-news/brexit-hate-crime-racism-reports-eu-referendum-latest-a7106116.html, accessed 7 October 2016.

Kettunen, Pauli, Sonya Michel and Klaus Pedersen, eds. 2015. *Race, Ethnicity and Welfare States: An American Dilemma?* Cheltenham, UK and Northampton, MA: Edward Elgar.

Mahon, Rianne and Fiona Robinson, eds. 2011. *The Global Political Economy of Care: Integrating Ethical and Social Politics.* Vancouver: UBC Press.

OECD. 2006. *International Migration Outlook 2006.* Paris: OECD.

OECD. 2015. *Labor Force Survey 2015.* Paris: OECD.stat https://stats.oecd.org/Index.aspx?DataSetCode=LFS_SEXAGE_I_R, accessed October 2016.

OECD-UNDESA. 2013. *World Migration in Figures*: http://www.oecd.org/els/mig/World-Migration-in-Figures.pdf, accessed 7 October 2016.

Parreñas, Rhacel. 2001. *Servants of Globalization.* Stanford, CA: Stanford University Press.

Parreñas, Rhacel. 2005. *Children of Global Migration: Transnational Families and Gendered Woes.* Stanford, CA: Stanford University Press.

Pillinger, Jane. 2011. *Quality Healthcare Workers on the Move.* Public Services International, International Migration and Women Health and Social Care Workers Programme. Ferney-Voltaire: PSI.

Polanyi, Karl. 1944/57. *The Great Transformation: The Political and Economic Origins of Our Time.* Boston: Beacon Press.

Razavi, Shahrashoub and Silke Staab, eds. 2012. *Global Variations in the Political and Social Economy of Care: Worlds Apart.* London: Routledge.

Sandel, Michael. 2012. *What Money Can't Buy: The Moral Limits of Markets.* London: Allen Lane.

Sassen-Koob, Saskia. 1984. "Notes on the Incorporation of Third World Women into Wage-Labor through Immigration and Off-Shore Production." *International Migration Review* 18: 1144–67.

Shutes, Isabel and Carlos Chiatti. 2012. "Migrant Labor and the Marketisation of Care for Older People: The Employment of Migrant Care Workers by Families and Service Providers." *Journal of European Social Policy* 22: 392–405.

UNHCR. 2013. *War's Human Costs. UNHCR Global Trends 2013.* (UNHCR: Geneva). http://www.unhcr.org/5399a14f9.html, accessed 7 October 2016.

WHO. 2010. *World Health Report.* Geneva: WHO.

Williams, Fiona. 2011. "Towards a Transnational Analysis of the Political Economy of Care." In Mahon and Robinson, *op. cit.*, 21–39.

Williams, Fiona. 2012. "Converging Variations in Migrant Care Work in Europe." *Journal of European Social Policy* 22: 363–375

Yeates, Nicola. 2009. *Globalizing Care Economies and Migrant Workers.* Basingstoke: Palgrave.

Fiona Williams is emerita professor of social policy at the University of Leeds, Honorary Professor at the Social Policy Research Centre, University of New South Wales, and Research Affiliate at COMPAS, University of Oxford. Her recent publications include "Converging Variations in Migrant Care Work in Europe" in the *Journal of European Social Policy* (2012) and "Critical Thinking in Social Policy: The Challenges of Past, Present and Future," in *Social Policy and Administration* (2016).

PART II

Everyday Realities and Cultures of Care

CHAPTER 3

Immigrant Women and Home-Based Elder Care in Oakland, California's Chinatown

Cynthia Cranford and Jennifer Jihye Chun

Immigrant women and women of color provide a disproportionate amount of paid care work in private homes in North America, including in the rapidly growing sector of publicly funded, in-home personal support work for elderly and disabled people. While studies have examined how the dynamics of racialized gendered servitude channel poor, Black, and immigrant women into positions of cleaning, cooking, and caring for others (Glenn 1992, 2010; Hondagneu-Sotelo 2007; Bakan and Stasiulis 2012; Parreñas 2015), we know little about how the entanglements of race, gender, migration, and class shape the social organization of paid care work within immigrant and racialized communities that are also experiencing increasing demand for home-based

We are grateful to the women who participated in this study, to Young Shin, Executive Director of Asian Immigrant Women Advocates (AIWA) for supporting and contributing to this project, and to AIWA staff MuTing Cen and Dennis Yee for facilitating the research. Graduate students Chi Cheng Wat and Justin Kong conducted interviews and Chi Cheng Wat, Justin Kong, Michael Lee, and Angela Hick transcribed, translated, and/or coded them. We would like to acknowledge the funding of the Social Sciences and Humanities Research Council of Canada Grant "Gender Migration and the Work of Care," No: 895-2012-1021.

C. Cranford (✉) · J.J. Chun
Department of Sociology, University of Toronto, Toronto, ON, Canada

© The Author(s) 2017
S. Michel, I. Peng (eds.), *Gender, Migration, and the Work of Care*,
DOI 10.1007/978-3-319-55086-2_3

41

elder care. Furthermore, we now have complex analyses of care work as a hybrid of labor and love that bridge the notion of love and money as "hostile worlds" and recognize the nurturant aspects of care work as a form of gendered labor (Zelizer 2000; also Constable 2009; Lan 2002; Stacey and Ayers 2012; Ungerson 1999). Yet, we lack knowledge about how the predominantly low-paid and racialized workforce of care workers negotiate and make sense of such hybrid conditions, especially as the state plays a more expansive role in funding and regulating care provider programs for low-income elderly people.

In this chapter, we examine how the complex social and institutional conditions of home-based elder care shape and reshape workers' understandings of care work as both paid employment and gendered labor. Two key questions drive our inductive analysis, which draws upon in-depth, semi-structured interviews conducted with Chinese immigrant women who provide publicly subsidized, home-based elder care to other Chinese immigrants in Oakland, California's Chinatown community. Whom do workers view as their employers when providing publicly funded, home-based elder care, including workers who are family providers? How does the state's role in partially subsidizing and regulating home-based care provision in private homes, including in collective bargaining negotiations with labor unions, influence workers' understandings of care work?

We focus on the low-income urban immigrant community of Oakland Chinatown to deepen understanding about how aging immigrant populations coincide with increasing numbers of immigrant women employed as personal support workers under California's In-Home Supportive Services (IHSS). The IHSS program, which began in the 1970s, enables poor, elderly, and disabled people to live independently in their own homes by subsidizing the cost of hiring personal support workers. IHSS recipients can hire family members or friends or find workers through non-profit or for-profit agencies to assist with activities of daily living, such as showering, shopping, cooking, cleaning, and visiting the doctor. For IHSS workers who care for aging parents and relatives, IHSS jobs provide a unique form of income, supporting the cost of home-based elder care while also serving as a source of wages. IHSS jobs represent a form of low-paid, precarious work in that IHSS jobs pay little, lack benefits, and expose workers to a higher likelihood of unpaid overtime, irregular schedules, and abusive working conditions. Interestingly, however, IHSS jobs also provide representation and benefits through the Service Employees International Union, which won the historic right to unionize California's

IHSS workforce in 1999, creating an unexpected source of unionization for workers who may have never previously joined a union.

The following case study contributes to broader efforts to conceptualize how the rapid expansion of the paid elder-care workforce both depends upon and reshapes the intersectional dynamics of gender, ethnicity, migration, and class. In doing so, it seeks not only to advance the importance of intersectional theorizing in the everyday lives of immigrant women of color but also to identify the potential for more just forms of work and organization through solidaristic collective action.

THEORETICAL FRAMEWORK

Scholars whose analysis builds from paid domestic work provided to White middle-class families by women of color and immigrant women interpret care work as a devalued form of reproductive labor that is gendered and racialized (Glenn 1992, 2010; Lan 2002; Bakan and Stasiulis 2012; Parreñas 2015). By showing how poor Black women and immigrant women of color in the USA were channeled into doing the "dirty" work of cleaning, cooking, and caring in private homes, researchers such as Glenn (2010, 7) provided foundational analysis about paid domestic work as a system of racialized gendered servitude that compels one party to provide services for another through *de jure* and *de facto* inequalities. Other scholars later globalized this framework, further theorizing how global economic and racial hierarchies between and among women in the Global North and Global South translated into an "international division of reproductive labor" (Parreñas 2015), a "new world domestic order" (Hondagneu-Sotelo 2007) and a "transnational political economy of care" (Williams 2011). While examining racial and gendered hierarchies within or across national spaces, scholars focus on how individualized employment relationships subject women in unequal relations of power and domination to tense and sometimes abusive relationships (Anderson 2000; Parreñas 2015).

The rapid expansion of the elder care workforce in the context of the soaring aging population shifted public and scholarly attention from studies of domestic work as a legacy of slavery and servitude to relational conceptualizations of care work. Many who theorize care as gendered labor place more emphasis on the interdependent and positive nurturing relations that, ideally, define quality care (Cancian and

Oliker 2000; Tronto and Fisher 1990). Inclusion of the nurturance dimension of gendered labor is especially important for analyzing state-funded care, given that it is provided to populations in need who are also generally poor, at least in the USA. However, as Duffy (2005) argues, the conceptualization of care as nurturance underestimates the implications of the racialization of care work—the fact that the most devalued forms are predominantly done by immigrant women of color. We thus draw on more recent work that bridges, conceptually, the "hostile worlds" of love and money (Zelizer 2000). Boris and Klein (2012, 19), for example, have shown how the position of publicly funded "visiting housekeeper" in the 1930s Works Progress Administration Program was constructed by state policy and funding as that of "neither nurse nor maid," but rather as a hybrid of work and welfare intended both to employ and provide household help to poor and needy mothers.

To embrace an intersectional analysis that examines care work as *both* coercive and nurturing, we build upon Glenn's (2010) two-dimensional framework, which identifies distinct yet overlapping systems of coercion in the social organization of care: racialized gendered servitude and gendered status obligations. While racial difference does not necessarily define the lived experiences of subordination between and among poor immigrants of color who occupy the role of both provider and recipient, the social dynamics of labor market inequality limit immigrant women workers' ability to access higher-paid jobs with job security and career mobility, thereby reproducing conditions akin to racialized gendered servitude rooted in extreme labor market inequalities of gender, ethnicity, migration, and class (Chun and Cranford 2016). "Status obligation," according to Glenn, is rooted in a system of coercion in which one's social status, such as that of wife or daughter, obliges women to provide unpaid care. Such gendered logics also work to devalue paid forms of care labor as informal and precarious.

In the case of Chinese immigrants, the gendered logics around filial piety—which traditionally view daughters-in-law as the main party responsible for serving elders in a hierarchical relationship—may be invoked to justify women's everyday responsibility for the direct care of aging parents (Lan 2002, 814, citing Liu 1998).[1] Even when family and household units are reconfigured through political and economic changes such as migration and globalization, filial duty can operate as a cultural ideal (Lan 2002; Zhan and Montgomery 2003). In her studies of Taiwanese families in Taiwan and California, Lan finds that many adult children have subcontracted the work of elder care to migrant women workers, yet they still maintain their fulfillment of filial obligations by keeping their parents at home and paying for care. Direct care is often provided by poor, migrant women subjected to low pay, irregular schedules, discretionary working conditions, and restrictive labor and citizenship rights, thus making filial duty compatible with exploitative forms of migrant labor.

The state's role in supporting elder care may perpetuate entrenched norms about gendered status obligation and filial duty. Stacey and Ayers (2012) argue that family providers are generally ashamed of receiving state funding to care for family members, reflecting the American logic of the "hostile worlds" of love and money and the stigmatization of welfare, but those active in the union often reframe their work as contributing to the public good as did non-family providers. Lan (2002) finds that poor Taiwanese immigrant families who receive state funding to take care of their elders view the state as the "filial son" that allows them to continue their gendered duty to care for elderly parents at home, thus transforming but not eroding the practices and meanings of filial duty.

In the empirical discussion that follows, we build on these studies to examine how migration intersects with state policies and programs to shape the meaning and practice of care work as both coercive and nurturing labor. Workers' views that the recipient is, or should be, the primary employer responsible for pay, hours, and conditions, are more in line with the coercive reproductive labor framework in locating conflict within an individual household employer-domestic servant relationship. In contrast, the notion that there is no employer, that this is not employment, or that the pay or hours of work are sufficient, could reflect either a coercive gendered obligation or care as nurturing. Thus, to evaluate the usefulness of these existing frameworks for understanding this work, we need to delve into the micro-relational level. The reproductive labor framework would consider workers' reports of disrespect or abuse from recipients as continuous with coercive relations of gendered obligation or racialized gendered servitude, for family and non-family providers respectively, whereas workers' reports of positive relationships and rewarding emotional work with recipients are more in line with the care-as-nurturance framework. In the following sections, we demonstrate that understanding the meaning of work in this case requires extending both of these frameworks to consider the state and the labor movement as key actors alongside providers and receivers of care. In doing so, we show how this work is made sense of by these women as a unique combination of labor-welfare-love.

RESEARCH DESIGN

Our empirical discussion draws primarily upon twenty in-depth, semi-structured interviews conducted with Chinese immigrant women workers who provide home-based elder care to other Chinese immigrants in or near Oakland Chinatown between 2014 and 2015. The interviews, which lasted approximately 60–90 minutes each, were conducted in a bi-lingual format by the co-authors through translators and in a mono-lingual Cantonese or Mandarin format by graduate student research assistants. All interviews were transcribed in the original languages, translated into English, and coded into NVivo. Pseudonyms are used to protect participants' identity. Cranford also conducted interviews in English with key informants from the IHSS, unions, and community groups supporting immigrant elderly and care workers to contextualize worker interviews.

Interviews were conducted in cooperation with our community research partner, Asian Immigrant Women Advocates (AIWA), who facilitated the outreach, recruitment, and coordination of the worker interviews and provided referrals to key informants. AIWA is a grass-roots community organization located in Oakland Chinatown that seeks to empower low-income Asian immigrant women workers to improve their living and working conditions through community organizing, popular education and grassroots leadership development (Chun et al. 2013; Chun 2016). AIWA works primarily with low-income Chinese immigrant women with limited English-language ability who do low-paid, insecure and socially devalued jobs in the ethnic economy. Since 2010, AIWA has focused on the growing in-home personal care work among its constituency and sought to understand how Chinese immigrant women can bring greater worker voice to improving the unstable and often arbitrary conditions of this work. Our interviews are part of a collaborative effort to better understand the complexities of IHSS home care work in the Oakland Chinatown community, a case about which the scholarly and policy communities have little research knowledge.

In-Home Personal Care Work in California's Oakland Chinatown

The social organization of care work in California's IHSS sector is shaped by a fractured employment relationship and confusion over the issue of exactly "who is the employer" (Chun 2009; Cranford 2005). As IHSS recipients, poor and elderly or disabled people are assessed by social workers and allotted a certain number of hours of care, and the state pays the worker directly, taking out income taxes, social security, and workers' compensation. IHSS work has some similarities to domestic work in that, in California, the recipient is considered a legal employer for the purposes of hiring, firing, and supervising workers. However, California's IHSS sector represents an innovative re-regulation of the fractured employment relationship (Delp and Quan 2002). Although IHSS recipients hire their own providers (whether relatives or friends or through an agency), they are not considered the sole employers. In 1999, after ten years of organizing workers and building coalitions with disability and senior movements, the Service Employees International Union (SEIU) won legislation at the state level that recognizes the multiple entities that shape working conditions. The person receiving services is considered the employer for the purposes of hiring, firing, and supervision, but the government is deemed the Employer of Record, thus allowing workers and unions to bargain collectively over wages and benefits. At the time of research, the union in Alameda County, where Oakland is located, was the United Long Term Care Workers Union (ULTCWU).[2] Importantly to its alliance with disability and senior movements, the union does not strike or bargain over conditions in home workplaces.

The employment relationship is additionally complicated in California because the state will pay one's family member to provide these services. In this way, the state activates a particular paid-unpaid hybrid. The IHSS program, which is housed within the county government's Department of Public Social Services, still assesses eligibility for services, determines the number of hours to be provided, and pays the workers upon receipt of time sheets submitted by the recipient-employer. It also operates a registry where workers/recipients can look for jobs/workers and provides some voluntary training to recipients as well as an orientation to workers. However, given the familial obligations that mediate the provision of parental care, the IHSS program relies heavily on informal kinship networks to secure paid, personal support workers. We interviewed four providers who had provided IHSS services only to family, four who had both family and non-family clients, and twelve who had only non-family clients. We interviewed seventeen women and three men and all of the men had only been family providers.

Adding another layer of complexity, the employer is marginalized as the recipient of state-funded services and through relations of disability and age (Cranford and Miller 2013; Twigg 2000). The racialized social location of the employer-recipients in this study further marginalizes them, making them even less akin to the traditional definition of an employer. Most elderly Chinese immigrants in our study reside in or near Oakland Chinatown, a historic region of racial segregation that continues to have disproportionately high levels of unemployment and poverty as well as poor housing and working conditions. All but a few of our respondents had arrived during or after the 1990s, yet all were tied to long chains of family migration linking late nineteenth- and early twentieth-century waves of Chinese migration to California with post-1965 flows that were reactivated after the elimination of race-based immigration quotas for Asians. The more recent Chinese immigrants had fewer English-language skills and relatively low social and human capital compared to some other immigrant groups that arrived after 1965. Despite extreme racial segregation in housing and public life, which resulted in the discriminatory development of ethnic economies, these immigrants also benefit from the residential and commercial infrastructure of ethnic communities such as Oakland Chinatown, which provide survival jobs and access to relatively autonomous businesses, civic groups, community organizations and, as we show here, care systems.

These dense community ties can be seen in the IHSS sector. Given their limited English and homogenous social networks, most elderly Chinese immigrants who reside in low-income urban ethnic communities such as Oakland Chinatown start receiving IHSS benefits only after the intervention of an immigrant service organization that provides crucial information about state benefits and programs. In many cases, this process is initiated by daughters or daughters-in-law who have already taken on the responsibility of providing home-based care for their elderly relatives and then learn, through a network of Chinese-speaking nurses, doctors and care professionals, that they are eligible for public subsidies under the IHSS program. Chinese elderly immigrants rarely access the IHSS registry to find personal support workers. Rather, they rely on informal family and neighborhood ties to find care providers.

Elderly Chinese immigrants in our study are marginalized within the broader IHSS recipient population, but, like other individual recipients, they have been designated by the state as employers for the purposes of hiring, firing, and supervision. As with most householder-employers, recipients of IHSS face little legal or social pressure to abide by existing legislation that regulates working conditions, and legislation covering this sector is also weak. Furthermore, research on ethnic economies suggests that ethnic employers might best be considered "middlemen" whose marginal social location within the broader racialized economy can in turn shape their exploitation of co-ethic workers and family (Bonacich 1973; Chin 2013; Kwong 1997). While exploitative co-ethnic employers are more common in places such as garment factories and ethnic markets and restaurants, they are not absent from the complex relationships between marginal employers and marginal workers, with state power layered on top, examined in this study.

The Work of In-Home Personal Care

The Fractured Employment Relationship

The issue of who is the employer within a fractured employment relationship, and the impact of this fracturing on labor market and income insecurity, were articulated strongly by the women we interviewed. Respondents understood that the government and the recipients were legally recognized as employers for different purposes but family and non-family providers differed in their emphasis on who was the main employer, indicating a different view of power relations.

Not one family provider felt the recipient was the primary employer, thus distinguishing this work from the direct power relation between householder and servant, yet they also did not view this work as not employment at all, or solely in the nurturance realm. Instead, most emphasized the state as the primary, but not only, employer, while a couple put equal emphasis on the state and the recipient in the employment relationship. A complex intermingling of welfare and love was evident in the narratives. For example, Jiaxuan was paid to take care of her mother and father and never had non-family clients. When asked if the government was her employer, she did not hesitate to say yes, stating: "[IHSS] gives me a small amount of money to care for my parents.... The employer is the one who gives me the work hours." When then asked if she considered her parents her employers in any way, she hesitated, laughed and said, "The employers...they...I don't know. They are both my parents and employers, sometimes!" Her hesitation reflects a discomfort with considering her parents as her employers, which is compatible with a view of this work as within the realm of coercive, gendered obligation, yet the role of the state in determining the hours of service allows Jiaxuan to simultaneously view her work as state-supported family welfare.

The views of non-family providers offer other perspectives on power and coercion within this fractured employment relationship. Non-family members included a few who viewed the elderly recipients as the predominant employer and a couple who viewed the state as predominant, but the majority emphasized both entities. Xuiyan, who had two clients and never worked for family members, felt "the elderly is not the real boss," though she acknowledged the power they have over workers since "they have the right to hire us and the right to fire us." She also felt, however, that since "the government pays,...the real employer is of course the government." Other non-family providers placed more emphasis on the power given to recipient-employers, even while they recognized that the government both determined the hours and paid them. Indeed, this program is designed to ensure that recipients have influence over who provides them such intimate services, but at the same time the state controls the amount of care they receive and how providers are compensated. As a result, these workers can also claim that the state should be considered the employer, which sets this work apart from the typical reproductive labor focused on householder-individual worker relations. Thus from the perspectives of both non-family and family providers on who is the employer, we might consider this work as a hybrid form shaped by state welfare. The complex meaning of this work is further evident in an analysis of working conditions.

Working Conditions

Our interviewees raised many issues regarding compensation and lack thereof. At the time of this study, the hourly wage for IHSS work in Oakland was $12.50. This wage increased with unionization and was higher than in most California counties. However, it was still well below the living wage of $15 per hour called for by economic justice advocates. Furthermore, given inadequate hours of work, issues of compensation include overall earnings and benefits.

One of the biggest issues raised by the women we interviewed was working hours beyond paid time. This was especially extreme among family providers. The amount of paid time received by family providers ranged from two to four hours a day, but they reported working much longer hours and a feeling of being on-call "24/7." Their narratives suggest that the intermingling of gendered duty with insufficient state welfare facilitates unpaid labor for the state. But their views also show that these women do not passively accept this work as only gendered duty and welfare, but value it as labor as well. Jiahua was paid up to four hours a day to take care of her mother, yet in actuality, she worked ten hours a day, seven days a week. She explained her situation as follows:

> The part that I do according to the time sheet is the job I work for the government.... Bonding, that is, filial piety, is separated from work. Overtime, that is, I extend the working hours because of filial piety.... In addition to the fact that it is a job, there is also an element of filial piety in doing this job. I'm not saying that I'm willing to do this job. It's that I need to fulfill our tradition of filial piety.... I must do this. If there is pay [though], it would definitely be better.

For Jiahua, working unpaid overtime is not a choice but a gendered filial duty, yet she also asserts that care work is valued labor that deserves adequate compensation.

Only three family providers used the language of filial piety to describe their family obligation to care, but others spoke of taking care of elderly relatives in a similar matter-of-fact way—as what daughters in Chinese families are supposed to do, despite the fact that the practice of filial obligation has changed with the changing organization of care, as indicated in other studies (Lan 2002; Qi 2014; Zhan and Montgomery 2003). Such changes are evident in our study as well: while two of the family providers were women taking care of their mothers-in-law, others were taking care of their own parents, and the sample includes two men providing the hands-on care for a mother, and a father-in-law. Xibi was paid approximately four hours a day to take care of her mother but she usually worked "twenty-four hours a day" without additional pay. When asked if she received sufficient hours, she pointed to the ways the state reinforced this gendered filial obligation, stating: "Oh, you can pretend that there are enough.... But the government only gives you so many so you have to work with [how many hours you get]." Even in the more traditional practice of a daughter-in-law taking care of a mother-in-law, as is the case with Zhaoli, insufficient funding provision results in a mingling of relations of love-welfare-labor. When Zhaoli told us of the recent cut of everyone's hours by 7 percent, we asked if this made it harder for her mother-in-law, or for her. She indicated her mother-in-law would still get what she needs:

> It's really a responsibility when I still have to keep an eye on her during my day off or holidays.... So you can't really count the hours. It's family, my family.... [But], it also is really like work, because other people have holidays and they can go outside to eat in a restaurant, but I still have to cook for her during holidays.

When asked if she resented this additional burden, Zhaoli indicated that she did not see work and family obligation as contradictory but rather suggested that both are part of filial duty. However, such duty did not prevent her from emphasizing the need for the state to strengthen its support for family care providers by providing more paid hours and higher pay.

Working over paid time was also pervasive among workers with non-family clients, but most of these workers identified its source as both the state and limited labor market opportunities. Unpaid overtime was particularly common for those caring for clients who needed 24-hour care, which the government did not fund. Sometimes the recipient's family supplemented IHSS paid hours with cash payments, but even if they did, the supplements generally did not cover all the hours worked. Chouyu described a client who needed 24-hour care but was allocated only 280 hours/month. She and another worker both worked approximately three hours a day over paid time to provide 24-hour care. According to Chouyu, the direct pressure to work unpaid overtime came from the adult children of her employer-recipient, yet the indirect pressure came from her lack of options in finding an alternative job. She stated matter-of-factly: "If you can't find anything [else], then you have to do it." Similarly, Yangfang explains that when she first began working as a home care worker:

> Some clients would exploit you because they knew you were not familiar with the regulations. For example, they might ask you to help them buy groceries but not count those hours as work hours. But buying groceries takes a lot of time. So I worked more hours than I was paid for.

These and other examples show how limited labor market opportunities for older Asian immigrant women combined with insufficient state funding to create conditions of care work that reflect an intermingling of coercive reproductive labor and state welfare.

The hybridity of this work was also evident at the interactional, emotional level, this time in the coupling of daily relations of coercing and nurturing. The vast majority of the respondents who had non-family clients reported affronts to their dignity instigated by the recipient-employer consistent with coercive relations of reproductive labor, namely in the form of "scolding" or biting critique, accusations of theft, or requests to do menial work beyond what most consider part of this job. Only two spoke of relationships with recipient-employers only in nurturance terms, emphasizing only affection, care, or mutual respect. Even if it was during paid time, most non-family providers resented being asked to do work that they felt was menial, especially since it was difficult to challenge requests to do work tasks that were excluded from the IHSS task list. Xueyan expressed resentment about a "very bad" employer who told her to "do laundry by hand and wash the clothes in the bath tub." She explained, "I know that doing laundry by hand violates regulations.... It should not be done by hand." Xiaoqing recalled a similar incident when her non-family client instructed Xiaoqing "to wash her grandson's clothes by hand." For Xiaoqing, and others, the fact that she was "treated like a maid" and expected to do such menial work suggest continuity with coercive reproductive labor in that blame is laid with the individual householder-employer.

At the same time, however, coercive relations intermingled with nurturing ones for non-family providers. Positive and rewarding relations with some recipient-employers were mentioned even by those who expressed deep resentment about unfair and coercive aspects of care work. Chouyu lucidly articulated this problematic, stating:

> Taking care of seniors, you have to take a lot of attitude. The mental and emotional pressure is great. If you meet the right senior, it is good. But, if the senior is not good, they scold you till you faint; nag you 'til you go crazy.... Sometimes they scold you to the point where you don't dare to disagree or talk back to them. You can only go outside and take a deep breath before you go back in to work... Some of them are good, some of them are troublesome. But usually they are good.

When asked how close she was to her current clients, Xiaoqing said, "they are pretty good, maybe because I am a caring person. I treat them with patience.... If they are happy, I am happy. No stress." Similarly, Yangfang, who spoke at length about her mistreatment and exploitation by previous recipients, said the following about her current client: "Since I know computers, I teach them to her. She also teaches me how to cook, and can cook really well. She often asks me to eat first, which makes me feel guilty. Overall, I am happy with the current situation."

Non-family providers' responses to affronts to their dignity, and the reasons behind them, pointed to an additional and more complex, intermingling of coercive and nurturing relations. Many put up with affronts to their dignity both because of lack of other opportunities in the labor market and empathy for older people that they, sometimes strategically, develop while doing this intimate work. When asked what defines a good home care worker, Aling said:

> Every time they ask you to do something, you should try to do it well. You'd not refuse to do anything. Some [workers] refuse to touch [the elderly] because they are dirty. However, people sometimes need a hug. Sometimes you touch their hands. Then you feel close to each other. Don't have like this type of boundary and they will feel like you are like kin....
>
> If you treat them like your mother and if they treat you like their daughter, then there will be fewer conflicts and misunderstanding.

Here the emphasis is squarely on nurturing relations. Yet, in another part of the interview, Aling revealed the need to foster nurturing relations to keep her job. She said:

> So, we can only explain to the elderly that we don't steal their belongings.... However, they didn't believe it. They told others and people introducing home care jobs that [I stole]. This is irritating and harms my reputation.... No matter how close you are to them, they are always closer to their own family.... They say you are their family, but in reality they don't treat you like their family. They treat you like a maid (工人). All elderly are the same. Having a close relationship with them only means that there is less conflict.... I believe that most home care workers don't argue back. In other words, I have a job while you have someone serving you.

Reputation is central because additional clients are secured through word of mouth within the Chinese immigrant community. Partly for this reason, some workers put up with poor treatment while others quit, but even quitting is difficult due not only to lack of other options but to the development of nurturing relations. Xueyan had come to accept the habit of her longtime recipient-employer who insisted on boiling all her food. Xueyan accommodated the habit even though she felt boiling food was less nutritious. Their good relationship, however, also allowed her to make suggestions on some issues as a sign of their intimacy and personal connection, a feeling of closeness she felt was mutual. She gave examples of socializing outside strict work boundaries, such as inviting each other to dinner when they had something to celebrate, which, she felt, was "quite comfortable for both of us." Engaging in an iterative process of developing nurturing, often familistic, relations with recipient-employers in order to do this job well was considered a key component of care work, which in turn was necessary for employment security.

Family providers' daily relations also reflected a hybrid of coercion and nurturing, this time coupling elements of gendered obligation and affection. Family providers spoke significantly about stress due to the 24/7 responsibility of providing home-based care, as alluded to above. When this was coupled with "scolding" by the recipient-family-employer, the situation was highly stressful. As Jiaxuan put it:

> This job is stressful because you don't know whether you can handle the job well. Because my parents are adults, they are less willing to compromise. But sometimes they behave like babies. When they scold you, you don't know where to vent your frustration. So caring for family members is the most difficult.

When asked about her relationship with her mother-in-law, Chouyu explained that even though her mother only has three paid IHSS hours, "she wants a lot of things," and the way she would ask for them led Chouyu to feel she was "not very nice." After recalling such difficulties, we asked Chouyu if the relationship was more like a working relationship or a family one. She responded: "It is both, I guess. If it was just a working relationship why would I do so much for her? We were thinking of hiring someone, but we couldn't find anyone, and she didn't want [anyone else] either." This quote suggests that insufficient state funding reinforces filial piety in terms of coercive gendered duty, and in doing so, can undermine the development of nurturing relations. Other family providers spoke of the stress of filial obligations in terms of being on call 24/7, but when they discussed daily relations, they did not relate extreme bossiness but instead emphasized flexibility and negotiation. Yet, one provider who interacted with many others, given a leadership position in the community, said the following, suggesting that Chouyu's experience is not that uncommon: "Some of the elderly recipients are demanding and even family members request a lot. 'You cannot take off Sundays, still need to come otherwise I don't want you.'" While our sample of family providers is too small to draw strong conclusions, collectively our evidence clearly indicates we should not assume that relations of nurturance are already present, or will develop, within filial obligations.

The fact that both family and non-family providers reported some good relationships with recipient-employers provides the basis for alliance between workers and recipients. Indeed, this alliance was essential to the re-regulation of employment to consider the state an employer alongside recipients, and it continues to be important in order to pressure the state for adequate funding (Cranford 2014; Delp and Quan 2002). We might expect solidarity among workers and recipients to be even stronger within an ethnically homogeneous community, but this is not automatically the case, given that both family and non-family providers also report difficulties with recipient-employers. This raises the question of what types of collective action are necessary to improve conditions at the relational level as well as in terms of security and compensation.

Improving Conditions Through the Union

The workers frequently sought to address problems arising from their employment individually, but they also spoke of the union as providing collective power. Several described their participation in mass demonstrations and protests at the county IHSS offices, the state capital and in other cities. For example, when asked about the benefits of unionization, Fuzhen said, "At least there is someone to speak out for us. Our voice becomes a bit louder. Our Alameda Home Care Union has more than eighteen thousand people."[3]

Collective voice and collective action made the women feel empowered. They experienced this empowerment as immigrant women and in reference to their experience and memory of China. Jiaxuan described the union like this:

We don't have this kind of union in China, in mainland China.... You could speak publicly at the protest. If not, you could follow the music and dance!... Okay, how the union has helped me? It works like a team! If you didn't have a leader, the rank and file would become a heap of loose sand. The union is like the leader, leading the members to take action.... SEIU, it's good! It unifies [the workers].

Collective action has not only made these women feel empowered, but also augmented their ability to change their conditions in meaningful ways. According to Hayin, "the union helps us win better wages and benefits." Hayin and others linked these wins to gaining power. Discussing her participation in protest, Yangfang was asked if the union had changed her. She replied, "I was timid in China, but I have become braver to fight for my rights since I arrived in the U.S. We succeeded at winning the pay rise after the protest in Alameda." This suggests linkages between empowerment as immigrant women and power to change one's conditions. Similarly, Jiahua was galvanized by a recent compensation gain due, in part, to protests:

Starting from January, the first of next year, we are given hours for [clients'] doctor's visit. We are also paid for the time spent on the road. These things have not existed for the past twelve, thirteen years or so. The union fought for these things for us. We went to the demonstration to fight for these things for ourselves.... We'll keep marching until the government gives us more hours.

In the context of funding cuts in California, workers and their union must keep up pressure on the state through ongoing mass protest. The women's experience of gaining power through protests was bolstered by specific gains—like the wage increase—but it went beyond that to broader, and longer, struggles for full compensation and reached deeper to personal transformations as immigrant women workers.

Women also spoke of the union as a source of help with navigating the home care system. They contrasted the fact that the union had Chinese speakers on staff and held meetings in Chinese and in Chinatown, with the lengthy process of trying to get a Chinese translator at the IHSS offices, which is 45 minutes by car or much longer by train and then bus from Chinatown. They positively evaluated the union for helping them intervene with the IHSS on issues such as late payments, and they felt union staff and other members helped in terms of being able to talk about difficult relations with recipient-employers and inform workers of their rights.

They also underscored, however, how the union was unable to challenge difficult recipient-employers, suggesting continuity with domestic work. For example Fuzhen, who lived with her non-family recipient-employer, went to the union when the employer and his family sought to restrict her ability to take a second job. She explained:

> I told the union how few hours I get from this senior.... The union got in touch with me and told me I was not infringing on IHSS policy,...that I could work 300 hours a month.... After I told them what the union said, the family was more reluctant to bring up this issue because I had the backing of the union.... They do, however, still say they can find someone who would work for less.

Fuzhen was hopeful that the union could assist her in enforcing IHSS policy, even in a live-in situation, but she also worried that doing so would get her fired. Similarly, as part of a conversation, Xueyan alluded to a particularly abusive recipient-employer for whom she had worked and who was notorious for firing workers:

> Filing a complaint almost means you will lose your job. How can the government solve this problem? How does the government control the elderly?...Talking to the union is also useless for something like this.... The union knows that the government stands on the side of the elderly so [these problems] cannot be resolved.

Similarly, Haiyin stated, "There is nowhere for us to make complaints, so our legal rights are not protected." Xiaoqing focused on the need for broader employment security: "There are many unemployed home care workers. However, the union hasn't found jobs for them, so it is not very helpful." Likewise, Chouyu simply said, "You want them to help you find a job but they don't do that." These interviews confirm the importance of the union's focus on the state (Delp and Quan 2002). Workers also indicated, however, the need for organizing on a more intimate scale to help foster good working relationships with recipient-employers.

Taking Action Through Community-Based Organizations

The women were asked if there were some problems a union could not help with but that a community organization could. Some women spoke of community organizations as providing important social support, to break the isolation of working one-on-one with elderly people in private homes. Yingzi, for instance, contrasted the social atmosphere in her previous Chinatown restaurant job with the isolation of home care and said this about her participation in AIWA, which included attending the home care workers' group: "[You work], face to face, never going into the outside world. So that is why I go often to AIWA, to see the people, to make myself a bit younger." Others emphasized how both AIWA and the union provided mutual support.

Several spoke of the value of community organizations as providing training and broader political education, and the linkages between the two. They valued training on health and safety, cooking, English, and computers. In contrast, they complained, neither the IHSS nor the union provided sufficient training that was accessible and in their language. The free classes offered through AIWA not only taught better English, computer skills, and how to avoid back injuries, but the immigrant women workers experienced them as a form of learning that challenged the disadvantages tied to their social location. For example, when we asked Yingzi why she was active mobilizing other workers through AIWA's home care workers group, she said:

> Well, because, when I came to the U.S. I didn't know anything, didn't know English.... Even social interactions, I lost that as well. By myself I felt really dumb, really slow. So the only thing I could do was participate in these community activities....

Thus, community-based worker organizations bring a specialized focus on immigrant workers.

Several of our informants emphasized the unique value of AIWA as an immigrant *women's* organization. Some focused on the political action coming out of personal gendered family and work relations, emphasizing that AIWA's focus on immigrant women allowed it to better address immigrant women's rights and broader issues of compensation endemic to home care work. Xiaoqing, complaining that the union was unable to help workers get compensation for unpaid overtime, felt that AIWA could help here because it "focuses on the rights and benefits of women." Jiaxuan suggested that community organizations add specific value for immigrant women, explaining:

> AIWA mainly serves women, while SEIU services both women and men . . . .
> You know, home care work is a demanding job. Caring at home makes me
> feel, as I keep doing it, that it is limiting my horizons. So I have joined
> AIWA to participate in their activities and to share experiences with other
> people, which is good.

Jiaxuan and others spoke of challenging the devaluation of home-based work through community organizing. AIWA's feminist lens makes it a site for imagining a more valued and less isolated form of care work (see also Chun et al. 2013).

Several workers suggested that a community organization might be better able to address problems with difficult recipient-employers than the union. For example, as part of a conversation about the union's inability to address "illegal or unreasonable" conduct by recipient-employers, Jiahua was asked if the workers needed a community-based organization to help address these problems. She replied:

> Yes, establish such an organization even if this organization cannot actually
> help, it can prevent clients from making threats and from harassing us. Some
> people are really bad, right? Or maybe some home care workers are not that
> nice either, right? . . . So [the] elderly should be able to have opportunities
> to complain about us, and we should be able to complain about them.

In order to probe the potential for more collectivized reciprocal relations, the women were asked if it would be good to have a community organization that brought together the elderly recipient-employers and home care workers. Several workers concurred, either implicitly or explicitly. Xiaoqing agreed with Jiahua, quoted above, stating that an organization that supported both workers and recipients could help resolve problems between them, beyond individual one-on-one negotiations. Fuzhen suggested that when home care workers and clients join together, they can "push the government" to improve the service and the work. The latter has been the basis of the alliance between the union and senior and disability movements (Delp and Quan 2002).

Others were not sure about bringing together workers and the elderly and instead emphasized community among workers. Yangfang said, "I want to have at least one or two annual gatherings that gather home care workers and facilitate exchanges of experience among workers on how to take care of the elderly." Yangfang was not sure whether a community organization or the union would be best to facilitate such an exchange, but AIWA's home care workers' group does just that. When asked if the elderly should be involved in this exchange, however, Yangfang said, "No, because the workers will become reserved and unhappy," thus suggesting that workers need a separate space to talk with one another about difficulties caring for elderly and strategies to address them. As Xueyan put it, "It's difficult to say whether or not one is on the same side as the elderly. Everybody has a different take, and it's hard to say whether or not there is solidarity [with the elderly]."

This suggests that a community organization that can incorporate an understanding of varied relationships is needed to improve the conditions of home care work.

CONCLUSION

We have examined the meaning and experience of care work for Chinese immigrant women who provide home-based personal care to elderly Chinese immigrants in one community. To understand the contours of this work, we asked whether it reflected the reproductive labor framework emphasizing coercive relations through racialized gendered servitude for paid work, or gendered obligation for unpaid work (Glenn 2010; Hondagneu-Sotelo 2007; Parreñas 2015; Bakan and Stasiulis 2012), or if state funding for poor, elderly citizens and co-ethnic relations served to initiate a significant shift toward positive and rewarding relationships between care providers and care receivers as emphasized in the care-as-nurturance framework (Cancian and Oliker 2000; Tronto and Fisher 1990). We analyzed how multiple actors shape the meaning of this government-funded employment by examining whom the workers considered to be their employers, whether they were paid enough and had sufficient hours, daily tensions or rewards at work, and how conditions at all these levels might be improved. Workers' views on these topics did not fit neatly into either of these two dominant frameworks. We thus argue that in order to capture the involvement of the state and the labor movement as key actors in the employment relationship, we need to extend both of these frameworks.

The meaning of work for Chinese immigrant women workers paid by the state to look after Chinese poor elderly immigrants points to a complex intermingling of relations of coercive work, welfare, and love obligation. Family providers' view of the state as the key actor responsible for ensuring work and paying for it modifies, but does not destroy, meanings of this work as obligatory gendered love by coupling it with the notion of this work as labor worthy of state welfare. Non-family providers' greater attention to the recipient-employer role alongside that of the state reflects a mixture of this work as tied to coercive labor for them yet also worthy of state welfare. Our analysis suggests that, despite an innovative regulation of this work to include the state as an employer alongside recipients, insufficient state responsibility for providing collective care to elderly citizens has created a unique integration of precarious reproductive labor, nurturing care and state welfare. Interview participants articulate how, despite the regulation and compensation offered by IHSS, insufficient funding exacerbates the insecurity, instability and stress of this fractured employment relationship. In addition to low pay, women were consistently working unpaid hours due to the kinds of care work that go uncompensated such as providing emotional support, working on call, and doing tasks that are not easily quantified. At the interactional-emotional level, non-family and family providers alike note a range of both tense and rewarding relationships with recipient-employers, suggesting a complex labor-love hybrid. Nurturing and rewarding relationships existed for most workers some of the time, but they often coincided with harsh critiques from recipient-employers, including family recipients. This underscores how co-ethnic relations do not necessarily shield workers from subservient treatment and points to the need for future research into the conditions under which marginalized employer-recipients attempt to transfer some of their oppression to care workers, and the conditions under which alliances between the two can be sustained.

The employment relationship of this state-funded personal care involves more actors and more variation among actors than other forms of care work, and this brings potential to challenge the inequalities of racialized gendered reproductive labor. Specifically, because the state is a key actor, not just regulator and funder but also (*one* of the) employer(s), the labor movement, along with the disability and senior movements, has been able to achieve a form of regulation that has improved the conditions of these workers by allowing for unionization. However, similarities with the conditions emphasized in the reproductive labor framework remain. This is in part due to workers' limited opportunities in a racialized and gendered labor market, due to a combination of the outsourcing of more stable and better paid manufacturing jobs, racial and age discrimination, limited English and low levels of education (Chun and Cranford 2016). In this chapter, we show how continuity with coercive conditions at the relational level is also related to insufficient state funding, as well as the inability of the union, and unwillingness of the state, to regulate daily relations in the home workplaces. Engagement in or support for collective action against the state is consistent with the view of this work as including coercive relations that are perpetuated by the organization of state welfare. Yet, the emphasis on the need for the state to regulate not only wages and employment but also relations with recipient-employers, including when they are family, suggests the fruitfulness of conceptualizing this work as a more complex intermingling of coercive labor-state welfare-love obligation, especially if we are to improve its conditions at all levels.

The conditions of paid home care work reflect persistent forms of social and economic subordination for immigrant women workers, but the unionization of home care work has created an important source of institutional support. The women we interviewed spoke of the power of the union to give them voice through mass collective action and win higher wages and important benefits. They understood this power as connected to empowerment as immigrant women workers. They also valued the union as an information conduit and as an advocate within the state bureaucracies that regulate and fund their work and, as employers, help determine their employment conditions. At the same time, the women noted the inability of the union to intervene with difficult recipient-employers. AIWA's feminist empowerment model, emerging from longstanding work with immigrant women workers, could help transform the most private of these troubles into public demands for quality care-work-family-community relations in the context of care for aging immigrants. More generally, the complex dynamics of both nurturing and coercive relations with co-ethnic recipient-employers, especially when they are parents, might be best tackled through ethnic community organizations—with ties, or potential ties, to both workers and recipient-employers.

NOTES

1. In China, from the 1950s to the 1970s, and especially during the Cultural Revolution, Confucian notions of sons' respect for parental authority and wives' submission to husbands and in-laws, were attacked in favor of loyalty

to the Party and an ideology of the broader collective. Yet because legislation and institutions continued to emphasize family obligations for welfare, gendered duty to parents remained, especially in rural areas, although responsibilities shifted from sons to daughters. The 1978 move away from a purely planned economy toward a more market-based one eroded nascent support for welfare in urban collective enterprises, and new notions of filial duty were mobilized (Qi 2014; Zhan and Montgomery 2003).

2. ULTCWU was an amalgamation of SEIU and American Federation of State and County and Municipal Employees (AFSCME) locals. At the time of writing, the union had amalgamated more locals into a new, larger entity— SEIU 2015—allowing them to bargain with the California government at a single table for all counties covered by the Independent Provider model discussed in this chapter, the dominant model in California.

3. The authors have been unable to confirm this number.

REFERENCES

Anderson, Bridget. 2000. *Doing the Dirty Work?: The Global Politics of Domestic Labour*. New York and London: Zed Books.

Bakan, Abigail and Daiva Stasiulis. 2012. "The Political Economy of Migrant Live-in Caregivers: A Case of Unfree Labor?" In *Legislated Inequality: Temporary Labor Migration in Canada*, edited by Patti Tamara Lenard and Christine Straehle, 202–226. Montreal: McGill-Queens University Press.

Bonacich, Edna. 1973. "A Theory of Middleman Minorities." *American Sociological Review* 38: 583–594.

Boris, Eileen and Jennifer Klein. 2012. *Caring for America: Home Health Workers in the Shadow of the Welfare State*. New York: Oxford University Press.

Cancian, Francesca M. and Stacey J. Oliker, eds. 2000. *Caring and Gender*. Walnut Creek, CA: Rowman Littlefield.

Chin, Margaret M. 2013. "Changing Expectations: Economic Downturns and Immigrant Chinese Women in New York City." In *Immigrant Women Workers in the Neoliberal Age*, edited by Nilda Flores-Gonzalez, Anna Romina Guevarra, Maura Toro-Morn and Grace Chang, 117–132. Urbana: University of Illinois Press.

Chun, Jennifer Jihye. 2009. *Organizing at the Margins: The Symbolic Politics of Labor in South Korea and the United States*. Ithaca: ILR Press.

Chun, Jennifer Jihye. 2016. "Building Political Agency and Movement Leadership: The Grassroots Organizing Model of Asian Immigrant Women Advocates." *Citizenship Studies* 20: 379–395.

Chun, Jennifer and Cynthia Cranford. 2016. "From Sweatshops to Homes: How Immigrant Women Became Paid Care Workers in Oakland, California's

Chinatown." Paper presented at international workshop on The Global Migration of Gendered Care Work, University of Vienna, Austria, July 5.

Chun, Jennifer Jihye, George Lipsitz and Young Shin. 2013. "Intersectionality as a Social Movement Strategy: Asian Immigrant Women Advocates." *Signs: Journal of Women in Culture and Society* 38: 917–940.

Constable, Nicole. 2009. "The Commodification of Intimacy: Marriage, Sex, and Reproductive Labor." *Annual Review of Anthropology* 38: 49–64.

Cranford, Cynthia. 2005. "From Precarious Workers to Unionized Employees and Back Again? The Challenges of Organizing Personal-Care Workers in Ontario." In *Self-Employed Workers Organize: Law, Policy, and Unions*, edited by Cynthia Cranford, Judy Fudge Eric Tucker and Leah Vosko, 96–135. Montreal: McGill-Queen's Press.

Cranford, Cynthia. 2014. "Towards Flexibility with Security for Migrant Care Workers: A Comparative Analysis of Personal Home Care in Toronto and Los Angeles." In *Migration and Care Labour: Theory, Policy and Politics*, edited by Bridget Anderson and Isabel Shutes, 173–191. Houndmills, Basingstoke, Hampshire: Palgrave Macmillan.

Cranford, Cynthia and Diana Miller. 2013. "Emotion Management from the Client's Perspective: The Case of Personal Home Care." *Work, Employment & Society* 27: 785–801.

Delp, Linda and Katie Quan. 2002. "Home Care Worker Organizing in California: An Analysis of a Successful Strategy." *Labor Studies Journal* 27: 1–23.

Duffy, Mignon. 2005. "Reproducing Labor Inequalities: Challenges for Feminists Conceptualizing Care at the Intersections of Gender, Race, and Class." *Gender & Society* 19: 66–82.

Glenn, Evelyn Nakano. 1992. "From Servitude to Service Work: Historical Continuities in the Racial Division of Paid Reproductive Labor." *Signs* 18: 1–43.

Glenn, Evelyn Nakano. 2010. *Forced to Care: Coercion and Caregiving in America*. Cambridge, MA: Harvard University Press.

Hondagneu-Sotelo, Pierrette. 2007. *Doméstica: Immigrant Workers Cleaning and Caring in the Shadows of Affluence*. Berkeley: University of California Press.

Kwong, Peter. 1997. "Manufacturing Ethnicity." *Critique of Anthropology* 17: 365–87.

Lan, Pei-Chia. 2002. "Subcontracting Filial Piety: Elder Care in Ethnic Chinese Immigrant Families in California." *Journal of Family Issues* 23: 812–835.

Liu, Z.-D. 1998. *Women's Medical Sociology*. Taipei: Feminist Bookstore.

Parreñas, Rhacel Salazar. 2015. *Servants of Globalization: Migration and Domestic Work, Second Edition*. Stanford, CA: Stanford University Press.

Qi, Xiaoying. 2014. "Filial Obligations in Contemporary China: Evolution of the Culture-System." *Journal for the Theory of Social Behaviour* 45:142–161.

Stacey, Clare and Linsey Ayers. 2012. "Caught Between Love and Money: The Experiences of Paid Family Caregivers." *Qualitative Sociology* 35: 47–64.

Tronto, Joan and Berenice Fisher. 1990. "Towards a Feminist Theory of Caring." In *Circles of Care: Work and Identity in Women's Lives*, edited by Emily K. Abel and Margaret K. Nelson, 35–62. Albany: State University of New York Press.
Twigg, Julia. 2000. *Bathing: The Body and Community Care*. London: Routledge.
Ungerson, Claire. 1999. "Personal Assistants and the Disabled: An Examination of a Hybrid Form of Work and Care." *Work, Employment & Society* 13: 583–600.
Williams, Fiona. 2011. "Towards a Transnational Analysis of the Political Economy of Care." In *Feminist Ethics and Social Policy*, edited by Rianne Mahon and Fiona Robinson, 21–39. Vancouver: UBC Press.
Zelizer, Viviana. 2000. "The Purchase of Intimacy." *Law and Social Inquiry* 25: 817–48.
Zhan, Heying Jenny and Rhonda J. V. Montgomery. 2003. "Gender and Elder Care in China: The Influence of Filial Piety and Structural Constraints." *Gender & Society* 17: 209–229.

Cynthia Cranford, an associate professor of sociology at the University of Toronto, is the co-author of *Self-Employed Workers Organize* and has published on migration, work and union renewal in *Gender & Society, Relations Industrielles/Industrial Relations, Social Problems, Work, Employment and Society* and elsewhere. She is currently writing a book comparing the organization of home care in Ontario and California from the perspectives of workers, recipients, advocates, government, and employers.

Jennifer Jihye Chun is an associate professor of sociology at the University of Toronto and director of the Centre for the Study of Korea housed at the Asian Institute in the Munk School of Global Affairs.She is the author of the award-winning book,*Organizing at the Margins: The Symbolic Politics of Labor in South Korea and the United States* (Cornell University Press, 2009). Her current research explores protest cultures in South Korea and global comparative approaches to studying informal and precarious worker organizing.

CHAPTER 4

Home Care for Elders in China's Rural-Urban Dualism: Care Workers' Fractured Experiences

Liu Hong

In the region of the Pacific Rim, China has customarily been considered a sending country with regard to migration and care work. Yet China alone had over 13 million domestic workers in 2013, constituting about one-fifth of the total 67 million domestic workers in the world (ILO 2015; see also Peng 2017). The large majority of these workers are internal rural-urban migrants (ILO 2015; Li 2008). In itself, the case of China resembles the whole region, sharing the same pattern of migration connecting economically disparate areas, with care workers moving from economically less developed provinces to coastal provinces and inland economic centers, and rural-urban and provincial boundaries acting like national borders. The *hukou*[1] or household registration system further reinforces these borders, creating barriers to equal citizenship access to resources and opportunities. For three decades since the 1980s, care work in those receiving regions has been characterized by an unregulated care market, disdained social status, and gender segregation. Deemed low-skilled work, care is labor-intensive and inevitably associated with low

L. Hong (✉)
Department of Social Work, Fudan University, Shanghai, China

© The Author(s) 2017
S. Michel, I. Peng (eds.), *Gender, Migration, and the Work of Care*,
DOI 10.1007/978-3-319-55086-2_4

wages, precarious employment, and rare opportunities for advancement (see Laliberté, this volume).

Over the past two decades, the government has intervened in more economically developed urban areas to reform the care sector, primarily in the domain of elder care. This chapter examines, through female care workers' accounts, the Home Care program, a personal assistance service initiative for home-bound older people in Shanghai. Because of Shanghai's pioneering role in China's care reform, this program serves as an exemplary case. On the surface, the program, which has been in operation for more than a decade, has gradually expanded to serve more clients, raised its financial support levels, and put in place sounder regulations regarding training and service quality. Nevertheless, the experiences of the female care workers reveal that the effort to formalize elder care has neglected care workers as key stakeholders in the process of care provision. Capitalizing on the abundance of migrant workers (but failing to address their needs and rights), the Home Care program has fallen short of lifting the value of care work and perpetuated the systemic rural-urban divide. As a result, care workers often find themselves left struggling to bridge the systemic chasm in everyday care work. To use the care workers' figurative expression, care work splits into "two worlds."

This chapter unravels three dimensions of the dualism in the domain of elder care. First, two systems of elder care co-exist in China, one in which elder care is traditionally seen as a moral duty and the other in which care is regarded as a kind of paid work. Migrant workers, who could not afford to fulfill their moral duties in the countryside, sell their labor, and take care of someone else's parents in the cities. A second dimension has to do with the identity of care workers. On the one hand, care is disdained as menial work for the lowly migrants, while on the other hand, care is regarded as valuable work for the caring person. The third dimension is associated with differential compensations for local and migrant workers. Migrants' labor is valued at a lower price than that of urban workers, while the denial of entitlement to social security institutionally prevents migrant care workers from truly settling in the cities.

The chapter is organized as follows: The first part introduces the co-existing care systems–moral duty and paid work–which are linked by migration. It also offers a case study of urban care reform in China and the Home Care program, setting the context for analyzing care workers' experiences.

The second part explores the dualism that exists at the psychological level. It begins by examining an association between care work and the social status of rural-urban migrants in the context of China's economic reform. Participants' narratives show that care has been depicted as demeaning labor performed by lowly migrant workers. Care workers thus often seek to avoid the identity of care worker. Meanwhile, however, they embrace care as intimate and valuable work for those in need which is accomplished by a caring self. Care workers construct these two contradictory but complementary identities in their interpretations of their own work.

The third part analyzes differential compensation for care work at the institutional level. It shows that the perceived value and status of care work can be elevated by societal recognition in the forms of decent wages and social security eligibility. However, the Home Care program fails to overcome the *hukou* impediments, with the result that migrant and local workers' labor are valued differently. Once again, two disjointed worlds of care present a contrast–in this instance, between the entitled and the deprived.

About the Study

Research Site

The data reported in this chapter were primarily collected during the summer and fall of 2013 as part of the field work for my PhD dissertation, which focused on long-term and intimate care relationships between care workers and their clients. Information was collected from three agencies in the Home Care program in Shanghai. The program targets people aged sixty or above and delivers personal assistance with Activities of Daily Living (ADLs), Instrumental Activities of Daily Living (IADLs), and other household chores in recipients' homes. The clients are entitled to government subsidies in the form of vouchers conditional on their age and demonstrated level of disability. The program's workforce comprises both migrant workers and local Shanghai residents. The care managers interviewed estimated that 80 to 90 percent of the employees in the three agencies I visited were migrant workers. This number could only be approximated because the actual number of migrant workers at each agency shifts constantly as people join and quit routinely. Most local workers were recruited through re-employment programs at the street-level government,[2] and many of them were previously employees laid off from state-owned enterprises. The large majority of the care workers are female. While city-wide data are unavailable, male workers constituted less than 5 percent of the workforce at the agencies I visited. The size of the care agencies varies depending on the service demand of the area, with each agency managing 100 to 300 care workers.

Data Collection

The original study followed grounded-theory methodology and employed an array of data collection strategies, including interviews, on-site observations, and archival research. The empirical findings reported in this chapter draw on 22 in-depth semi-structured interviews with female care workers as well as key informant interviews with local social welfare department officials and care managers, which typically lasted 1.5 to 2 hours. All interviews were conducted in Mandarin Chinese or regional dialects and were audio recorded and transcribed in the Chinese language by myself. The coding and analysis of the transcripts were facilitated by NVivo. Agency records, care policies, job guidelines, and brochures prepared for service users gathered at local government and the care agencies are used to draw a picture of the Home Care program. While official data on the program are not available, the figures reported in this chapter are based on policy documents and program data gathered for this study.

Participants

Among the 22 participants, seven are of local origin and the remaining fifteen are migrant workers. The majority of the non-local participants are from Anhui and Jiangsu, two provinces near Shanghai. On average, the participants were 48.3 years of age at the time of interview. Most had lower levels of education; only three are high school graduates, and the rest had nine years or less of education. The participants did, however, have experience in the care industry. At the time of the study, the participants had been employed in the Home Care program for 6.4 years on average. About half of them, mostly migrant workers, had worked in some kind of domestic service jobs prior to the Home Care program, with an average of seven years' experience in that type of work. Because the large majority of the study population were women, I will use female pronouns to refer to care workers throughout the rest of this chapter.

DUALISM IN THE CARE SYSTEM: MORAL DUTY AND PAID WORK

The organization of elder care in China in the early years of the economic reform (1979–present) largely capitalized on the traditional Chinese filial norm, which assigned responsibility for seniors' old-age care to the younger generations. Care was seen primarily as a moral duty and entirely a familial concern. This principle straddled both sides of the *hukou* system, unifying the world of care despite differential arrangements between rural and urban areas when it came to other types of social welfare.[3] Care responsibilities fell on family members, and such responsibilities toward older people were enshrined in the Chinese national and local legislations. For example, the Law on Protection of the Rights and Interests of the Elderly and the Marriage Law both stipulated that family members are responsible "to provide for, to take care of, to comfort, to meet basic needs of, to pay medical expenses for, to arrange housing for, and to farm for" their seniors who have lost the ability to do so. Not only are spouses and adult children primarily liable, the senior's siblings and grandchildren all share some responsibility. In practice, care activities in Chinese families were and continue to be gendered. It is women–both daughters and daughters-in-law–who undertake most of the care tasks for seniors in families (Whyte and Qin 2003; Zhan 2005).

For the majority of older people, institutional care was not an option before the 1990s. Such service was reserved only for elderly populations who fit the "three-nos" (no family, no work, and no income) criteria. Their counterparts in rural areas were covered by the "five-guarantees" (food, clothing, housing, medical care, and funeral expenses [Chen 1996]). While the majority of older people who needed care remained at home, they lacked formal services to support them, even if their caregivers were absent.

Since the 1990s, urban residents have begun to "contract out" their elder care duties under the pressure of population aging and shrinking household size (Chen and Liu 2009; Gu and Vlosky 2008; Sun 2002; Zeng and Wang 2003), whereas in rural areas dependence on family members continued. In the cities, care became a kind of work performed outside of family boundaries.[4] In richer urban regions, the practice of hiring live-in maids (*bao mu*) to take care of elders became more popular (Chappell 2008). On the public front, the number and variety of publicly financed or subsidized care services has been expanding gradually in urban areas in the past two decades (Bartlett and Phillips

1997; Chen 1996; Wu et al. 2005). The ongoing urban care reform carried out under the banner "socialization of care" suggests that care has been recognized as a business not only of the private domain but of the whole society. Typical government support includes subsidies for capital investments in and favorable policies to encourage building retirement homes, nursing institutions, and community care facilities. Other efforts involve consolidating, subsidizing, and regulating brokers or care management agencies and creating benefit schemes to reduce older people's out-of-pocket expenditures for care services. The care reform measures can be interpreted as government efforts to formalize care work by publicly supporting certain care activities that have been traditionally provided within the family or through other private means.

One pivotal link in the urban care reform is the workforce. The reform coincided with emergence of an abundant supply of rural migrant labor. While the number and proportion of migrant workers working in the care sector are difficult to count accurately, a 2004 national survey recorded a total of 120 million rural-urban migrant workers in China, slightly over 10 percent of whom worked in the social service sector (Li 2008). These migrant workers are currently hired through various formal and informal channels, working in environments from homes to institutions. Table 4.1[5] shows a list of the care-related occupations typically held by women.

In this study, participants used the terms *a yi* and *bao mu* most frequently and consistently, although they sometimes used all of these words interchangeably to refer to themselves and care workers in general. Up until the fifth edition of the *Contemporary Chinese Dictionary*, published in 2005, *bao mu* had been defined as "a female person hired to care for children, or to do housework." The word for "the old" was first added in the 2012 edition, recognizing the reality that care for the old can be performed outside of the family context and in an employment relationship. Furthermore, the gendered nature of care is reflected in the female root of these Chinese characters. Today, a male caregiver is sometimes referred to as a "male *bao mu*" in Mandarin Chinese.

It should be noted that the terms for care-related occupations in various forms, whether formal or informal, such as *bao mu, jia zheng*, and *zhong dian gong*, came into existence *before* the initiatives for the "socialization of care." In fact, many participants in this study had been employed previously in these kinds of care and domestic jobs. As the government formalizes the care sector, a *bao mu* previously hired through private

Table 4.1 Chinese words for care-related occupations

Chinese word	Definition[6]	Notes
bao mu (保姆)	A woman hired to care for children, seniors, or patients, or to do housework.	Definition did not include "seniors" in earlier versions of dictionaries.
a yi (阿姨)	A yi in some Chinese dialects means a sister of one's mother. It can generally be used by a child to refer to a non-kindred female person about the same age as his or her mother. Another word for bao mu.	This term was the most frequently used word by the participants.
ji a zheng (家政)	Homemaking, housekeeping—the business of managing housework, usually excluding personal care.	This word refers to an occupation rather than a person.
zhong dian gong (鐘點工)	Hourly work; an hourly employee.	This term has been used to mean housekeeping and care work performed and paid on an hourly basis, and it is gender-neutral.
hu gong (護工)	A personal aide hired to take care of patients, typically in a ward.	This word may refer to either a male or female person. This word began to appear formally in hospital settings.
hu li yuan (護理員)	Care worker.	This word may refer to either a male or female person. This is often the formal title that appears in official documents in the domain of care.

channels may now become an employee in the Home Care program and receive the formal title of *hu li yuan*.

Researchers have observed that frontline workers were typically not trained in early years of formal care services (Chu and Chi 2008; Gu and Vlosky 2008). To raise the quality of services, in recent years local governments have rolled out measures to mandate training for care workers and set practice standards for elder care services. For example, to qualify for the Home Care program, care workers must hold a government-issued professional certificate and receive continuing training. In this way, more migrant workers have been converted to be professional caregivers in the city.

As the rural-urban wage difference is predicted to continue to persist as an incentive for migration (Herd et al. 2010), "two worlds" of care

are thus created. In the urban world, care is rendered as a kind of service that can be sold and purchased. In the rural world, care remains a family responsibility, although those who undertake such responsibility are now selling their care labor in the cities. A professional care worker in the urban world might previously have been a daughter or daughter-in-law taking care of her elderly relatives in the rural world, but now she is leaving her own seniors behind and taking care of someone else's. In rural China, unmet elder care needs are placing great pressure on families (Giles et al. 2010; Wu et al. 2009). Emerging evidence is showing the negative impact of adult children's out-migration on left-behind older parents' mental and physical health (Ao et al. 2016; Zhou et al. 2015; Guo et al. 2009). The lack of care and of ongoing family care relationships are also considered critical risk factors in suicide among older people, which has increased sharply since the 1990s (Dong et al. 2015; Liu 2013). The world where care is paid work and the one where it is a moral duty are, ironically, connected by migration: care work in urban China is performed by those who cannot afford to perform their own family duty.

DUALISM IN CARE WORKER IDENTITY: THE DEMEANED AND THE CARING

Care as Menial Work for the "Provincials"

At the time the Home Care program was introduced, privately hired *bao mu* or *zhong dian gong* were largely rural-urban female migrant workers. These titles carry social meanings beyond naming the kind of care-related job. They become social labels applied to these migrant women and whomever undertakes such jobs. In early years of the loosened restrictions on internal migration, migrant workers were derogatorily called "peasant workers" and "provincials," terms that, to urban residents, implied inferiority and persons who were "uneducated and treacherous." *Bao mu*, the lowest status among the city jobs, is relegated to this marginal group. Recalling her experience of settling in this unwelcoming city in the early 1990s, Gu commented on the local reception of migrants:

> We were from out of town. And [migrant workers] had made a negative impression on Shanghai [people], not a very positive image. One thing is theft and another is robbery. Very bad image.... Our work [as *bao mu*] is

the lowliest, the lowliest job in Shanghai.... People were kind of looking down [on this job]. I said to a senior, "Your granddaughter doesn't seem to care to talk to me. Does she despise me?" [The senior] said, "Maybe somewhat. First, you are from out of town, and second, doing this kind of work is very, very miserable, pitiable."

The status of care work is so tightly affixed to the image of a migrant worker that for local (Shanghai) people, doing the "pitiable" work of care can mean disgracefully lowering oneself and aligning one's own status with that of the lowly migrants. As one local worker said, she felt humiliated to be a care worker:

Doing this kind of work is after all embarrassing.... You'd be ashamed to tell other people.... Because it was all those migrants being *zhong dian gong*, now doing it as a local is like a cut below [a city person].

Not only an intra-psychic struggle, this humiliation can bring about tangible consequences. Many care workers face strong pressure from within their own families. Mei, a woman married to a local man, complained:

My husband doesn't like me doing this line of work.... He said, like this kind of work is losing [face]. Shanghai people, you know, Shanghai men are touchy about their face. But what can I do? I have a child [to take care of]! It is not that I want to do this. I have a child, I have no choice.... Sometimes he fights with me, not letting me go [to work]. What could I do if he doesn't let me go? [I] just called [clients] and asked for leave.... Sometimes [he]...loses his temper: "What kind of job is this? What a terrible job!" Blah, blah. "[The job] sounds awful, pays little, and is a drudge. Why do you have to do this?" If I had other choices....

Resistance to the identity of a care worker prevails among both locals and migrants. Care workers typically try to hide their occupation from relatives and neighbors, keeping only the immediate family informed about their work. Some even avoid working for clients living in the vicinity. One participant said she would seek clients a few kilometers away from her own neighborhood so she would not be recognized by acquaintances. Others who failed to hide their trade might feel embarrassed when their care worker identity was publicly revealed. One confessed that when she first started the job, she would walk her clients in wheelchairs in the neighborhood with her head lowered, her chin tucked in, constantly being anxious that neighbors whom she knows might spot her. "I was so afraid they recognized it was me!" she said.

By concealing the care worker identity, participants resist being associated with the demeaning label "care worker" and the image of a migrant worker. The person who is doing the care work is not "recognized as me," and the "care worker" is kept apart from where "I" live and whom "I" know. This concealment in public is a matter of degree that depends on how reflective and sensitive the person is to the prevailing view toward care work, and how much pressure she bears from her immediate social groups, such as families, friends, and neighbors.

Care as Valuable Work for a Caring Person

Many care workers, facing deep-seated stereotypes about migrant workers and *bao mu,* may start their careers with an unsettled mind, questioning the value of the work they do: "if I had another choice," as Mei put it. Yet after years in this line of work, many care workers begin to reconcile with it. They manage to resolve the disquiet associated with doing what is portrayed as a menial job and restore the value of work found in their daily relationships with seniors.

To begin with, care workers make downward comparisons between their own socioeconomic condition and that of their clients. Since many clients' economic and living conditions are lower than the prevailing standard of the society, describing the situations of impoverished older people can be "heartbreaking." Their hardships evoke a strong sense of sympathy on the part of the care workers, which, in turn, shores up the value of the care they provide. Gu, describing her clients as "poor people," said:

> We don't despise the poor. We'd rather think how to help them, to give them something, because we lived a hard life. It hurts when others look down on us. You know? ... We always thought, one day if we got richer, we wouldn't look down on the poor.

The hard life of a migrant worker is now a source of compassion and care. As a care worker makes such downward comparisons, the thought that she is better off than the client summons a desire to extend altruistic help.

Care work is thus regarded as being more valuable than "just any work such as that of a shelf stocker or a bottle washer."

Similarly, the value of care work also lies in the perception that care workers are much needed by the clients. Participants portrayed their work as meeting the needs of elderly clients who would have otherwise been left unattended. Fang elaborated on this point:

> I can't take a day off. Seniors have been used to you coming routinely. They think, "she is going to come today"–they are used to that.... Seniors look forward to you. Some neighbors told me: "You see, he [a client] has been sitting there, looking to the direction you come from. He was waiting for you, so anxiously." Seniors count on you to help them with housework. They need us. They really need us.... They would ask you to come earlier, so after the work is done you can talk to them. When you have to leave for the next home, they wouldn't want you to go.... These seniors are lonely. They want someone to talk to, to be company. Families are close, but they [seniors] can't count on them [families]. So they have to count on us. Right?

Care workers feel that they are "important" to the older people and are "counted on." For them, the perception of being needed enhances the perceived value of their work, which counterbalances the disdain inflicted by the lowly social labels. Moreover, the important care work is suited for those who know how to do it. For the workers, caring is an essential quality for doing good care work. Chao was very proud of her own work and claimed to be the "best *bao mu*" in her neighborhood because she "cares":

> Wherever I work, I get along with people. You care about her with your conscience. If you don't mind dirty and smelly work, and are hard-working, she will be happy. I have very good relationships with the seniors. Among so many *bao mu* in this neighborhood, I am the best! Why? Everyone likes me because I have a positive attitude. I don't mind [that] they are dirty and I am caring for them. So your relationships will last long!

Care workers depict themselves as caring: they do not mind dirty and smelly work, they are observant of seniors' needs, they are responsive to clients' requests, and they often go beyond the call of duty to help the elders. They weave *caring* into their narratives about themselves and relationships with clients.

For some, this quality originates from their "conscience," for others, from their "sympathy." Yet more people drew on filial relationships in describing caring as a moral disposition. Yun told me she is the "most filial" among her four siblings:

> I cared for my parents out of my conscience. I wanted to treat them well. You can never repay your parents' kindness. Right? So to the elders [clients], I am the same. I do the same.

Treating the seniors the same way their parents were cared for, Chao thinks she upholds a high standard of caring. This example illustrates how filial morality finds its way into care workers' accounts of everyday experience of providing care. Lin echoes this point:

> I treated [clients] like my parents. Both my own parents passed away. I was working in Shanghai, and [my parents] were in the country. I could not take care of them by myself. I feel very guilty about this. Now I care for [clients] from the bottom of my heart, just like caring for my own parents.

In Lin's words, we can see not only a direct parallel between parents and clients, but also that she tried to compensate for the unfulfilled duty to care for her own parents through her relationships with seniors at work. Being a caring person thus produces a morally desirable character that evokes a sense of fulfillment.

The prolonged contact between the carer and the cared for can sometimes nourish a relationship that embodies meanings so rich and powerful that the care worker's menial trade can be glorified. Care workers restore value to these care experiences and construct narratives in which their self-image is not spoiled by the label placed on them. They construct another world in which care becomes valuable work for the care-giving person, to counter the one in which care is regarded as menial work for the "provincials." Thus "two worlds" of care, contradictory but co-existing, are depicted in care workers' interpretations of their own experiences.

Dualism in Compensation: The Entitled and the Deprived

Care can have radically opposing meanings for the care-giving person or for the provincial, but in the world where care is a kind of work, its status and value are reflected in how it is compensated. For care workers, higher pay symbolizes higher social status of the job. As Fang recalled it: "[It would be better] if the salary was higher. People would think more highly of you. I don't talk to people about my work. If I had a better salary, people would say it's not bad." While the standard of what makes for a decent salary may vary for different people, it is certain that a higher perceived status is associated with a higher income. Yun felt that the status of her work had risen with increased income over the past decade:

> People are practical, very realistic, because home care now pays okay.... After all, it's about salary. Now this line of work pays okay, so you think, "it's not too bad." We are not like *bao mu* in the olden times. Our social status, I should say, is higher than before. Financially, the income is okay, four or five thousand [yuan] a month is okay.

Many participants who worked as *bao mu* before joining the Home Care program recalled the days in the 1990s when privately hired domestic workers were largely underpaid and at risk of being exploited by employers. In the Home Care program, a minimum hourly rate is implemented and updated every year to reflect the city's minimum wage standard. Although far from being a high-paying job, domestic care work in the public program secures the participants an income close to, if not on par with, the city average. At the psychological level, better compensation works to shield care workers from the prevailing negative views toward care work, restoring dignity for the workers. Being able to "win our own bread in a respectable way" also imparts a sense of control as the care workers become economically viable through work. Consider what Jun has to say about her pride in living off her own labor:

> [Those who] don't do this kind of work always feel superior. Right?... Like I said, no matter you look down on me or look up to me–I do my own work, and I am not begging from you.... Those people on social assistance, they play mah-jong at home all day. How comfortable they are! You live your comfortable days, I do my work. At least I earn 100 yuan from work today. You play mah-jong and you are on social assistance, but you earn nothing. I can go eat at a restaurant today if I feel like it. Can you afford that? You can't. You can despise me all you want, but I'll do it.

A decent salary is conducive to self-reliance, which redresses the socially imposed sense of inferiority. Some care workers routinely tried to distinguish themselves from the "provincials." They hold the view that in today's Shanghai, no one should feel ashamed of her job as long as she earns a decent salary through her own labor, not through "theft and robbery," which again are offenses stereotypically associated with migrant workers.

While both migrant and local care workers stress the importance of income, they are facing two different wage structures. Income for local workers is made up of two parts: an hourly wage starting at 12.5 yuan per hour and a fixed-rate monthly payment funded by the local government. For example, for a full-time equivalent local care worker who works forty hours a week, the typical income is 3,000 to 4,000 yuan per month, which is slightly lower than the city average, but higher than minimum wage. Migrant workers, however, are not entitled to the fixed-rate payment and are only paid the hourly wage. To reach the same level of income, they would need to work extra hours. Most of the migrant workers participating in this study worked more than eight hours a day, seven days a week. Working "six-to-six," from 6 AM to 6 PM with or without a lunch break, is not unusual for migrant workers.

In addition to the income gap, there are other differences in compensation. Local workers are entitled to health insurance and old-age security, the premiums for which are covered by the government. Migrant workers, though working in the same public care program, are excluded from these benefits. Because the government pays their premiums, local workers often view home care as a public or government job. The perceptions that their employer is the government and that they are entitled to social security give rise to higher "credibility" for the job compared to the kinds of *bao mu* and *jia zheng* work found in the traditionally unregulated market. Care workers would introduce their job as "home care for the government" to show that it was not just any kind of work. "I am sent by the street [-level government], and I contribute to social security," said Lian. The significance of the meaning attached to these two "perks" can be further understood in Lian's words:

> People consider this a job! People look at you differently. You are doing this for the social security, like those who do cleaning work, security guards, or work in supermarket. Same idea. They do it for social security and for a better life. Different, really different. So I appreciate this job a lot.

Being a "public job," for the local workers home care warrants respect. The prevailing attitude that portrays care work, be it *jia zheng, bao mu,* or *zhong dian gong,* as low-status, precarious, and informal can be shaken up when care work is recognized as a formal job associated with benefits equal to those of other occupations.

Migrant workers, finding themselves in a different world of compensation, often complained about the injustice of their exclusion from social benefits. Huo explicitly expressed her discontentment toward the differential treatment of migrant and local workers:

> We'd appreciate if they gave us benefits. For example, when we get old, we will [need to] have some security. Without security, we are uncertain about the future.... People from out of town like me have done this work for so many years. To be fair, I think, I have my opinion. Why is there such a big difference between us? They get benefits and we don't regardless of how well we do. We can't compare to the locals. We are discontent.

This inequality between the two groups may in part explain why migrant workers are more likely than local workers to present themselves as hardworking. In fact, they do tend to work longer hours at the risk of their own health. Migrant workers, who do not have old-age security, not only universally feel a sense of injustice, they also hold a bleak outlook on the future—an "uncertain" future, as in Huo's words. Working with older people becomes a reminder of the fact that "one day I will be like them." Migrant workers often disclosed worries about their own old age:

> I want to have a secure life for the future. We only have one child. When we get too old to work, what do I do? I often think about this. I wonder if they would give us a pension. Some security. Even the minimum would be good, better than nothing.

When Jian voiced these thoughts, she had already given up on staying in Shanghai, the city where she spent more than half of her life, yet where a secure old age could not be provided. She continued:

> I like it here. I am used to the life style here. We rarely visit our hometown, not every year.... I am used to the life here, the food and everything. I feel I am more used to being here than back there.... But without security, how can you stay here? I think I will go back.

The public care program in Shanghai fails to overcome the institutional bias against migrants, leaving migrants and local workers' care differentially compensated. For the locals, health care benefits, a pension, and a guaranteed income are entitlements, whereas for the migrants, these entitlements are denied. The world of the entitled and the world of the deprived are kept apart institutionally.

CONCLUSION

Care in China splits into "two worlds" on different dimensions, the impact of which is rather palpable down to the personal level of everyday care work, as we see from the case of the Home Care program in Shanghai. While the chasm in care work can be traced back to China's urban-rural dualism, itself expressed most visibly through the *hukou* system, the reliance on migrant care workers is not unique to the Chinese context. It remains to ask ourselves: what lessons can we learn from this case?

To begin with, in the face of fast-growing elder care needs and declining capacity to care in urban Chinese families, a rapid expansion of care service coverage at lower costs seems to be in line with the national government's general strategy for the development of social security and health care systems: "wide coverage at lower standards." This strategy thus creates a strong disincentive for the government to mitigate the systemic dualism and raise pay levels for migrant care workers. With an abundant supply of migrant workers from poorer areas in the country, care work is expected to continue to be "work for the provincials." We have seen a similar phenomenon at an international level. For several decades now, developed care markets across the world—in North America and Europe as well as Asia—have been drawing migrant, mostly female, care workers from economically less developed countries to provide elder care in homes (Bettio et al. 2006; Fujisawa and Colombo 2009; Huang et al. 2012; Michel and Peng 2012). Its implications can be dire.

First, the logic of cost containment unbridled by deliberate regulation runs contrary to the reality of the care market. Costs are not actually reduced but made invisible by being shifted from the underprivileged to the more underprivileged, and specifically from "local women" to "foreign women," as migration reinforces the gendered and racialized/ethnicized nature of care (Browne and Braun 2008; Razavi and Staab 2010; Yeates 2012). For example, Shutes and Chiatti's (2012) research in the UK and

Italy demonstrated that in both home and institutional care for elders, migrant care workers are those who have been compelled to accept low wages and poor employment conditions, and thus absorbed the impact of cost reductions. In this way, cost containment measures lead to the further devaluation of care. The Home Care program in Shanghai is unfortunately trapped in this pitfall. Nationally, rural migrant workers' wages have been rising since the turn of the millennium, steadily until 2007 and in double digits after 2008 (Yao 2014). Wages in publicly funded care work also increased during this period, but they still lag behind increases in other sectors. Migrant workers are persistently denied social security enrollment in care programs. The impact of cost depression falls on the backs of the migrant workers. Overwork and health issues may bog down some migrants, but the rural-urban wage disparity continues to provide an incentive for more of them to come to cities to fill the vacancies. At the same time, care work will continue to be linked to low social status and, in the worst case, devaluation of care and the disdain for migrant workers will reinforce each other.

Second, a picture of care is incomplete without considering the welfare of the care workers. Care ethicists may say that when migrant care workers leave their families behind and care needs go unmet in their country of origin, the "surplus care" (Hochschild 2000) provided in the destination country is undesirable due to its implicit exploitation of the migrants. Care work, intersecting with the divides between paid and unpaid work and between rich and poor countries, connects people across the globe. Taking into consideration migrant workers' needs "as both carer and cared [for] in the destination and origin countries" seems to be a premise of genuine good care (Kofman and Raghuram 2009, 16). Care work in Chinese cities is performed by those who cannot afford to fulfill their filial duties in their hometowns. Like the average worker in a cellphone parts factory in southern China who cannot afford its products, the care worker cannot afford to purchase the services she is providing strangers for her own family, nor can she afford to stay at home and provide them in person. One can live without a cellphone, but when it comes to the lack of care, the consequences are dire. This is not to suggest that the problem can be resolved by constraining workers from migrating from their hometowns, but only to show that the "two worlds" of care are in fact one within the same country. Problems in one will inevitably affect the other.

Third, care can be viewed as a social process subject to a series of economic and moral conditions in a society. As Razavi (2007) rightly pointed out, the question is not so much about whether monetization and marketization are deleterious to care, but how a market of "rich and complex social relationships, aspects of reward, appreciation, reparation, gift and so on" may be sustained (Folbre and Nelson 2000, 133–134). For many, an answer lies in a policy commitment to create an environment conducive to good care, which entails legitimizing care work, both by recognizing it as a social good and valorizing it through policy support (Daly 2001, 49). We have seen that the world of work and the world of duty are not mutually exclusive. Duty finds its way into work through the powerful representation of care relationships in the language of cultural and moral principles. In a broader sense, as care workers embody the image of menial work suitable only for provincials and valuable work for those being cared for, they are also (perhaps unwittingly) bridging the world where care is a paid work and the one where it is a moral duty.

This is not, however, to suggest that all care relationships in the Home Care program are rosy and problem-free. Much of the emotional work (Chichin 1993; Griffin 1983; Hochschild 1983/2003; James 1992; Neysmith and Nichols 1994) that falls on care workers' shoulders in adjusting interpersonal care relationships—for instance handling friction and tension—could easily go unseen and uncompensated. More importantly, moral commitment and its concomitant emotional investment should not result in a wage penalty (England and Folbre 1999) for those who are "caring"; neither governments, nor agencies, nor clients and their families should take advantage of care workers' sense of duty or attachment to those they care for by underpaying them. Programs like Home Care in Shanghai are likely to capitalize on filial norms and retain at a lower cost care workers who dedicate themselves to long-term relationships.

Throughout this chapter, we have seen care workers as isolated agents repairing systemic gaps. They invoke the value of care to counterbalance the demeaning social status attached to care work, they work hard to bridge the income and social security gap, and they may, unconsciously, unite paid work and moral duty. Arguably, as the Home Care program is organized and valorized by the government, it is possible to close the gaps caused by the *hukou* system or at least to mitigate it. However, if care work continues to be viewed as marginally important and worth only minimum investment, the problem will be perpetuated. Migrant care workers who have served in the program for almost a decade are still excluded from proper coverage of social security. At the intersection of the rural-urban divide and gendered segregation in the labor market, predominantly female care workers suffer a double inequity. Public care programs could perpetuate the dual-world of care as long as care is considered an independent area isolated from other policy realms, such as social protection entitlements. On an optimistic note, public programs also offer opportunities to bridge the "two worlds," if the government foregrounds the challenges of care and turns them into a window for addressing social justice issues that have been long brushed aside.

Notes

1. The household registration (*hukou*) system is a pivotal institution in China through which the Chinese government controls the migration of people and organizes welfare provision. This system was introduced in the 1950s. It categorizes Chinese citizens into "agricultural" (i.e., rural) and "non-agricultural" (i.e., urban) classes.
2. Street-level government is the lowest level of government in Shanghai. The population of the streets varies from thirty thousand to almost two hundred thousand people in Yangpu, the district with which this study is concerned.
3. The *hukou* system institutionalized contrasting urban and rural administrations. In the former, the government was responsible for providing welfare benefits, usually through employment, to the residents, e.g., rationed food, housing, health care, and education; whereas in the latter, people were expected to be self-sustaining or rely on collective cooperation. China's post-reform social policy development clearly prioritized the urban areas. Rural migrants were long treated as "second-class citizens" in terms of denied welfare benefits and public services in cities where they work and live. In recent years, efforts have been made to mitigate the rural-urban gap by developing universal social programs, but their practical success is yet to be assessed (Hong and Kongshøj 2014).
4. This is hardly a new idea, for servants and maids have always existed in Chinese culture, for example as depicted in the Chinese literary classic, *Dream of the Red Chamber*. However, the forty years of socialism should have, in theory, reset class differences, eradicating such servitude.
5. This is not an exhaustive list because local variations in dialect may exist.
6. Definitions were translated from the fifth and sixth versions of the *Contemporary Chinese Dictionary*.

REFERENCES

Ao, Xiang, Dawei Jiang and Zhong Zhao. 2016. "The Impact of Rural-Urban Migration on the Health of the Left-behind Parents." *China Economic Review* 37: 126–39.

Bartlett, Helen and David Phillips. 1997. "Ageing and Aged Care in the People's Republic of China: National and Local Issues and Perspectives." *Health & Place* 3, 3: 149–59.

Bettio, Francesca, Annamaria Simonazzi and Paola Villa. 2006. "Change in Care Regimes and Female Migration: The 'Care Drain' in the Mediterranean." *Journal of European Social Policy* 16: 271–85.

Browne, Colette V. and Kathryn L Braun. 2008. "Globalization, Women's Migration, and the Long-Term-Care Workforce." *The Gerontologist* 48, 1: 16–24.

Chappell, Neena L. 2008. "Comparing Caregivers to Older Adults in Shanghai." *Asian Journal of Gerontology & Geriatrics* 3, 2: 57–65.

Chen, Feinian and Guangya Liu. 2009. "Population Aging in China." In *International Handbook of Population Aging*, edited by Peter Uhlenberg, 157–72. Dordrecht: Springer Netherlands, 2009.

Chen, Sheying. 1996. *Social Policy of the Economic State and Community Care in Chinese Culture: Aging, Family, Urban Change, and the Socialist Welfare Pluralism*. Brookfield, VT: Avebury.

Chichin, Eileen R. 1993. "Home Care Is Where the Heart Is." *Home Health Care Services Quarterly* 13, 1–2: 161–77.

Chu, Leung-Wing, and Iris Chi. 2008. "Nursing Homes in China." *Journal of the American Medical Directors Association* 9: 237–43.

Daly, Mary. 2001. "Care Work: The Quest for Security." In *Care Work: The Quest for Security*, edited by Mary Daly, 33–56. Geneva: ILO.

Dong, Xinqi, E-Shien Chang, Ping Zeng and Melissa A Simon. 2015. "Suicide in the Global Chinese Aging Population: A Review of Risk and Protective Factors, Consequences, and Interventions." *Aging and Disease* 6, 2: 121–30.

England, Paula and Nancy Folbre. 1999. "The Cost of Caring." *The Annals of the American Academy of Political and Social Science* 561: 39–51.

Folbre, Nancy and Julie Nelson. 2000. "For Love or Money–Or Both?" *Journal of Economic Perspectives* 14 (4): 123–40.

Fujisawa, Rie and Francesca Colombo. 2009. "The Long-Term Care Workforce: Overview and Strategies to Adapt Supply to a Growing Demand." OECD Health Working Papers, No. 44. Paris: OECD Publishing.

Giles, John, Dewen Wang and Changbao Zhao. 2010. "Can China's Rural Elderly Count on Support from Adult Children? Implications of Rural-to-Urban Migration." *Journal of Population Ageing* 3, 3: 183–204.

Griffin, Anne. 1983. "A Philosophical-Analysis of Caring in Nursing." *Journal of Advanced Nursing* 8, 4: 289–95.

Gu, Danan, and Denese A. Vlosky. 2008. "Long-Term Care Needs and Related Issues in China." In *Social Sciences in Health Care and Medicine*, edited by Janet Garner and Thelma Christiansen, 51–84. Hauppauge, NY: Nova Science Publisher.

Guo, Man, Maria P. Aranda and Merril Silverstein. 2009. "The Impact of out-Migration on the Inter-Generational Support and Psychological Wellbeing of Older Adults in Rural China." *Ageing and Society* 29: 1085–1104.

Herd, Richard, Vincent Koen and Anders Reutersward. 2010. "China's Labour Market in Transition: Job Creation, Migration and Regulation." OECD Economics Department Working Papers, No. 749. Paris: OECD.

Hochschild, Arlie Russell. 2000. "Global Care Chains and Emotional Surplus Value." In *On the Edge: Living with Global Capitalism*, edited by Hutton Will and Anthony Giddens, 130–46. London, UK: Vintage, 2000.

Hochschild, Arlie Russell. 2003. *The Managed Heart: Commercialization of Human Feeling*, 2nd ed. Berkeley, CA: University of California Press.

Hong, Liu, and Kristian Kongshøj. 2014. "China's Welfare Reform: An Ambiguous Road towards a Social Protection Floor." *Global Social Policy* 14, 3: 352–68.

Huang, Shirlena, Leng Leng Thang, and Mika Toyota. 2012. "Transnational Mobilities for Care: Rethinking the Dynamics of Care in Asia." *Global Networks* 12, 2: 129–34.

ILO. 2015. "ILO Global Estimates on Migrant Workers: Results and Methodology - Special Focus on Migrant Domestic Workers." Geneva: International Labour Organization.

James, Nicky. 1992. "Care = Organization + Physical Labor + Emotional Labor." *Sociology of Health & Illness* 14: 488–509.

Kofman, Eleonore and Parvati Raghuram. 2009. "The Implications of Migration for Gender and Care Regimes in the South." Social Policy and Development Programme Papers, No. 41. Geneva: UNRISD.

Li, Shi. 2008. "Rural Migrant Workers in China: Scenario, Challenges and Public Policy." Working Paper, No. 89. Geneva: ILO.

Liu, Yan-wu. 2013. "The Suicides of the Rural Elderly and the Crisis Intervention in China: 1980–2009." *South China Population* 2013, 2: 57–64.

Michel, Sonya and Ito Peng. 2012. "All in the Family? Migrants, Nationhood, and Care Regimes in Asia and North America." *Journal of European Social Policy* 22: 406–18.

Neysmith, Sheila, and Barbara Nichols. 1994. "Working Conditions in Home Care: Comparing Three Groups of Workers." *Canadian Journal on Aging* 13: 169–86.

Peng, Ito. 2017. "Transnational Migration of Domestic and Care Workers in Asia Pacific." Geneva: International Labour Organization.

Razavi, Shahra. 2007. "The Political and Social Economy of Care in a Development Context." Programme on Gender and Development, Paper No. 3. Geneva: UNRISD.

Razavi, Shahra and Silke Staab. 2010. "Underpaid and Overworked: A Cross-National Perspective on Care Workers." *International Labour Review* 149: 407–22.

Shutes, Isabel and Carlos Chiatti. 2012. "Migrant Labour and the Marketisation of Care for Older People: The Employment of Migrant Care Workers by Families and Service Providers." *Journal of European Social Policy* 22: 392–405.

Sun, Rongjun. 2002. "Old Age Support in Contemporary Urban China from Both Parents' and Children's Perspectives." *Research on Aging* 24: 337–59.

Whyte, Martin King and Xu Qin. 2003. "Support for Aging Parents from Daughters versus Sons." In *China's Revolutions and Intergenerational Relations*, edited by Martin King Whyte, 167–96. Ann Arbor, MI: Center for China Studies, University of Michigan.

Wu, Bei, Mary W. Carter, R. Turner Goins and Chunrong Cheng. 2005. "Emerging Services for Community-Based Long-Term Care in Urban China: A Systematic Analysis of Shanghai's Community-Based Agencies." *Journal of Aging & Social Policy* 17, 4: 37–60.

Wu, Bei, Zong-Fu Mao and Renyao Zhong. 2009. "Long-Term Care Arrangements in Rural China: Review of Recent Developments." *Journal of the American Medical Directors Association* 10: 472–77.

Yao, Yang. 2014. "The Lewis Turning Point: Is There a Labour Shortage in China?" In *Oxford Companion to the Economics of China*, edited by Shenggen Fan, Ravi Kanbur, Shang-Jin Wei, and Xiaobo Zhang, 388–92. Oxford, UK: Oxford University Press.

Yeates, Nicola. 2012. "Global Care Chains: A State-of-the-Art Review and Future Directions in Care Transnationalization Research." *Global Networks* 12, 2: 135–54.

Zeng, Yi, and Zhenglian Wang. 2003. "Dynamics of Family and Elderly Living Arrangements in China: New Lessons Learned from the 2000 Census." *China Review* 3, 2: 95–119.

Zhan, Heying Jenny. 2005. "Aging, Health Care, and Elder Care: Perpetuation of Gender Inequalities in China." *Health Care for Women International* 26: 693–712.

Zhou, Yicheng, Linyi Zhou, Changluan Fu, You Wang, Qingle Liu, Hongtao Wu, Rongjun Zhang, and Linfeng Zheng. 2015. "Socio-Economic Factors Related with the Subjective Well-Being of the Rural Elderly People Living Independently in China." *International Journal for Equity in Health* 14: 1–9.

Liu Hong, is an assistant professor of social work at Fudan University in Shanghai. Before earning his PhD from the Faculty of Social Work at Wilfrid Laurier University in Waterloo, Ontario, Canada, he studied social welfare and social work in Hong Kong and Shanghai. His current research relates to social care for children and older people in China, with a focus on understanding how care relationships are shaped in service, policy, and cultural contexts.

CHAPTER 5

Caring for Your Children: How Mexican Immigrant Mothers Experience Care and the Ideals of Motherhood

Gabrielle Oliveira

In the spring of 2010 I started my fieldwork in the city of New York. I lived in New York City (NYC) and my neighbor, Marin, was a busy mother who had a nanny helping her take care of her two-year-old toddler. One day Marin asked what my research was about and I told her I wanted to learn more about maternal migration and how it influenced the lives of children and youth on both sides of the Mexican-US border. "Well," she replied, "what kind of migration are you talking about? I live in the same country, city, and house as my daughter and she is not being raised only by me. Sara, my nanny, is from Mexico and she has a kid there, and a kid here, and she takes care of Nina. You should talk to her" (Marin, February 2010). As the US media debate whether women can "have it all"–that is, a successful career and a family—migrant women like Sara wonder how they can *care* for them all: for their children in Mexico, children they have brought over to the United States, children who were born here, and children they care for professionally.

While Sara saw her work with Nina as a direct conduit to the life she was providing for her children both in NYC and in Mexico, the constant

G. Oliveira (✉)
Lynch School of Education, Boston College, MA, USA

© The Author(s) 2017
S. Michel, I. Peng (eds.), *Gender, Migration, and the Work of Care*,
DOI 10.1007/978-3-319-55086-2_5

91

contradictions of daily life filled her with doubts and questions about how to be a "good" mother to her children, spending long hours with Nina and not being around her own young sons as much. At the same time, the sadness she felt about leaving her child, Agustín, in Mexico was balanced by the newfound love she had for teaching Nina Spanish and seeing her grow. Her relationship with her employers was based on the premise that she had the flexibility and skills to take care of Nina and that it was only with Sara's help that her boss Marin could continue to be a successful professional. Sara thought she did her job well and she was very firm with Nina, but she had doubts about how "good" she was for her own sons.

In this chapter I explore how women like Sara, an undocumented Mexican migrant mother of two, thought about this care dilemma and made sense of her role as both a mother of children in NYC and in Mexico and also as a professional caregiver to other people's children. I first present a conceptual framework for the discussion of transnational motherhood and the care chain crisis as well as relevant literature on how women make sense of their relationships with these groups of children. After a brief description of the methods used in this research, I present the story of Sara in detail, addressing the topics of sacrifice, care, education investment, and everyday routines. Sara's story is typical of a pattern I have observed in data collected over a three-year period with twenty families who are organized transnationally—between Mexico and NYC—as well as over fifty interviews with migrant Mexican mothers who were cleaning ladies, nannies, salespeople, cooks, night nurses, elder-care providers, cashiers, and stay-at-home mothers in NYC. Out of the 53 women interviewed, 42 were nannies or had been professional caregivers at some point in their lives.

Although sometimes synonymous, professional caregiving carries larger expectations when associated with ideals of mothering. I argue that ideals and practices of caregiving are made and remade as women try to navigate the reality that they simultaneously care for different sets of children, some of whom may not be geographically, culturally, or economically close. Even though these ideals and practices may seem at odds, they are actually adaptations of what the women consider to be "good" and "caring" motherhood and caregiving. For migrant women, the very act of leaving represents a break in the "nexus" of motherhood, which, with regard to some of their own children, has included physical presence but has to be adapted and recreated in order to fulfill their ideals of what care should be like now that they are apart. On the other hand, their physical presence becomes the main feature of their nanny careers, whereby, in contrast to their relationship to their own children, they experience the everyday routine and growth of children who are not their own. And, to complicate things further, some, like Sara, also have children of their own in the United States. Thus, I ask: how do Mexican migrant mothers reconcile their labor as professional caregivers and their perceived duties as mothers of children in NYC (some of whom are US citizens, some undocumented) and in Mexico? In addition, how do women's relationships with each group of children differ or overlap in this context?

GENDER AND MIGRATION

More than half of the migrants in the world today are women (United Nations 2013). In different countries where women are the principal wage earners for themselves and their households, many are driven to migrate, leaving their families and children behind in search of a living wage (Castles 1999; Forbes Martin 2003). Gender, historically, has not been an important factor in the dominant economic and sociological theories of migration, but recent ethnographic research has demonstrated the significance of gender by revealing power differences within households and families. Cerrutti and Massey (2001) have found that in the past most women migrants left their country of origin to follow a husband or a parent (196), but this pattern is changing. In Mexico, for example, an increasing number of female migrants are departing for the United States alone, leaving their children behind in the care of relatives or friends (Fernandez-Kelly 2008). Although mothers leaving children behind is not a new phenomenon, the number of years mothers migrating to the United States remain separated from their children has increased due to longer periods of settlement abroad. This is because immigration restrictions make it difficult for many migrant women, who are considered unskilled, to obtain visas and enter the country legally.[1] To reduce the risks of exit and undocumented re-entry to the United States, they extend their stays once in the country.

Although some women migrate to reunify with other family members, Hondagneu-Sotelo and Avila (1997) found that 40 percent of their sample of undocumented mothers were working to support children left behind in the country of origin. Studies suggest that transnational migration challenges norms and ideals of family life, which involve entrenched gender hierarchies (Coe et al. 2011), especially gendered roles and the division of household labor. However women's roles inside and outside the home vary tremendously according to social and geographical locations (Dreby and Schmalzbauer 2013). Only recently have scholars begun to examine the life experiences of children of migrant parents, especially children of migrant mothers, in their home countries (Bernhard et al 2005; Dreby 2010; Boehm 2011; Hamann and Zúñiga 2011; Fresnoza-Flot 2013).

Maternal migration may economically benefit children, as mothers tend to be more regular remitters even though they typically earn less than male migrants (Abrego 2009). However, the emotional costs of "transnational mothering" may affect children differently when compared to the absence of fathers (Hondagneu-Sotelo and Avila 1997; Ehrenreich and Hochschild 2002; Parreñas 2005). Because the mother is seen as a nurturing and caring figure in Mexican society and her role is socially valued, mothers are often primary caregivers (Hondagneu-Sotelo 2003; Hirsch 2003; Paz 1985; Lewis 1959); hence, the consequences of maternal absence may be heightened in this instance. At the same time, maternal migration may prompt changes in traditional understandings of gender, motherhood, and caregiving. Mexican migrant women, in contrast to their male counterparts, reportedly continue to remit and stay in touch with children even after long periods of separation, yielding new transnational parenting and shared childrearing practices that have been largely omitted from the literature on transnationalism and migration (Dreby 2010). However, ideologies of motherhood are slow to adjust accordingly. In her studies of transnational Filipino families, Parreñas (2005) found that the care children received from relatives or other caregivers became obscured because it was not performed by their mothers. She argued that the resulting "gender paradox" harms "children's acceptance of the reconstitution of mothering and consequently hampers their acceptance of growing up in households split apart from their mothers" (92).

Women in developing nations often resort to migration as a means of family survival (Schmalzbauer 2005), and transnational mothers struggle with the paradox of having to leave their children in order to care for them. In Mexico and other Latina societies, when women migrate and grandmothers, aunts, sisters, elder daughters, or female friends assume the role of caregiver for their children, their maternal role is called into question. Transnational Latina mothers find themselves negotiating family bonds through remittances, gift sending, and various transnational connections.

Although women migrate to provide for their families, the question of how much remittances and migration help migrant families in

Mexico is a matter of debate. Remittances can actually exacerbate economic inequalities in the sending society (Smith 2005). Families with migrant members enjoy economic advantages over those without migrants (Kandel and Massey 2002; Cohen 2004). For example, children with a US migrant parent have better grades than children in non-migrant households; this trend is assumed to be associated with an increase in overall financial resources for families with a migrant parent (Kandel and Kao 2001). However, parental migration exerts a heavy emotional toll. Suárez-Orozco and Suárez-Orozco (2001) find levels of depression to be higher among immigrant children in the USA who experienced separation prior to migration than those who migrate with their parents. Others find that in countries with a longstanding tradition of US migration, the departure of a caregiver, including the mother, is associated with academic or behavioral problems and emotional difficulties among children (Jørgen et al. 2012; Heymann et al. 2009; Lahaie et al. 2009).

TRANSNATIONAL CARE IN CONTEXT

The feminization of migration brings to the forefront of migration studies an important discussion regarding everyday "care" practices (Dwyer 2004). How is it done? Who is involved? And, finally, what do these practices mean to mothers, caregivers and children? On the one hand, women are socialized to attach certain ideals and meanings to motherhood and care; on the other hand, they interpret, transform, and complement such gendered ideals as they perform the actions of care. The ideals of motherhood, some have suggested, are especially challenged when mothers migrate as family breadwinners (Hondagneu-Sotelo and Avila 1997). In her study of children of migrant mothers in the Philippines, Parreñas (2005) describes how a "gender ideology" determines the impact of maternal emigration on the children who stay behind. She explains that the ideology of women's domesticity in the Philippines has been recast to be performed in a transnational terrain by migrant mothers, meaning that tasks mothers have at home in the Philippines are also being performed in the host country (168).

To fully understand transnational motherhood, we must look not only at the children in the country of origin, but also at the children brought to the United States by the same mothers, those born in America, and the children they care for professionally. Previous studies have theorized the concept of "care chains" (Ehrenreich and Hochschild 2003; Sassen 2002, 2010; Yeates 2005) and focused on the migrant women on one side of the border; some scholars have moved further to also consider the families they left behind (Parreñas 2010; Dreby and Stutz 2012; Dreby 2010, 2009a, 2009b; Madianou and Miller 2012; Yarris 2011). Yet with their focus on structural factors, these studies do not acknowledge the empowering potential of migration for women as they assume a normative and universal perspective of biological motherhood that is performed in the context of co-presence (physically living in the same household). Ethnographically-based studies such as those by Aguilar et al. (2009) and Dreby (2010) demonstrate that both the global feminist discourse employed by Parreñas (2001) and globalized ideas about women's responsibilities have to be complemented by grounded studies within specific countries, which may reveal very different and more nuanced expectations about mother-child relationships.

CHILD CARE AND IMMIGRATION

Nannies form a sector of workers that has been largely excluded from workers' rights laws. A 2007 study entitled "*Behind Closed Doors*," conducted by Mujeres Unidas y Activas among 240 household workers in California, found that 94 percent of workers interviewed were Latina, and the majority, 72 percent, were immigrants who sent money back to their families in their home countries. Twenty percent said they had experienced physical and verbal abuse and 9 percent said they had experienced sexual harassment. Because many migrant women workers are compelled to either enter the country illegally or overstay tourist visas due to immigration restrictions, their status is highly vulnerable and exposes them to exploitation since they are fearful of complaining.

METHODS

Data for this chapter is a sliver of a larger multi-sited ethnographic study that seeks to "follow the people" and their stories (Marcus 1995, 106). Data was collected through my engagement with members of what I refer to as "transnational care constellations" made up of mothers, their children, and children's caregivers. I used multi-sited methods to be able to explain more fully the social phenomenon of transnational motherhood. As such, I traveled between different states in Mexico and parts of NYC numerous times over a 32-month period in order to capture the dynamism of communities that are both "here and there." In Mexico I did research in the states of Puebla, Hidalgo, Vera Cruz, Mexico State, Morelos and Tlaxcala, spending most of my time in the state of Puebla. In the United States I did research in the NYC neighborhoods of East Harlem (Manhattan), Sunset Park (Brooklyn), Jackson Heights (Queens), and the South Bronx. The irony of the fact that I was able to travel back and forth between family members who were, effectively, barred from seeing each other face-to-face was not lost on me.

Drawing on ethnographic method as well as surveys, I examined transnational caregiving practices among women with mixed-status (both undocumented and US citizen) children in New York and Mexico. After recruiting twenty families to participate in my study, I established three levels of engagement with participants. Eight transnational care constellations constituted the center of my qualitative research. I spent time with them in Mexico and in New York and tracked half of them for over three years. The second level of engagement took place with the other twelve families, whose members I interviewed and observed in NYC but visited fewer times in Mexico. From the transnational care constellations, I interviewed and observed thirty children in Mexico (fifteen females and fifteen males, ranging in age from seven to eighteen) and 37 children in NYC (twenty female and seventeen male, ranging in age from four months to eighteen years). Finally, participants who belonged to the third level of engagement comprised forty mothers in NYC, as well as fathers, caregivers, and over sixty children and youth in Mexico who were not part of any specific constellation. In all of the interviews with migrant Mexican mothers in NYC, their work conditions and experiences were discussed and recorded. In addition, I was able to do participant observation with ten women and their bosses at the site of their work over the period of the ethnography, which in this case meant that I observed them caring for other children in someone else's home.

Sara

Sara, a Mexican migrant from a small rural town in the state of Hidalgo, was my first interviewee in this research project. After my neighbor Marin had told me about Sara's situation, I asked Marin if she could set up a time for me to come by and meet Sara. Marin was hesitant. We truly got along and I had babysat for her a few times myself, but she said, "Let me speak to her and I'll let you know." A day later, Marin sent me a text message and told me to come on over. I went to their apartment and sat on the couch with Sara, while Nina and Marin were walking around the living room. I asked Sara if she would allow me to do an interview with her and explained to her my research project, my studies toward a doctorate, and my intended trip to Mexico to meet children whose mothers were in NYC. Sara's eyes lit up when I told her I was headed to Mexico in the summer. She immediately told me she had a son, Agustín, whom she had left in Mexico seven years ago. I asked if she was willing to talk to me about her experiences of mothering from afar and her relationship with Agustín and with Nina. She did not hesitate, as she seemed excited about the prospect of me taking some gifts to her son on my upcoming trip to Mexico, and she instructed me to come to her house in the following days to meet her US-born son, Felipe.

During this entire first visit, Marin, who did not speak any Spanish, and Sara, who barely spoke English and communicated with Nina only in Spanish, kept looking at each other as if they were checking in on each other to see if everything was going well. Marin interrupted me a few times to tell Sara that she did not need to speak with me at all, that she did not want Sara to feel pressured into talking to me because her boss set it up. The truth was, it was a power struggle and I did everything I could to make sure Sara knew of my intentions for research and that whatever her decision was, it would not affect my or her relationship with Marin.

A day later, upon her invitation, I went to East Harlem to visit Sara in the one-bedroom apartment that she shares with her husband and Felipe. As we sat in the kitchen and enjoyed some really spicy guacamole, I asked Sara about her crossing. Sara, like all other mothers who participated in this study, is undocumented. She had crossed into the United States by foot across the Arizona border, which got her to the city of Phoenix. From there, Sara and many others were put into trucks and vans that took them across the country to destinations such as North Carolina, Chicago, New Jersey, and NYC. As it was for other women in this research, her crossing was difficult, painful, and something that she hopes never to have to do again. Sara became dehydrated during her four-day crossing and passed out in the middle of the Sonoran desert. She remembers members of her group discussing if they should leave her behind and continue their journey. One man, who was a friend of her family, carried her for miles until the group found a place to hide from the border patrol. The crossing cost over $4000. Sara's sister, Rosa, already in NYC, helped her cover half of the cost. Sara paid part of the other half with her savings and got the remainder from her other sister, Gloria, also in the United States.

A single mother, Sara migrated alone, leaving her son Agustín behind with his maternal grandmother, Clarisa. Sara later met and started to live together with Marco in NYC, and together they had a son, Felipe, now five. I asked Sara how it was for her to be away from her child in Mexico but also have a child in NYC and care for a third one professionally. She responded: "One feels divided, you are here, but your heart sometimes is there. I know I left him with the best care I could ask for and...now I have a child here, with another man. It's hard...but I think it's better this way...and I also take care of Nina, who sometimes I spend more time with than with Felipe" (Interview, Sara, March 2010). When he wasn't in school, Sara took Felipe in to work at least twice a week, and when he wasn't with her, her sister took care of him and his cousins. Her sister lived upstairs in the same building, which made it easier for her.

Sara, Agustín, and Felipe

As Sara talked to me, she also checked her phone, only to find a text message from her fourteen-year-old son Agustín in Mexico that read: "hi I want to go out with my friends." Sara paused. She took a deep breath and typed a response while uttering the words out loud: "It's late already, what did your grandmother say?" Agustín texted back: "She said it is ok as long as you allow me to go." Sara responded: "You can go, but you need to text me when you come back home. It can't be after 9 p.m., tomorrow you have school." Agustín responded: "Ok, thank you." A couple of hours later Sara sent a text message to her cousin to confirm Agustín's whereabouts. Agustín did not come back at 9 p.m. and his grandmother, instead of calling Agustín on his cellphone, called Sara in New York and asked her to call Agustín, because she was worried.

In between the exchange of text messages and my interview with Sara, Felipe showed up in the kitchen crying because his cousin did not want to share her Spiderman toy with him. Sara tried, unsuccessfully, to convince him that he had so many other toys to play with that he did not need his cousin's action figure. When he kept insisting and crying, Sara told him, "Felipe, if you keep being like this I will send you and your cousin to Mexico to be with your *abuela*."

At that moment, I observed one of the many daily actions related to "care" that pertained to this particular transnational care constellation. In the few hours I spent at Sara's house during my first interview, I could see that the small town in Hidalgo and the reality in East Harlem were intrinsically connected. The constant communication among caregivers, children, and mothers regarding everyday decisions and daily discipline made the physical border between Mexico and the United States more fluid. In a split-screen moment, I was able to visualize Agustín going to school in San Nicolás, a town in Hidalgo with 300 residents, and Felipe getting on a bus to attend a public school in NYC. During my fieldwork I was able to accompany both Felipe and Agustín as they got up and went to school. They both woke up before 6 a.m. and ate breakfast before they left. They both complained on the way to school and wished they could have slept another ten minutes. Agustín received money from Sara every week and all his school costs were taken care of, but he wanted to drop out of school as soon as he finished junior high school. Even though Sara did not want Agustín to drop out of school, she felt she had no control over the matter. Alternatively, with Felipe, Sara was confident that dropping out of school was never an option as she felt completely in control. I reflected: when and where was school important? How did Sara's absence influence or shape Agustín's choices? Conversely, did Agustín's choices influence Felipe? And why did Sara feel powerless to affect Agustín?

Sara took center stage in her care constellation because of her decision-making power. This power was attributed to her by her sons and her mother but also claimed by her at times. Her role as the biological mother, or, as she described it, "the one who birthed him," was celebrated for better or for worse. She was the one who got asked for permission, she was the one who sent financial support, she was the one who bought gifts, and she was the one who made decisions about school-related activities. However, when she did not deliver on the practices related to care that were expected from her, she was criticized; she was blamed for everything that went wrong; she felt guilty and many times helpless.

Sara and other mothers I interviewed played a large role in the academic and educational lives of their children. Mothers and children had a tough time communicating about feelings, love life, personal desires, and dreams. However, when the discussion was about schooling—homework, classes, teachers, uniforms, books, summer classes, field trips, grades, parent-teacher conferences—the mothers were able to communicate their desires and assert their authority by giving children orders. Providing a better education was the topic that participants in the constellation thought to be the most important reason behind familial separation. The act of talking about school, according to another mother, meant that Agustín and Clarisa (Sara's mother) shared a relationship that Sara respected and did not try to compete with. As Sara said, "I left him with my mother. I can't fight with my mother and tell her off.... If she lets him do things that I do not agree with, sometimes I have to let it go. I know at this point he loves her more than he loves me. But that's all right. She is the one that *takes care of him*" (Interview, Sara, March 2010).

In my interviews with Clarisa in Mexico, she seemed concerned about not "going over Sara's head" in regard to Agustín's life. She stated: "Whenever she is ready, she should come back to enjoy her son.... They are only young for a certain period in their lives... and those are the most beautiful years. She should really enjoy him" (Interview, Clarisa, June 2010).

Sara and Marin

Marin was a successful physical therapist and her husband, Bob, was a chef and restaurateur. They had met later in life, and they adopted their daughter, Nina, when she was a few weeks old. Nina was born in Kenya, and Marin and Bob went to the country to pick her up. Nina has biological siblings who were adopted by other families in the United States and in Europe, and both Marin and Bob make sure she stays in touch with them via Skype and phone calls. Sara originally had a job cleaning the restaurant where Bob worked, and after a while she started cleaning Marin's house and then became Nina's caregiver when Marin went back to work full-time. Marin and Sara had a good relationship, in part because the existent language barrier prevented them from fully understanding each other and the tones used. When communication took place between them, there was a lot of smiling and pointing from both parties. Sara received $500 a week in cash to work full-time, five days a week, at Marin and Bob's house. Marin also provided a subway card for Sara and allowed her to bring her own son a couple of times a week when he was not in school. When I met Sara, she had been working with Marin and Bob for over a year. Sara spoke in Spanish with Nina, and Marin appreciated that.

The relationship had its bumps, however. Marin complained to me once about Sara using the washer and dryer to wash her own clothes without asking her first. She told me,

> You know, it's hard to figure out how to navigate domestic work . . . . I went to put my clothes in the washer and all her clothes and Felipe's clothes were in there. She obviously brought them here to wash them . . . but what do I do? If I tell you that I don't want her doing that I will sound petty. But the point is, I just wish she had told me before she used it.

She did become impatient with Sara multiple times about which food to give Nina and when and what to feed the dog. Marin could come off as abrasive, but she was a direct person who did not dance around an issue. Sara appreciated that she was never surprised or blindsided by Marin, but she also felt intimidated by her boss. Sara told me in an interview,

> All you want is someone that is just and nice. And she is. It's still hard because I work in her house, with her daughter, with her dog, it's her money that supports me and my two sons. Sometimes I feel like there is nothing that is . . . that is mine. There I am all the way from my *pueblito* in Mexico, working at this house in New York City, taking care of a girl that is not mine, so I can take care of my own?

Marin was aware of this struggle and she had Sara only do things in the house that pertained to her daughter. Unlike other cases I observed, where domestic work became a synonym for taking care of all things around the house. Marin had a job that allowed her to come home once or sometimes twice during the day to check in. Sara thought that Marin did not trust her in the beginning because she kept showing up at random times without warning. When I asked Marin about it, she told me, "I could come because I had breaks, but what if it was random? Isn't that for me to decide?" But Sara perceived it differently: "This is what I do, this is what I know how to do . . . why can't she trust me?" Most first-time mothers would agree that leaving your child with someone else to care for them may be a hard thing. For Sara, however, being undocumented, having left her child in Mexico, not speaking English and depending on that weekly salary to pay rent and buy food, put her in a tough spot when it came to negotiating or standing her ground regarding her skills.

Marin tried to help Sara at different times in her life. After coming back from a summer in Mexico for research, I received a call from Marin. "Can you come here to our house?" she asked. She seemed worried. I said yes. By then I had been doing research with Sara's family for over six months. When I arrived at Marin's apartment, Sara was sitting there looking upset and in shock. Marin asked me, "Can you translate what is going on? I think her husband did something bad to her, but I can't understand." I sat next to Sara and she told me:

Sara: He cheated on me and, Gabi, I found out.... I looked on his cellphone and I saw all the messages between him and that whore. I saw all the messages.... They were planning to see each other that same night. So I confronted him holding the cellphone in my hand. He told me I was crazy and that I had to stop screaming. He said, "If you don't stop screaming I'm going to call the police and then they will take Felipe away from you and deport you." I kept screaming, Gabi.... I held on to a knife and looked at him and I said, "I'm going to kill you," but I didn't mean it.... My sister came downstairs and she started screaming at me, calling me crazy. How could she take his side?

Gabi: Then what happened?

Sara: He called the cops and they showed up. I thought they were going to take my son. I was about to lose another one.... I just dropped down on the floor and cried. The police said for me to calm down and I explained to them what happened.... They just said "Everyone calm down" and then they left.

Gabi: Then did you talk to Marco?

Sara: Yes, and he said, "I recorded you threatening me and I will use this recording and show it to your boss and to the police. You will never work with Nina and see Felipe."

At this point Sara was in tremendous distress, and we took a quick break. Marin asked me to translate for her and, with Sara's consent, I did. Marin was shocked and upset. She immediately grabbed her cell phone and called a friend:

Marin: Arnold, hi, how are you? Good, good.... Listen, sorry to be quick, but can we come by this afternoon? I have a legal question.... It's urgent.... It's for my nanny, we need to help her. Ok...2:30, thanks so much.

Sara continued,

Sara:	Can you imagine all this happening? Can he have recorded me?
Gabi:	Sara, I don't understand how it would be possible since you had his phone the entire time. But I don't know....
Sara:	What if he tells the police and I am deported? What I am going to do?
Gabi:	Sara, I think Marin just made an appointment with a lawyer who is her friend. He will help us figure out what to do next, ok?
>*Sara:*	Ok...but then (her voice cracked)....
Gabi:	Then what.... What would you like to tell me?
Sara:	After he said I was going to be deported, he made me...he made me have sex with him.... He said you are still my wife and I can do this....
Gabi:	That was last night?
Sara:	Yes....
Gabi:	Would you like to go to the hospital and get counseling and checked out?
Sara:	No, no...no way.

I again translated the interaction to Marin, who became enraged. She said she was going to find this guy and teach him a lesson. This entire time Felipe and Nina were playing in the room. We got all the kids and headed to the subway to go meet the lawyer. When we arrived there, we were ushered into a conference room. Felipe and Nina were around us and Nina was skipping from chair to chair. She eventually fell hard on her face and cried loudly. Sara and Marin were both trying to console her. Marin apologized to Nina for not making a big deal when she was indeed hurting. Sara kept saying, "You're ok, you're ok." Nina was divided. She took turns going to her mom and going to Sara, while the lawyer patiently waited for us to tell him what was going on. Marin said, "You both stay here and tell Arnold what is going on while I entertain the kids outside. Once you have recommendations, Arnold, call me back in."

Sara told me the whole story again and I told the lawyer in English. Arnold said that Marco was definitely not recording Sara, so she could calm down about it. He also told her that the fact that Marco was having an affair and forced himself onto her would give them a strong case if he decided to pursue anything against her. Arnold called Marin back in and told all of us, "Listen, you are going to let this guy know that you have support and that you are not alone in this fight. I am not telling you to threaten him, but let him know that your boss and a lawyer are aware of what happened. Take my business card and hand it to him. If something changes, call me, and we will deal with this." Sara thanked him and thanked Marin. She was grateful, but she also told me she was embarrassed for having brought up an issue that was so personal.

Marco moved out the next day and agreed to pay Sara $600 a month to help with rent. She took a hit financially and had to look for another, cheaper, apartment that she could share with other family members and their children. Marco moved in with his new girlfriend and she became pregnant a few months after. Sara and Marco ended up being civil because of Felipe, who spent one night with his dad every other week.

Sara and Nina

"I finally have a girl" Sara told me in the first day I spent with her and Nina. Unlike other observations I had made of caregivers and the children, Sara was very firm with Nina. She had no problem telling her no and asking her straight questions like, "Do you want to go to the bathroom now before we leave? If you don't go now, you will have to hold it in." Nina ran to bathroom before we headed out. She had been potty-trained already (by Marin), and Sara followed Marin's tone when speaking to Nina. With her own son she was more permissive—there was hardly a "no" being said—but with Nina, Sara was determined: "She is such a fast learner, you teach her once and she knows.... She respects me and loves me and doesn't challenge me like Felipe or worse, like Agustín.... Sometime I think about how far I am to how I was raised and how far I am from my children and how close I am with a stranger who becomes dependent on me" (referring to Nina).

"Sara, Sara" called Nina, "look, *uno, dos, tres,*" counting in Spanish and pointing at pigeons in the park. Sara responded, "Great job, your Spanish is great," and Nina smiled. They were not very affectionate with each other in terms of hugs, kisses and cuddling because Marin was not like that, and Sara took her job very seriously to follow the mother's lead. At the same time, her interactions with Nina represented her attempts to correct how she had raised and was raising her other two sons. Sara never screamed at Nina, though Marin did. Sara hardly got scared when Nina ran in front of her in NYC sidewalks; Marin, on the other hand, had intense episodes of panic and fear whenever her daughter would get remotely close to the streets. Sara was proud of her relationship with Nina, and she described her impact on Nina's life as a positive one:

> She [Nina] sees me for who I am. She doesn't know about with or without papers, she doesn't know I don't speak good English, she doesn't know the house I live in is so small, and that I make so little money and that I haven't seen one of my sons in eight years and that my mother is sick. But she still loves me. That's nice. I think because she also came from a different country and she was also separated from the one [who] gave birth to her, she connects with me.... Don't you think?

CARING FOR THEM ALL

How do Sara and the other mothers interviewed experience care with each child? Sara asked me once, "How many children do you think you could fit in your heart?" I asked her why she was asking me that, and she responded, "I think I can fit my three right now...like there's no more room.... I mean they are each different, because with Agustín I am far away but I can send him things and money, with Felipe he is now here in the US, and with Nina...I make sure everything is correct, you know?"

As women establish transnational arrangements of familial ties, their roles become more fluid since they are constantly negotiating everyday decisions regarding children in Mexico and children in the United States, both their own and the ones they care for professionally. To say that their roles are completely transformed once they arrive in the United States and that these women become "empowered" through the process of migration because of their breadwinner status is to disregard the constant reconciliations they must make with what they have learned growing up about what a good mother and a good woman "should" be. At the same time, to state that women only reproduce the gender roles present in the host society is to ignore the active and creative ways in which mothers care "for them all" here and there.

Many of the migrant women I interviewed saw professional caregiving as an opportunity to "get it right" when raising children. Thus, part of their commitment to raising children like Nina was that they felt at one point that they were being valued for a set of skills they had: to care for and mother a child. However the contradiction was not lost on them. The very skill they found so valuable was the one they left in Mexico to migrate to this country, namely caring for a child every day. Dora, another mother I interviewed, told me, "when you go to an interview they ask you, 'What experience do you have with caring for children' and then you say, 'Well first of all I have children of my own,' they are like 'Oh, great, are they here?' and you say, 'No, I left them with my mother in Mexico'...so you will give me a job even though I left my own child at home in Mexico?" Forty-six other mothers responded in similar fashion when asked about going to interviews and discussing personal life and experiences with future employees. They explained that the supposed beneficiaries of their migration, their children in Mexico, were the ones who had provided them with firsthand experience to be a professional caregiver in NYC. Over forty women interviewed agreed that saying that they had children of their own helped them land the first few caregiving jobs they had in NYC.

Getting along with your employers while doing domestic and care work is not always easy (cf. Hondagneu-Sotelo 2001). Migrant women described "good" families as "*suerte*" (luck), but more often than not, domestic workers, including nannies, described situations where employers "pressed their buttons" and used their predicament as immigrants who support an entire family at home (in Mexico) as a way to get more out of them. One mother, Gemma, explained to me, "It's like they know we care about their children and that for us is a big deal to be far away from our own, so they know we need that job, not just because of the money, but because we care about the children."

The biggest fear for women working as professional caregivers is the fact that children grow up and go to school; all of a sudden, your employer doesn't need you for a full-time job. As Marta, a professional caregiver and migrant mother told me

> You play a movie in your head to convince yourself that your sacrifice is worth it. You play that over and over. And then your employer tells you, now she is two and she will go to part-time school, so you get a cut in hours and pay.... The movie breaks into pieces and you can only think: my own children are not with me and there I go [to] find another child to love and care for.... Sometimes it makes me sick.

CONCLUSION

When I began this study looking for transnational practices of families' everyday lives, I did not understand in detail how the concept of care worked across transnational boundaries or how the nature of kinship relations would shift in the context of global political economy, increased migration, and the gender hierarchies that are characteristic of a highly integrated and globalized world. Although I am not arguing that maternal migration necessarily provokes a shift in familial power structures, as have other researchers, I have discovered a marked shift in familial dynamics, through transnational care constellations and the structures of care that influence the lives of children involved.

My research shows how women such as Sara make sense of their roles as mothers as well as professional caregivers. Authors like Arlie Hochschild and Barbara Ehrenreich (2002) as well as Pierrette Hondagneu-Sotelo (2001) have discussed free-market forces and how they affect domestic work. My interviews with Sara, Marta, Gemma and others open up a different—emotional—dimension of women's paid jobs as they provide a window into their own identity as mothers. These women constantly try to justify to themselves the reasoning behind doing this work. Employers such as Marin, who were also working mothers, were helpful and genuinely interested in trying to assist their nannies. However, the fact that care in this context is a commodity and part of a much larger chain of labor and globalization meant that employers limited their involvement to the point where they thought they could handle it, and where it did not interfere with meeting their own needs. Care workers were at their employers' mercy, grateful when they "found a good family" but having little control over their working conditions beyond that.

As this chapter shows, the ideals and practices of caregiving are made and remade as women try to navigate the reality that they are simultaneously caring for different sets of children, some of whom may not be geographically, culturally or economically close. Even though these ideals and practices may seem at odds when viewed from the perspective of conventional US norms, they are actually adaptations of what the women consider to be "good" and "caring" motherhood and caregiving.

Behind many care workers and most remittances, there is a separated family, a situation that makes things even more complicated. In the case of migration from Mexico, women not only leave some children behind but bring others with them, and then also sometimes give birth to more children in the United States, creating "mixed-origin" families of children who have both mixed backgrounds and also mixed citizenship status. The layers that contribute to the predicament these women find themselves in deserve closer attention. A macro view of how domestic labor is regulated in the United States as well as other countries is important; however, we cannot ignore the different micro contexts where nannies, caregivers, and domestic workers come from, and where they live as migrants. These micro contexts tell us much about the bigger picture we crave to see as they reveal the complicated, layered, and multi-factor struggles women go through, and they allow us to expand our view from individual experiences to entire constellations.

NOTE

1. Employment visas to the United States are allotted mainly for "skilled" labor.

REFERENCES

Abrego, Leisy. 2009. "Economic Well-being in Salvadoran Transnational Families: How Gender Affects Remittance Practices." *Journal of Marriage and Family* 71: 1070–1085.

Aguilar, Filomeno V., Jr., John Estanley Penalosa, Tanya Belen Liwanag, Resto Cruz and Jimmy Melendrez. 2009. *Maalwang Buhay: Family, Overseas Migration and Cultures of Relatedness in Barangay Paraiso.* Quezon City: Ateneo de Manila University Press.

Bernhard, Judith, Patricia Landolt and Luin Goldring. 2005. "Transnational, Multi-Local Motherhood: Experiences of Separation and Reunification among Latin American Families in Canada." *Early Childhood Education Publications and Research. CERIS Working Paper* No. 40. Toronto: Ryerson University.

Boehm, Deborah A. 2011. "Here/Not Here: Contingent Citizenship and Transnational Mexican Children." In Coe et al., 161–73.

Castles, Stephen. 1999. "International Migration and the Global Agenda: Reflections on the 1998 UN Technical Symposium." *International Migration* 37, 1: 5–19.

Cerrutti, Marcela and Douglas S. Massey. 2001. "On the Auspices of Female Migration from Mexico to the United States." *Demography* 38: 187–200.

Coe, Cati et al., eds. 2011. *Everyday Ruptures: Children, Youth, and Migration in Global Perspective.* Nashville: Vanderbilt University Press.

Cohen, Jeffrey H. 2004. *The Culture of Migration in Southern Mexico*. Austin: University of Texas Press.

Dreby, Joanna. 2009a. "Negotiating Work and Family over the Life Course: Mexican Family Dynamics in a Binational Context." In *Across Generations: Immigrant Families in America*, edited by Nancy Foner, 190–218. New York: New York University Press.

Dreby, Joanna. 2009b. "Transnational Gossip," *Qualitative Sociology* 32: 33–52.

Dreby, Joanna. 2010. *Divided by Borders: Mexican Migrants and Their Children*. Berkeley: University of California Press.

Dreby, Joanna and Leah Schmalzbauer. 2013. "The Relational Contexts of Migration: Mexican Women in New Destination Sites." *Sociological Forum* 28:1–26.

Dreby, Joanna and Lindsay Stutz. 2012. "Making Something of the Sacrifice: Gender, Migration and Mexican Children's Educational Aspirations." *Global Networks* 12, 1: 71–90.

Dwyer, James. 2004. "Illegal Immigrants, Health Care, and Social Responsibility." *Hastings Report* 34, 5: 34–41.

Ehrenreich, Barbara and Arlie Hochschild, eds. 2002. *Global Women: Nannies, Maids and Sex Workers in the New Economy*. New York: Metropolitan Books.

Fernández-Kelly, Maria Patricia. 2008. "Gender and Economic Change in the United States and Mexico, 1900–2000." *American Behavioral Scientist* 52: 377–404.

Forbes Martin, Susan. 2003. *Refugee Women*. Lanham, MD: Lexington Books.

Fresnoza-Flot, Asuncion. 2013. "Cultural Capital Acquisition Through Maternal Migration: Educational Experiences of Filipino Left-Behind Children." In *Refugees, Immigrants, and Education in the Global South: Lives in Motion*, edited by Lesley Bartlett and Ameena Ghaffar-Kucher, 238–52. Hoboken: Taylor and Francis Routledge Research.

Hamann, Edmund T. and Victor Zúñiga. 2011. "Schooling and the Everyday Ruptures Transnational Children Encounter in the United States and Mexico." In Coe et al., 141–60.

Heymann, Jody et al. 2009. "The Impact of Migration on the Well-Being of Transnational Families: New Data from Sending Communities in Mexico." *Community, Work & Family* 12: 91–103.

Hirsch, Jennifer H. 2003. *A Courtship after Marriage: Sexuality and Love in Mexican Transnational Families*. Berkeley: University of California Press.

Hondagneu-Sotelo, Pierrette. 2001. *Doméstica: Immigrant Workers Cleaning and Caring in the Shadows of Affluence*. Berkeley: University of California Press.

Hondagneu-Sotelo, Pierrette, ed. 2003. *Gender and U.S. Immigration: Contemporary Trends*. Berkeley: University of California Press.

Hondagneu-Sotelo, Pierrette and Ernestine Avila. 1997. "I'm Here but I'm There: The Meanings of Latina Transnational Motherhood." *Gender & Society* 11: 548–560.

Jørgen, Carling, Cecilia Menjívar and Leah Schmalzbauer. 2012. "Central Themes in the Study of Transnational Parenthood." *Journal of Ethnic and Migration Studies* 38, 1: 55–72.

Kandel, William and Grace Kao. 2001. "The Impact of Temporary Labor Migration on Mexican Children's Educational Aspirations and Performance." *International Migration Review* 3: 1205–1231.

Kandel, William and Doreen Massey. 2002. "The Culture of Mexican Migration: A Theoretical and Empirical Analysis." *Social Forces* 80: 981–1004.

Lahaie, Claudia et al. 2009. "Work and Family Divided across Borders: The Impact of Parental Migration on Mexican Children in Transnational Families." *Community, Work & Family* 12: 299–312.

Lewis, Oscar. 1959. *Five Families: Mexican Case Studies in the Culture of Poverty.* New York: Basic Books.

Madianou, Mirca and Daniel Miller. 2012. *Migration and New Media: Transnational Families and Polymedia.* New York: Routledge.

Marcus, George E. 1995. "Ethnography in/of the World System: The Emergence of Multi-Sited Ethnography." *Annual Review of Anthropology* 24: 95–117.

Mujeres Unidas y Activas [Day Labor Program, Women's Collective of La Raza Centro Legal]. 2007. "Behind Closed Doors: Working Conditions of California Household Workers." San Francisco: Mujeres Unidas y Activas Data Center, March.

Parreñas, Rhacel Salazar. 2001. "Mothering from a Distance: Emotions, Gender and Intergenerational Relations in Filipino Transnational Families." *Feminist Studies* 27: 261–290.

Parreñas, Rhacel Salazar. 2005. *Children of Global Migration: Transnational Families and Gendered Woes.* Manila: Ateneo de Manila University Press.

Parreñas, Rhacel Salazar. 2010. "Transnational Mothering: A Source of Gender Conflicts in the Family." *University of North Carolina Law Review* 88: 1825–1856.

Paz, Octavio. 1985. *The Labyrinth of Solitude and Other Writings.* New York: Grove Press.

Sassen, Saskia. 2002. "Global Cities and Survival Circuits." In Ehrenreich and Hochschild, 254–74.

Sassen, Saskia. 2010. "Strategic Gendering: One Factor in the Constituting of Novel Political Economies." In *International Handbook of Gender and Poverty: Concepts, Research, Policy,* edited by Sylvia Chant. Cheltenham: Edward Elgar.

Schmalzbauer, Leah. 2005. *Striving and Surviving: A Daily Analysis of Honduran Transnational Families.* New York: Routledge, New Approaches in Sociology, Studies in Social Inequality.

Smith, Robert C. 2005. *Mexican New York: Transnational Lives of New Immigrants.* Berkeley and Los Angeles: University of California Press.

Suárez-Orozco, Carola and Marcelo M. Suárez-Orozco. 2001. *Children of Immigration.* Cambridge, MA: Harvard University Press.

United Nations. 2013. "Population Facts." http://www.un.org/en/develop ment/desa/population/publications/pdf/popfacts/popfacts_2013-1.pdf

Yarris, Kristin E. 2011. "Living with Mother Migration: Grandmothers, Caregiving, and Children in Nicaraguan Transnational Families." PhD dissertation, University of California, Los Angeles.

Yeates, Nicola. 2005. "Migration and Social Policy in International Context: The Analytical and Policy Uses of a Global Care Chains Perspective." Paper presented at Arusha (Tanzania) conference on "New Frontiers of Social Policy," December.

Gabrielle Oliveira, from São Paulo, Brazil, received her PhD in applied anthropology from Teachers College, Columbia University, where she became a lecturer in the Department of International and Transcultural Studies. Her research focuses on female Mexican migration to the United States with a specific focus on transnational motherhood, separated siblings, childhood, and education. She was a Spencer Foundation Dissertation Fellow and finished her post-doc at the University of Wisconsin's School of Education. She is now assistant professor at Boston College's Lynch School of Education.

PART III

All (Global) Politics are Local

Responses to Abuse Against Migrant Domestic Workers: A Multi-scalar Comparison of Taiwan, Hong Kong, and Shanghai

André Laliberté

Migrant domestic workers (MDWs) in Hong Kong, Taipei, and Shanghai suffer from a variety of abuses from their employers, often in complicity with brokers. How have governments and civil society responded? This chapter reports on a comparative survey of the measures taken by governments and private sectors to address abuses against such workers in Taiwan, the Hong Kong Special Administrative Region (HKSAR), and Shanghai. This multi-scalar comparison identifies the most efficient ways in which governments can intervene to prevent abuse against domestic migrant workers. The three locations have similar demographic and socioeconomic characteristics, but the authorities examined here represent three different levels of government: national, semi-autonomous, and

An earlier version of this chapter was presented at the ILO-sponsored 4th Conference on the Rights of Domestic Workers, "Developing and implementing policies for a better future at work," July 8–10, 2015, Geneva, Switzerland

A. Laliberté (✉)
School of Political Studies, University of Ottawa, Ottawa, ON, Canada

S. Michel, I. Peng (eds.), *Gender, Migration, and the Work of Care*,
DOI 10.1007/978-3-319-55086-2_6

municipal. The locations also represent three different forms of political system: liberal democratic in Taiwan, "consultative authoritarian" in Shanghai, and a hybrid between the two systems in Hong Kong. This chapter, based on fieldwork in all three locations, identifies the actors in government, the agencies that recruit and place domestic workers, and the organizations that advocate the protection of their rights, and assesses their relative influence and resources. I analyze the role of governments, employment agencies, civil society, and faith-based/communal organizations in promoting/guaranteeing and/or respecting the rights of domestic workers.

Research Design

The three areas have most similar conditions with respect to demographic structure, levels of social and economic development, exposure to international trade, integration into the global economy, and role as major sources of economic, commercial, and political influence within their respective country. Most importantly, the Republic of China (ROC) (Taiwan)[1] the HKSAR, and the Special Municipality of Shanghai[2] are primarily urbanized areas with wealthy middle classes which rely on an unusually high number of MDWs.

People in all these three areas share the same cultural heritage, broadly defined here as "Chinese," with markers of identity such as a language using characters,[3] allegiance to worldviews/religions with specific concepts about life after death, retribution for sins, social norms and expectation, and obligations throughout generation, in the tradition of Confucianism, Taoism, and Buddhism. Central to these and relevant here is the value attributed to the concept of filial piety, which entails an obligation toward one's parents and grandparents.

There are, however, key differences that could help explain variations in outcome in these locations: levels of government with unequal powers, and differences in political regime. For example, Taiwan is a fully sovereign state,[4] the HKSAR enjoys a large degree of autonomy within the People's Republic of China (PRC), under the framework of "one country, two systems,"[5] and Shanghai is a Special Municipality within the PRC, with important political clout, but no measure of autonomy. This chapter assesses whether level of government influences the ability–or the willingness—of authorities to comply with the international labor standards for domestic workers adopted by the International Labour Organization

(ILO). Turning to the other significant difference, the nature of political regime, Taiwan is a full-fledged multi-party democracy and Hong Kong is a hybrid regime of multi-party democracy with limited representation, while Shanghai is a constituent entity within an authoritarian party-state whose leaders consider democracy a "dangerous idea." The differences in political regimes are superimposed on the differences in level of government in terms of political autonomy: Taiwan's government is the most autonomous and the most democratic among the three entities considered here. The Shanghai government has the lowest political autonomy and is also the least democratic of the three.

This chapter asks whether the differences in level of governments and in the position on the democracy-authoritarian spectrum, which imply varying degrees of responsiveness to pressures from international organizations, have any impact on governments' willingness to implement the rights of MDWs and can trump the other factors that are likely to foster similarities in the approach of each government in its treatment of MDWs. I address this question as follows: after presenting a short historical outline of the MDW presence in Taiwan, Hong Kong, and Shanghai, I compare the labor condition and workplace abuses suffered by MDWs in the three locations, paying attention to the differences and similarities that need to be explained. I outline the two key differences in terms of level of government—multi-scalar differences—and of political regimes in the three cases. Moving to the outcomes, I present the responses of the governments in the three locations to international and domestic pressures from civil society in addressing the situation of MDWs; this will serve to underline the effects, if any, of the two explanatory variables that we expect to effect change.

The chapter relies on fieldwork conducted during the summer of 2015 in Hong Kong, Shanghai, and Taipei, with a follow-up in Taiwan in the spring of 2016. This included interviews with over fifty civil servants, NGO activists, scholars, journalists, in English and Mandarin. It also comprised participant observation with NGOs involved with promoting the rights of workers, in Hong Kong and Taiwan.

Who Are the MDWs?

This chapter focuses on a small portion of the global market for migrant care workers, albeit in a region that is poised to see a significant increase in the demand for such labor in years to come, especially in China's big cities.

Economists have argued that the entry of native-born women in the labor force of Hong Kong and Taiwan has generated demand for live-in foreign labor doing domestic work and providing child care (Cortes and Pan 2013). Similar dynamics in Shanghai have created a demand for migrant workers from Chinese provinces who are already living in the city to help women working outside the household. But there are differences in the legal provision surrounding the work of MDWs: the range of services that MDWs can provide in Hong Kong and in Shanghai is greater than that in Taiwan, where the law forbids caregivers working for elders to perform any other tasks such as household chores and child care.[6] As the discussion below reveals, however, these legal differences may not matter much because of the widespread practices of employers who ignore the law, and the inability—or unwillingness—of authorities to enforce it.[7]

MDWs in Taiwan and Hong Kong are known officially as "foreign domestic workers," but both employers and government officials use euphemisms to conceal the reality of their condition. In Taiwan they are known as foreign domestic "caregivers,"[8] while in Hong Kong they are officially labeled as foreign domestic "helpers,"[9] an identity that robs them of their rights as workers.[10] In both cases, foreigners represent a majority of all MDWs, and local domestic workers represent a minority of the workforce that is relatively better-off than the foreigners yet resentful of the latter, whom they see as "stealing their jobs."[11] Local domestic workers, as citizens, are fully protected by the local labor laws in Taiwan and Hong Kong. Not so foreign domestic workers, who are extremely vulnerable in their condition as temporary workers without any chance of becoming citizens in Taiwan or securing the right of abode (other than their employers') in Hong Kong. Local residents in Taiwan and Hong Kong, on the other hand, shun hiring local domestic workers, whom prospective employers consider too expensive and too demanding.[12]

In Shanghai, the distinction between foreign and local domestic workers is irrelevant. Most of the MDWs are fellow Chinese nationals, i.e. internal migrants from rural regions, and as such they are protected by the labor legislation of the PRC. One specific characteristic of China, however, makes the situation of MDWs in Shanghai not so different from that of their counterparts in Taiwan and Hong Kong in terms of social exclusion: the residence permit.[13] Under the so-called *hukou* system, all Chinese citizens and their dependents are entitled access to free social services in health care, education for their family, and elderly care in the location where they are born. The residency requirement, however, limits their eligibility for social services when they move to another province, and most importantly, from the countryside to the city. As a result of this system, Shanghai MDWs who want to benefit from the free or low-cost social services they are entitled to as citizens must return to their native places, as indicated in their residence permits, unless they are willing to pay or accept lower-quality services provided at a lower cost in situations of gray legality.

In Taiwan, MDWs represent a significant proportion of all foreign workers, who are roughly divided into two distinct categories: workers in industry and factories, and domestic workers.[14] According to the Ministry of Labor (MOL), in May 2015 there were 349,000 workers in "productive industries" and 225,000 in the sector of social welfare, mostly MDWs.[15] Both categories of foreign workers are excluded from general employment statistics in Taiwan, but detailed statistics provided monthly by the MOL give information about their national origins and locations in each of Taiwan's municipalities and counties, as well as the nature of their work, disaggregated into nineteen categories for specific types of activities for factory workers,[16] and into two separate categories for MDWs: mostly nursing (98 percent of the total), and housemaids. Most MDWs in Taiwan are located in the three largest cities: the greater Taipei area, Taichung, and Kaohsiung.

In Hong Kong, MDWs are invisible as far as the government is concerned. Fact sheets produced by the HKSAR government do not indicate numbers of immigrants relative to the native-born population, and labor force statistics broken down by industry lump together "public administration, social and personal services," the category most likely to include MDWs.[17] The Immigration Department does not help either, as it does not provide numbers for MDWs but only notes that 28,300 individuals were admitted to the HKSAR through a program encouraging overseas professionals to apply for work if they have special skills, expertise, and experience lacking in Hong Kong.[18] The Labor Department mentions two other programs for the importation of labor: a supplementary labor scheme (SLS), which allows employers to import staff, and a program for the recruitment of Foreign Domestic Helpers (FDH), but the department does not provide specific numbers for the people who make use of them.[19]

In Shanghai, the number of foreign workers is relatively modest; they are mostly employed by expatriate residents, and not all of them employ FDW.[20] This may reflect the fact that at least until 2009, FDW were not allowed in the country (ILO 2009). Informants have mentioned the existence of such foreign domestic workers, but their numbers are negligible. However, the proportion of MDWs coming from other provinces in Shanghai's labor force is important: according to one estimate, this figure is over 300,000 people (ILO 2009, 2)—50 percent more than the number of registered MDWs observed in Taiwan, but a smaller proportion of the total workforce than that observed in Hong Kong. By 2013, this number has reached 490,000 (*Insight* 2014). MDWs coming from other provinces to Shanghai, most of my informants have claimed, are likely to work for several employers and do not have to live at their employer's residence, unlike MDWs in Taiwan and Hong Kong.[21]

In both Taiwan and Hong Kong, most of the MDWs come from two countries—Indonesia and the Philippines—although the dynamics of migratory flows from the sending countries has changed considerably since they began arriving in these two locations. Filipinas came first, but over the years, their increasing ability to assert their rights and fight back against the abuse they suffered from a few unscrupulous employers and agencies made them less likely to be hired. Many employers have looked to people of other nationalities who are perceived as less demanding and more docile.[22] Indonesian women, who do not speak English and are seen as being more "modest" and subservient, have become favorite employees for Taiwanese. According to the Taiwan Labor Department, in 2015 there were over 170,000 Indonesian MDWs in the country, compared to only about 20,000 Filipinas. In Hong Kong, the Census and Statistics Department indicated that in 2011, 48 percent of the MDWs came from the Philippines and 49 percent from Indonesia (Hong Kong CSD 2012; AI 2013), revealing the beginnings of a similar shift.[23]

The MDW labor market is now shifting again, following the scandal caused by a horrific case of abuse in Hong Kong, against Erwiana Sulistyaningsih, an Indonesian MDW who suffered six months of physical abuse by her employer. The crime prompted the Indonesian government to clamp down on MDWs' movement out of the country (albeit temporarily).[24] The particular case, however, represented the tip of the iceberg of a more systemic problem, one that revealed the vulnerability of MDWs in general, who are often isolated because of their inability to speak the local language and therefore cannot communicate with people who could help them. However, the governments of the receiving countries, rather than questioning the nature of the labor market conditions that enable such abuses in the first place, have simply decided to look elsewhere for a supply of labor and have entered into negotiations with other sending countries to offset the anticipated labor shortage that the Indonesian decision is likely to create. Hence the New Taipei City Labor Department and the Hong Kong Equal Opportunity Commission, in anticipation of trends to come, have both prepared documentation in Vietnamese and other languages to help recruit MDWs from other countries. Both are actively cooperating with governments or employers' agencies in other countries in South and Southeast Asia.

The migration of domestic MDWs to Shanghai is more recent than in Taiwan and Hong Kong, having increased in the 1990s following a rise in the demand for their services, as the middle class became ever more important. The MDWs come from neighboring provinces, especially the poorer ones. Cultural differences with respect to language dialect, culinary habits, and customs, are important enough to set the migrants apart from the native Shanghai population.[25]

Main Source of Abuses Against MDWs

In all three locations, MDWs represent extremely vulnerable segments of the population. As foreigners in Taiwan and Hong Kong and outsiders in Shanghai, they are subject to abuse coming from three different sources. First, *employers*, some of whom are themselves in relatively deprived socio-economic categories, regard the MDWs as an expendable source of labor (in some of the worst cases, employers impose on their employees virtually slave-like working conditions, as I document below). Second, *placement agencies*, which impose fees on employers in exchange for finding them the most compatible employees, also often extract from the latter "training fees," exploiting the opportunity offered by an expanding labor market that has yet to be fully regulated. Finally, MDWs suffer from *regulations* that seriously harm their rights and limit their opportunity for redress in cases of abuse. MDWs in Taiwan, Hong Kong, and Shanghai confront similar forms of abuse, but their ability to address them differs from one locale to another. On the one hand, the media in Taiwan and Hong Kong have been instrumental in attracting attention to the most egregious cases of abuse and eventually shaming all parties concerned. In Shanghai, Chinese Communist Party rules limit the media's ability to expose abuses, making it more difficult to measure the extent of bad treatment against the MDW in that city. Moreover, as I discuss below, the possibility of a sustained mobilization by civil society actors, in particular religious institutions, in Taiwan and Hong Kong, enables a kind of redress that is less likely in Shanghai, where civil society has less autonomy.

Workplace abuses at the hands of employers are the most obvious source of suffering endured by MDWs. We know much about the cases of bad treatment reported in Taiwan and Hong Kong thanks to the advocacy work performed by civil society organizations, some reporting by the media, and major scholarly investigations about the life and work of foreign domestic workers (Liang 2014; Tseng and Wang 2013; Lin and Bélanger 2012; Pan and Yang 2012; Lan 2002). In both Taiwan and Hong Kong, the main source of exploitation rests on the requirement that migrant caregivers and domestic helpers live in their employers' homes. Differences in the labor legislation between the two locations, however, explain the specific forms of mistreatment in each place. The residency requirement, known in Hong Kong as the "live-in rule," was originally meant to ensure that employers fulfill the obligation to find their employees a place to live. But in practice, this rule has come to mean confinement and limited opportunities to communicate outside of the employer's home, leaving the latter total control over the life of his/her employee. The space set aside for MDWs in many employers' home is tiny and affords them little to no privacy. In Taiwan, the live-in requirement is made all the more stringent by a rule forbidding employers to hire MDWs for anything other than care for the elderly; this rule is often flouted by employers, putting their employees in a constant state of anxiety.

For too many MDWs, one immediate consequence of the obligation to live in is that they are on-call 24 hours a day, all year long in the case of the most abusive employers. In 2015 Taiwan's Ministry of Labor found that 70 percent of caregivers worked 365 days a year and only 30 percent were given one day off a month (Hsiao 2015). In Taiwan and Hong Kong, employers must, according to the law, provide one day of rest to their employees each week. For MDWs, these breaks are important to socialize, send remittances to their family, and simply get a well-deserved rest. However, some employers limit even this time off, out of fear that their employees would take the opportunity to escape. In the worst cases, the lack of rest resulting from demands for overtime work has led to death from sheer exhaustion.

The restriction on free time not only violates workers' right to rest, but also prevents their possibility of having any form of social life outside of work —or joining a union or other DW rights organization. In the worst cases of ill-treatment, the absence of a private space for domestic workers make them vulnerable to physical abuse, sexual abuse, and other forms of harassment (Pan and Yang 2012). An especially egregious form of restrictions on MDWs' rights is employers' practice of confiscating employees' passports, thus preventing them from leaving to find an employer elsewhere.[26]

We know much less about the treatment experienced by MDWs in Shanghai because, relative to the other two locations, the PRC bars the exposure of abusive conditions that free media and a robust civil society can provide. Without guarantees that independent NGOs can work without fear of retribution from authorities and given the constraints on the media, there is no way to confirm that media silence on abuse against MDWs reflects the reality of their situation. Few scholarly studies of the situation of MDWs in China pay specific attention to Shanghai (Shen 2015; Qiu 2013; see also Hong, this book). A rare exception is a 2009 ILO report that sheds light on the fate of domestic workers, mentioning that they suffer from conditions similar to those that affect their counterparts in Taiwan and Hong Kong, including long working hours and overtime without compensation, risks of sexual or physical abuse, low adherence to labor contracts, and lack of access to social insurance (ILO 2009, 5). There is little reason to believe that the situation in Shanghai is better than elsewhere in China, as the study by the ILO covered that city along with others of a comparable size.[27]

The second source of abuses affects both employees and their employers. Brokers and placement agencies charge prospective immigrants for finding them good employment opportunities in Taiwan and Hong Kong. These fees can represent up to three months of salary, which basically means that MDWs are working as indentured laborers—without pay—for the first few months in their new workplaces. Aggravating the situation are the fees charged to employers, which can be passed on to the employees.[28] Moreover, some unscrupulous brokers in Taiwan and Hong Kong impose additional fees for training and the cost of relocation, which can result in more unpaid wages. Brokers also fail both employees and their employers when they omit to notify appropriate authorities about mistreatment on the part of abusive employers. More concerned with keeping their business, some brokers and placement agencies prefer to ignore mistreatment on the part of employers and continue to lead unaware MDWs to them. In both Taiwan and Hong Kong, the market for placement agencies is highly competitive and poorly regulated. As I discuss below, reforming this market has become a priority for NGOs concerned with the welfare of foreign workers.

Throughout China, the ILO concluded in its 2009 report, there are over 600,000 placement agencies for domestic workers. In Shanghai, however, there are "only" 1000 registered agencies, despite the fact that the city's population counts for 1/55 of the country's total. This number is all the more remarkable since its population is one of the most likely to resort to MDWs of all of China's cities. The relatively small number of placement agencies—comparable to Taiwan and Hong Kong—simply reflects the maturity of the market for this kind of firm. A handful of placement agencies are operating in many of the city's districts, and the most important of them are in fact oligopolies that act as federations of smaller agencies. I could not find studies of placement agencies in Shanghai,[29] but my own fieldwork revealed an extraordinary variety, including large enterprises catering to the entire municipality and small local firms serving the neighborhood. I have not been able to establish a correlation between size and good corporate practice in terms of relations to employers and provision of protection to employees when they have to deal with abusive employment situation. The 2009 ILO report mentioned five major issues: exclusion from the labor code, undervaluation of domestic services, confusion as to whether domestic workers' disputes should be handled under labor laws or civil laws, low awareness of domestic workers' rights, and lack of data on their numbers and conditions (ILO 2009, 9). Lack of data makes it difficult to ascertain whether there has been progress since 2009 on most of these issues. One certainty is that significant gaps remain on the issue of rights awareness within the context of a political climate that is already hostile to rights advocacy.

Finally, in all three cases, MDWs have to contend with restrictions to their rights derived from government actions or inaction. In most instances, the labor laws, by determining working conditions, empower employers at the expense of those they hire. In both Hong Kong and Taiwan, there is lack of oversight over brokers and placement agencies, and no institution fills that role in Shanghai either. In Taiwan and Hong Kong, as we have seen above, the state is indirectly complicit in creating the conditions for some of the worst forms of abuse against MDWs, with the live-in requirement that limits their rights not only to privacy and security but also to find alternative employment. In Taiwan, moreover, the state does not fulfill its obligations to MDWs with regard to labor laws and regulation, which recognize them not as workers but as temporary caregivers.[30] Finally, the rule according to which MDWs in Taiwan can only deliver care for the elderly is not enforced in practice. In the name of respect for privacy, government inspectors rarely investigate private citizens to ensure that they adhere to this aspect of its regulations. As a result employers can with impunity ask the MDW to do much more than what the law allows them to do.[31] In addition to the restriction mentioned above in Hong Kong, a "two-weeks rule" imposed on employees allows them only this short period of time to find a new job if they quit or are dismissed, before they are deported.[32] In sum, in all three locations MDWs suffer a wide range of abuses. How much can different levels of governments in Chinese society make a difference in addressing them?

MULTI-SCALAR AND REGIME DIFFERENCES AND THEIR POSSIBLE EFFECTS

As mentioned before, the three locations considered in this chapter represent different levels of government and forms of political regime. Which of these levels is more likely to address the issues affecting domestic workers, and does the nature of the political regime reinforce the observed differences, if any? The first level considered here is Taiwan's central government, national in scope and sovereign, with the capacity to determine policies and the power to implement them. As a political democracy, Taiwan also offers more political space for NGOs to express their grievances (Cooper 2003). This is followed by the semi-autonomous/quasi-sovereign central government of the HKSAR (Holliday, Ngok and Yep 2002), a city-state whose situation of relative autonomy under the one country, two systems arrangement gives it some powers to manage its own affairs, but within the limits imposed by the central national government in Beijing, including restrictions on the space for civil society. Finally, we look at what a second-tier, municipal-regional level of government can achieve, namely the Special Municipality of Shanghai, wherein the activities of civil society are more restrained relative to the regime of civil liberties found in Taiwan and the HKSAR (Chen 2009). I examine the extent to which the respective powers of these different levels of government make a difference in regulating, enforcing and monitoring regulations and laws relevant to the rights of MDWs, paying attention in all three cases to how civil society responds to pressure for change in the absence of pressure from within the governments of these three entities. For each of these three levels of government, I introduce the agencies responsible for the management of MDW affairs, spell out the main issues, identify the actors pressuring governments to address them, present governments' responses, and briefly review remaining obstacles.

The Rights of Foreign Caregivers in Taiwan

Are higher levels of government in Chinese societies more likely than the lower tier of governments to respond to pressure concerned with the welfare and the rights of MDWs coming from international organizations such as the ILO? A brief examination of Taiwan's central government policies on MDW offers a good starting point. The ROC operates as a centralized state like the PRC, but on a much smaller scale, with no province-level government, with the exception of special municipalities.[33] Taiwan counts three other local levels of government: county (Xian), district-township (Xiang-Zhen), and community-village (Licun), in descending order. All policies are determined at the center: the representatives for the main political parties in the Legislative Yuan usually debate the laws submitted to them by either fellow representatives, members of the Executive Yuan, or other sources. Once these laws are adopted, lower levels of government are expected to implement them.

At the central level, the main agency responsible for foreign caregivers is the Ministry of Labor (MOL), which is responsible for a wide range of services for all workers, including the enforcement of labor standards, promotion of gender equality, supervision of labor relations, management of services ranging from welfare and retirement, etc. To address the issue of labor shortages in key sectors of the economy, the MOL has established a Workforce Development Agency (WDA) to recruit workers, including foreigners, to fill gaps in the labor force. For foreign caregivers, the WDA has created two specific structures: the Cross-Border Workforce Management Division and the Cross-Border Workforce Affairs Center. Most local administrations have a Department of Labor Affairs that implements MOL regulations through two bureaus, one for foreign workers inspection and one for foreign labor consultation services.[34]

As noted above, one of the most significant sources of abuse for foreign caregivers in Taiwan is the live-in requirement that puts them in situations of extreme vulnerability. But foreign caregivers are also excluded from labor regulations that protect workers' rights such as workplace safety because they are expected to be in Taiwan only on a temporary basis. Conversely, foreign caregivers must abide by very rigid regulations that confine them to the task of providing elderly care at home or care for the disabled when no relative is available.[35] Regulations rarely allow Taiwanese households to hire a caregiver to look after a senior below the age of eighty and strictly forbid Taiwanese employers from hiring foreign caregivers to serve as maids, nannies, or home-helpers. Exceptions are possible only when a very strong case is made by the employer that a senior under the age of eighty is seriously incapacitated and no one in the household is available to help her/him. There are countless cases in which employers ignore these rules, and many of the caregivers end up caring for babies, doing household chores, gardening, etc.—practices that draw them into situations of illegality against their will.

By putting foreign caregivers in these situations, often knowingly, many recruiting and placement agencies become the most serious offenders. Agencies present themselves as intermediaries between people looking for work as caregivers and their eventual employers. They offer job seekers employment as "au pairs, nannies, babysitters, pet sitters, housekeepers, tutors, personal assistants, and senior carers," suggesting a wide range of attractive jobs, but they do not mention the legal prohibitions against most of these types of positions. Moreover, employers and caregivers depend on recruiting agencies and brokers based on both sides—in the sending countries, as well as in Taiwan. Sending countries' agencies can pay for the airfare, preparation of relevant documents—passports, vaccine certificate, etc.—for admission in the receiving country, while agencies in Taiwan charge fees for training as well as instruction about the local culture, laws, and regulations. These fees, unregulated, can add up to the equivalent of months of the caregivers' salary. In many cases caregivers have gained too little knowledge about local regulations and their rights, despite having paid fees for that purpose.

To prevent abuse against foreign caregivers, many actors have come forward in Taiwanese civil society over the years to express their solidarity with care workers, moved by some *cause célèbre*, directly witnessing abuse, acquaintance with a victim, or simply concerned citizenship. The Awakening Foundation, which in 1982 established the *Awakening Magazine* to promote women's rights and awareness, represents one of the best-known of these organizations. In 2007 and 2009 it promoted the Amendment to the Immigration Act to protect the rights of women immigrants in Taiwan. The Taiwan International Workers Association (TIWA), along with its main mandate to support the rights of workers to workplace safety in factories, has since its founding in 1999 campaigned to organize caregivers into trade unions. The process was made all the more difficult because most foreign caregivers are in Taiwan for a limited period of time and do not see the benefit of the kind of long-term involvement needed for organizing. Meanwhile, as mentioned above, some native-born Taiwanese domestic workers resent possible competition from outsiders. Finally, religious groups have been quite active in helping caregivers in difficulty. The Garden of Hope, a non-denominational Christian NGO, has become directly involved, providing shelter and counseling to caregivers who are victims of abuse. The Presbyterian Church is doing advocacy for individuals, even taking up legal cases. The Catholic Guangchi communication broadcasting service reaches out to university students and sensitizes them to the situation of caregivers by organizing face-to-face meetings.[36] In all of these ways, concerned and aware citizens in Taiwan have organized and advocated changes in the laws and regulations affecting foreign caregivers.

Taiwan authorities are certainly aware that shaming by transnational NGOs for their mistreatment of foreign caregivers—by omission rather than by action—seriously undermines their efforts to generate support and gain recognition from the international community. The situation is becoming critical, as shaming is now coming from countries considered friendly to Taiwan. Hence, in its 2015 annual report on human rights, the US State Department broke with the previous tradition of generally giving Taiwan a high rating regarding respect for human rights and criticized both the exploitation of domestic workers and the government's lack of effort to address the issue (Lowther 2015). The Filipino government has reacted to reported cases of abuse in Taiwan by increasing awareness of Filipino migrant workers about the risks attending their work, following an investigation's findings that poor knowledge of government regulations made them highly vulnerable to abuse (Battistella and Asis 2011). Indonesia's decision to phase out and restrict migration after the *cause célèbre* of Erwiana Sulistyaningsih in Hong Kong has put Taiwan in a difficult position. This is all the more so as the lack of diplomatic recognition for Taiwan makes it difficult to achieve internationally recognized and binding agreements with other potential sending countries such as Vietnam, which the MOL considers enlisting.[37]

The government's timid response to cases of abuse is mediated by the confluence of many conflicting interests, ranging from brokers and employers' associations concerned with costs and profit margins to trade unions, some of which prefer to terminate reliance on foreigners and instead recruit local caregivers. Among the few responses that the government has undertaken—one that did not risk offending too many constituencies—has been the institutionalization of a mechanism to provide emergency assistance to foreign caregivers in distress, including those suffering abuse at the hands of their employers. To that end, the MOL has since the 1990s subcontracted to the NGO Garden of Hope the task of providing shelter to foreign caregiver victims of abuse. More potentially substantive responses, such as passing the Domestic Worker Protection Act in late spring 2015, after twelve years of active promotion by NGOs, turn out to be merely symbolic, according to local observers.[38] In sum, despite its capacity to improve the situation of foreign caregivers, the Taiwanese state has not acted decisively, likely captured or distracted by too many divergent interests.[39] The next section examines whether a lower tier level of government could do better.

The Rights of Foreign Domestic Helpers/Workers in Hong Kong

The HKSAR stands in an intermediate position, between Taiwan and Shanghai, in terms of political autonomy. According to its Basic Law, a quasi-constitution that determines its powers and obligations to the PRC, the HKSAR represents a special case of local government administering its territory with a large degree of political autonomy, but always with a possibility of censure from above. Hong Kong does not have its own foreign policy—a responsibility of the PRC—but as a major hub of international trade and finance, it has a special status in many international organizations and institutions with an economic objective, such as the International Monetary Fund and the World Trade Organization. As far as the ILO and workers' rights are concerned, Hong Kong is considered a part of the PRC and does not enjoy representation in that organization. This does not, however, prevent independent trade unions in the HKSAR from organizing, even when the target of the organizing is foreign domestic workers. Finally, and even if the HKSAR is responsible for the management of its workforce and its own immigration policy, as Taiwan is, decisions on the granting of citizenship must defer to the central authority in Beijing.

Three organizations in the HKSAR government are especially relevant for the welfare of foreign domestic workers/helpers. The Labor Department, as the executive arm of the Hong Kong Labor and Welfare Bureau, primarily looks after issues of health and safety in the workplace and provides some information about foreign domestic helpers' rights and protection ordinances. To that end, it publishes for the benefit of employers and foreign domestic workers a list of their rights and duties.[40] Besides this service, the Labor Department refers to the Hong Kong Immigration Department, which processes visa applications for prospective foreign domestic workers and provides employers basic instructions about the eligibility of potential applicants. Finally, the Equal Opportunity Commission, while not a government agency but a public institution, monitors abuses against employees and reports to relevant HKSAR authorities. Its mandate is to monitor compliance with HKSAR governments' ordinance on gender and racial discrimination, but it does not look specifically at cases of discrimination against domestic workers, simply because no ordinance has been produced for that particular group.

All the above agencies are aware of the problems caused by the proliferation of placement agencies and offer information useful to employers and, ultimately, to MDWs. The Labor Department, for example, provides a monthly gazette with a list of employment agencies licensed to place foreign domestic helpers, along with a list of the agencies that have lost their authorization and one of institutions that benefit from an exemption to the rules. However, as mentioned above, rampant abuse by brokers and placement agencies, and some of the regulations, such as the two-weeks rule and the live-in requirement, are problems related to labor regulations that only the authorities have the ability to solve. According to most of my interviewees, this is not a priority for the administration, and only a minority in the Legislative Council (Legco) is willing to tackle such issues. Like caregivers in Taiwan, foreign domestic helpers/workers are not protected by Chinese or Hong Kong labor laws because of their status as non-citizens and because they are not considered qualified workers in the same way that foreign teachers, bankers, and professionals are. Thus, they remain an extremely vulnerable component of the Hong Kong labor force.

As observed in Taiwan, many actors in Hong Kong civil society have risen to support the rights of foreign domestic helpers. The labor movement has been quite active and able to maintain its independence from the official and CCP-dependent trade unions in the PRC. Hence, the Hong Kong Confederation of Trade Union (HKCTU) and its affiliates, the Federation of Asian Domestic Workers (FADWU), the Union of Filipina Workers (UNIFIL), the Thai Migrant Workers Union (TMWU), etc., have sought to encourage foreign domestic workers to join force, despite the opposition of many native-born domestic workers. Perhaps the bigger obstacle to organizing for collective action, however, is the isolation at the workplace imposed by employers of live-in workers. Besides the labor movement, NGOs such as Amnesty International, which considers labor rights violations a *human* rights violation, contributes to bringing to the attention of the outside world the situation that prevails in Hong Kong.

The legal profession has been especially active in the promotion of domestic workers rights. Many lawyers have agreed to defend cases on a *pro bono* basis, despite the enormous difficulties they face. One of their biggest hurdles is when cases are dropped because the aggrieved party has left the HKSAR before a ruling can be issued by courts. In addition to prosecuting or advocating for foreign domestic workers, some lawyers have even sought to tackle the problem of abusive and unscrupulous brokers by setting up their own data bank and organizations to name and shame the unlicensed and problematic placement agencies, helping both employers and employees. Finally, as observed in Taiwan, churches have been extremely active in providing advocacy, counseling, and basic humanitarian support to the foreign domestic workers. Anglicans, Catholics, and Protestant denominations have housed or supported financially institutions such as the Christian Action, Mission for Migrant Workers and Pathfinders, who see solidarity with foreign domestic workers as an expression of their faith.

An important event in the spring of 2015 bringing together most of the above institutions, noted local politicians, and even foreign representatives, signaled that some progress was possible. The "Domestic Workers Roundtable," sponsored jointly by the Center for Comparative and Public Law at the Faculty of Law (University of Hong Kong), and the Hong Kong Public Interest Law and Advocacy Society, brought on board the ILO and the International Organization for Migration as observers. On this occasion, participants considered the creation of an Inter-Governmental Working Group to provide an informal framework for dialogue on domestic workers. The mobilization orchestrated by these organizations has contributed significantly to bringing the plight of domestic workers to the attention of society at large, and at the time of writing, the roundtable is being institutionalized, with ongoing activities to promote legal change, defend specific cases, and inform public opinion.

But the obstacles to change remain daunting. The Hong Kong Labor and Welfare Department has long resisted attempts to change the law with respect to foreign domestic workers, despite the vigorous pressures mentioned above. Immigration Department officials do not believe that they have any power to change rules for the right of abode or the granting of citizenship to foreign domestic workers, as they believe that such matters can only be determined in Beijing. The Equal Opportunity Commission, while mandated to monitor compliance with a number of ordinances related to racial and sexual discrimination, is deprived of a specific ordinance that would aid in addressing specific problems affecting foreign domestic helpers, and thus it cannot do advocacy on their behalf. A small ray of hope at the time of writing is that change is being debated within the Legco, as a direct result of the roundtable convened in the spring of 2015. At the end of the day, however, many issues related to immigration depend on the agreement of central authorities in Beijing.

Maids, Nurses, and Home Workers in Shanghai

The Special Municipality of Shanghai is an entity with the responsibilities of a provincial government. It is important to keep in mind, however, that the PRC is not a federal state, and Chinese provinces do not have their own powers according to the constitution, in contrast to federal regimes such as the United States, Canada, or Switzerland. Even though Shanghai has discretionary powers for spending and administering its own affairs in areas as diverse as tourism, communication and religious affairs, any degree of autonomy is ultimately determined by decisions from the center, which has the authority to grant more powers or withdraw them at any time. This is even truer when one considers the CCP, the ultimate source of power in China. Although the Party Secretary for the CP Municipal Committee of Shanghai is a member of the Political Bureau, the highest and most powerful source of authority in the political system, the Shanghai Party Secretary cannot impose his will on his peers, and can be shuffled—or demoted—to any other position by the CCP. In other words, Shanghai is a lower level of government, even though an important one, relative to Hong Kong and even Taiwan, in terms of population, as we have seen before, but also in terms of economic activity. It has clout, but not the final say on most decisions.

Because the composition of the MDW labor force in Shanghai is primarily made up of fellow Chinese, not foreign workers, one would expect differences between Taiwan and Hong Kong, on the one hand, and Shanghai, on the other, in the state's approach to MDWs. In Taiwan and Hong Kong, authorities have shaped and framed the issue of foreign caregivers and foreign domestic helpers as a problem outside the bounds of the national community. Since migrant workers in Shanghai are Chinese and not foreign workers, how could municipal authorities adopt the same approach? Yet, as we have seen before, the residence permit system imposed by the central government, by entrenching differences in the social and economic sphere, produces results that are not different from those observed in Taiwan and Hong Kong: in all three cases, domestic workers—overwhelmingly women—are "intimate strangers": living among the middle-class family who employ them,[41] but yet seen as "alien," because of their different culture. In Shanghai, the shared Chinese identity fails to overcome the view that migrants are different, because of their lower levels of education and their mores. In other words, many of the *nouveaux riches* try to reinforce their class position in what they see as ethnic/regional stratification.[42]

Several agencies in the Chinese central government are responsible for looking after issues that directly affect domestic workers, such as social security, population policy, labor regulation, and health. The ILO report on the conditions of these workers in China has revealed, however, that the problem has long been a lack of integration between these agencies and the absence of a unified set of policies targeting this specific population across different provinces and municipalities (ILO 2009, 5). At the time of that report, the agencies enforcing, regulating, and monitoring aspects of migrant workers' lives were the Ministry of Human Resources and Social Security, the Ministry of Commerce (domestic service is seen as a form of "consumption"), and the State Administration of Industry and Commerce, which licenses the recruiting and placement agencies. In 2012, reflecting changes in the higher level of government, the Shanghai Bureau for Human Resources and Social Security, in coordination with ten other commissions and GONGOs (government-organized NGOs), issued a series of measures meant to regulate the industry of domestic workers, and two years later, the Shanghai Department of Commerce adopted new rules to regulate the placement agencies. To what extent these measures have made a difference is not clear.

While China is not a "free market economy"—state-owned enterprises represent an important source of economic activity and employment— some aspects of its labor market evoke unfettered capitalism, with all its dangers for vulnerable workers. The fact that most MDWs in Shanghai are not foreign nationals may mitigate some of the worst aspect of the situations faced by Taiwan and Hong Kong MDWs. For one thing, if MDWs want to leave their employers, they do not have to fear deportation. For another, there are no established limitations on the kind of work that MDWs can do. Chinese migrant workers can choose to be maids, house-keeper, elderly caregivers, baby sitters, etc. Most of my informants, in employment agencies as well as in NGOs, claimed that MDWs have the ability to negotiate their working conditions and leave if they are unhappy with their employers, and they can work part-time for more than one employer. Moreover, there is no requirement to live in the employer's house. Despite these differences, in the absence of systematic data about their welfare it is extremely difficult to assess whether Shanghai MDWs are better off than their Taiwanese or Hong Kong counterparts. In theory, however, they do seem better protected by a variety of regulations.

In contrast to Taiwan and Hong Kong, many of the domestic workers in Shanghai find employment in this sector through their contacts—either relatives or former co-workers—or as part of the efforts by the All-China Federation of Trade Union (ACFTU) to find employment for laid-off workers. However, as is the case in Taiwan and Hong Kong, there is a considerable number of placement and recruiting agencies, but in a con-text of limited space for activist NGOs, little pressure on government to regulate and oversee the proliferation of such agencies and prevent abuses of the kind observed in Taiwan and Hong Kong. The limited evidence available suggests that there are efforts at self-regulation, such as the Association of Shanghai Family Service Trade (上海市家庭服务业行业协会), along with many efforts to consolidate the industry. In 2014, Shanghai counted 6,117 agencies (Insight 2014), and many of them run their own websites. A cursory look at sites advertising their services opens a window to the nature of these operations: candidates are listed, with their photographs, details about their age, height, level of education, cultural background, ethnicity, and matrimonial status (http://www.198526.com/). In their sordid presentation of vulnerable women anxious to make a decent living via menial work, these advertisements evoke human trafficking. Owing to the contrast between Taiwanese liberal democracy and its regime of rule of law, and Shanghai's consultative authoritarian politics and the regime of rule by law prevailing in China, we would expect that the landscape of civil-society associations promoting the rights of MDWs in Shanghai to differ considerably from those of Taiwan and Hong Kong. One of the most important by-products of the PRC approach to civil society—its opposition to it, in fact, under Xi Jinping—is the prevalence of GONGOs. Some of them, such as the

All-China Women's Federation, or the ACFTU, are united-front work organizations, closely working with the CCP. The same is true for associations such as the YMCA, connected with the officially-recognized Protestant Church of China, even if it appears somewhat distant from the Party-state. Besides these GONGOs, however, a few genuinely independent NGOs do exist in Shanghai, but it is difficult to find them.[43] However, their chances of effecting change are limited. Like their counterparts in Taiwan and Hong Kong, they are advocating for redress on behalf of populations that have little power and few allies. Moreover, it is almost impossible to trace the process of state response to these civil society pressures because of the opaque nature of the policymaking process in the PRC.

Concluding Discussion: The Remaining Obstacles

We have seen that higher levels of government are not necessarily more likely than governments at lower levels to address the issue of abuse against MDWs. In other words, the level of government does not matter much. This is especially relevant to entities that belong to centralized states such as Taiwan and the PRC, in contrast to federal states, where constituent provinces or states can have the power to intervene on specific policies such as immigration and labor that are relevant to the welfare of MDWs. However, the evidence does not show that the higher level of government in Taiwan's centralized state would be more likely to act than lower-level ones in Hong Kong, and Shanghai, two subordinated components of another centralized state. This suggests that agents of the state, regardless of the level of government, are simply not interested in dealing with the issues faced by domestic workers, oblivious as they are to the gendered nature of this work on which they depend.

The evidence from Taiwan and Hong Kong leaves us also with some surprising findings. Hong Kong and Taiwan both see a greater and more robust presence of civil society organizations relative to Shanghai. We can observe a similar discrepancy between these societies with respect to the media, which are much more likely to shame governments over the issue of MDW in Taiwan and Hong Kong than in Shanghai, where the issue is not discussed as often. However, these discrepancies in the vigor of civil society in Taiwan and Hong Kong, on the one hand, and its weakness in Shanghai, on the other, do not seem to have generated significant differences in outcome; governments in Taiwan and Hong Kong have been extremely slow in responding to pressure. In other words, we end up with the realization that even the nature of political regimes may not make a big difference, and that across these differences, there exists a shared belief that care work does not merit much attention.

The sobering conclusion to the question raised at the beginning of this chapter about the effect that levels of government can have on the promotion and enforcement of MDW rights and the improvement of their conditions is that it is limited or non-existent. In Taiwan, Hong Kong, and Shanghai, MDWs face social, economic, and political marginalization, and monitoring efforts by local governments to enact laws ensuring that they enjoy basic rights remains limited and inconsistent. At one end of the spectrum, we found that Taiwanese authorities at the central, municipal, and county levels have the greatest latitude and ability to enforce laws and regulations that could affect the rights of domestic workers, but they do not act. At the other end, Shanghai, which is subordinated to the Chinese central government, has less autonomy than the two other entities. Hong Kong, which has considerable autonomy under the regime of one country, two systems, is, in principle, able to decide on internal matters, but it does not want to intervene on the status of MDWs, because the issue of nationality is interpreted as the responsibility of Beijing. And yet, despite these differences, all three locations appear equally determined not to change the status quo too much.

In sum, political differences do not appear to matter much when they are weighed against the forces of market and the cultural resources that governments deploy to give legitimacy to their preference for these forces. The current policies provide the veneer of the natural—if not that of the sacred—when they suggest that the reliance on domestic workers is deemed "necessary" to fulfill the filial piety "obligations" of dutiful sons and daughters. Questioning this cultural logic stands out as a categorical imperative. Meanwhile, the urgent issue aggravated by that cultural logic remains the dismal conditions that millions of women face as they get trapped into the political economy of care for the aging population of post-industrial East Asia. Enhancing their rights is an urgent and pressing issue too important to ignore, as the demand for this category of workers is very likely to increase significantly along with the rates at which these societies witness an unprecedentedly rapid aging of their populations. Moreover, the hiring of MDWs, often construed as liberating women who seek work outside the household, can merely reproduce patriarchy and unequal relations of power, as mothers still feel a disproportionate sense of responsibility, and fathers conceive of hiring an MDW as a "gift" to their wives (Groves and Lui 2012).

The reliance on MDWs in Taiwan, Hong Kong, Shanghai, and elsewhere, ultimately, reveals antecedent policy choices that are problematic. The reliance on domestic workers is "naturalized" as a "need" in these societies where Confucian values such as filial piety are supposed to constitute the foundation of moral, social, and political order, in spite of the fact that younger generations repudiate them. This naturalization of Confucian values is suddenly becoming difficult to resist, as it has received endorsement from some hitherto unlikely places. Hence, Xi Jinping, as leader of the Communist Party—an organization that has perhaps done more than any other in history to "relegate Confucianism to the dustbin of history"— is promoting the revival of that tradition as a key element of his China Dream that it must nurture. The task of future research will be to document such strategic deployment of cultural resources by the state and its agencies, as well as by the corporate sector, in the tug-of-war between the social forces that refuse further expansion of state provision of social services, and those who struggle against this policy of retrenchment.

NOTES

1. For the sake of simplicity I will refer throughout to Taiwan.
2. This designation of "Special Municipality" means that Shanghai has powers equivalent to that of a province in China.
3. The majority in each of the three locations speak a native tongue that is unintelligible to each other: Cantonese in Hong Kong, Hokkien in Taiwan, and Wu in Shanghai. However, in the latter two, the language of instruction at school is Mandarin, which is taught in Hong Kong alongside English and Cantonese.
4. Albeit the PRC has successfully managed to convince most UN member states to deny it this recognition.
5. This autonomy is nominal for the election of the chief executive and the members of the legislative council, but the media and civil society enjoy more liberties than in the rest of China.
6. Although my informant mentions that this requirement is very often breached.
7. An additional difficulty in Shanghai is the inability of workers to protest.
8. 外籍家庭看護工 (Waiji jiating kanhugong)

9. 外籍家庭傭工 (Waiji jiating yonggong)
10. As a member of the equality opportunity commission explained, this is more "friendly," an approach which people I interviewed in an NGO and in a trade union rejected strongly.
11. My informants in Taiwanese and Hong Kong's trade unions both reported the presence of that bias.
12. From interviews 7, 8, 29, and 33 in Hong Kong and Taipei.
13. Hukou 户口.
14. Foreign professionals in business, higher education, etc., are not included in these statistics and not subject to the same restrictions.
15. http://statdb.mol.gov.tw/html/mon/c12010.pdf.
16. Most of them are employed in "3 D" industries, which are "dirty, dangerous, and demeaning."
17. http://www.gov.hk/en/about/abouthk/factsheets/docs/statistics.pdf.
18. http://www.gov.hk/en/about/abouthk/factsheets/docs/immigration.pdf.
19. http://www.labour.gov.hk/eng/plan/iw.htm.
20. Interview 27.
21. To put these numbers in perspective, as of 2016, Hong Kong has 7.5 million people, while Taiwan and Shanghai count 23 million each.
22. This perception overlooks the fact that migrant workers anticipate that their stay in Taiwan and Hong Kong will represent a major improvement over their lives back home, and also a way to look after their extended families through remittances.
23. For more recent data, see Peng (this volume).
24. This reminds us that we need to take into account sending country regulations as well.
25. MDWs are also moving to cities other than Shanghai, mostly wealthy cities in the East, where the middle class is large, such as Beijing, Shenzhen, and Guangzhou (ILO 2009, 2)
26. This was mentioned to me time and again by my informants in NGOs, churches, and even in government, in both Taiwan and Hong Kong. Although a minority of employers engage in these behaviors, they do considerable damage to both locations' reputations.
27. In the rare case of an NGO defending MDWs in a Chinese city, see the case study of the Northwest city of Xi'an, presented by the China Development Brief, a well-respected NGO that monitor NGO activity in China (Han 2013a; Han 2013b).
28. Employers deduct these fees from MDWs' wages.
29. Chinese colleagues at Fudan, Shanghai and East China Normal Universities confirmed to me that they did not know of such surveys at the time of my visit, in May 2015.

30. The implication of this approach is that Taiwan's labor code does not apply to MDW, who lack an instrument for redress in case of violation of their labor rights.
31. Interview 29.
32. Thereby losing the fees they have paid for travel, training, etc.
33. The ROC constitution states that there is a provincial-level government, but the ROC being limited to the province of Taiwan and a small district of the province of Fujian, the provincial government has been streamlined to avoid redundant administration.
34. http://www.labor-en.ntpc.gov.tw/_file/1413/SG/29365/40830.html.
35. These rules were put in place because while there was a shortage of nurses who could look after the elderly, the Taiwanese government also wanted to address popular anxieties over immigration.
36. Sunday Mass offers an important occasion to reach out to Filipina domestic workers and help them as well. Hence, as I have witnessed at masses attended by mostly Filipina worshippers, the ceremony often concludes with Church lay people providing all assembled worshippers a phone number to reach if they need help in case of abuse.
37. Interview with a government official on June 10, 2015, Taipei.
38. This was the view expressed by Taiwanese colleagues in legal and political studies, a few weeks after the passing of the law.
39. The Long-Term Care Services Act, passed in May 2015, will take effect only in 2018, so at the time of writing it is too early to speculate on its consequences.
40. http://www.labour.gov.hk/eng/public/wcp/FDHguide.pdf.
41. In Taiwan and Hong Kong, we have seen that migrant domestic workers live in the household of their employers, but that is not always the case in Shanghai.
42. This is not unique to Chinese society: in Italy, for example, employers of domestic workers take pains to present them as "part of the family." I am grateful to Sonya Michel for this insight.
43. At the time of writing, the climate of fear instigated by the regime against foreign NGOs makes it extremely difficult to make international linkages. I have been unsuccessful in liaising with three of the four that the Canadian consulate knew of because of cooperation problems with Chinese authorities.

REFERENCES

AI (Amnesty International). 2013. *Exploited for Profit, Failed by Governments: Indonesian Migrant Domestic Workers Trafficked to Hong Kong.* London: Amnesty International Ltd., Peter Benenson House.

Battistella, Graziano and Maruja M. Asis. 2011. *Protecting Filipino Transnational Domestic Workers: Government Regulations and Their Outcomes* (No. DP 2011–12). Makati City, Philippines: Philippine Institute for Development Studies.

Chen, Xiangming and Zhenhua Zhou, eds. 2009. *Shanghai Rising: State Power and Local Transformations in a Global Megacity.* Minneapolis: University of Minnesota Press.

Copper, John Franklin. 2003. *Taiwan: Nation-State or Province?* Boulder: Westview Press.

Cortes, Patricia, and Jessica Pan. 2013. "Outsourcing Household Production: Foreign Domestic Workers and Native Labor Supply in Hong Kong." *Journal of Labor Economics* 31: 327–371.

Groves, Julian M. and Lake Lui. 2012. "The 'Gift' of Help: Domestic Helpers and the Maintenance of Hierarchy in the Household Division of Labour." *Sociology* 46: 57–73.

Han, Hongwei. 2013a. "An Interview with Wang Wei of the Xi'an Domestic Employees Union." *China Development Brief* 58 (Summer), http://chinadeve lopmentbrief.cn/articles/domestic-workers-manage-their-own-organization-interview-with-wang-wei-of-the-xian-domestic-workers-union/

Han, Hongwei. 2013b. "Domestic Workers Set out Rules for their Employers." *China Development Brief* 58 (Summer), http://chinadevelopmentbrief.cn/articles/domestic-service-workers-give-employers-set-rules-rights-advocacy-case-marginalized-group/

Holliday, Ian, Ma Ngok, and Ray Yep. 2002. "A High Degree of Autonomy? Hong Kong Special Administrative Region, 1997–2002." *Political Quarterly* 73: 455–464.

Hong Kong CSD (Census and Statistics Department). 2012. "Nationality and Ethnicity." *2011 Population Census,* http://www.census2011.gov.hk/flash/dashboards/nationality-and-ethnicity-db-203-en/nationality-and-ethnicity-db-203-en.html

Hsiao, Alison. 2015. "Groups Slam Foreign Labor Rule." *Taipei Times* (10 February), 3.

ILO (International Labor Organization). 2009. *Situational Analysis of Domestic Work in China,* http://www.ilo.org/wcmsp5/groups/public/—asia/—ro-bangkok/documents/publication/wcms_114261.pdf

Insight (Zhongguo Chanye Dongcha wan 中国产业洞察网). 2014. "中国家政服务行业发展分析+重点城市市场分析。(Analysis of the domestic workers' trade development by cities)." *Insight* (Zhongguo Changye Dongcha wan 中国产业洞察网), http://www.51report.com/article/3051737.html

Lan Pei-chia. 2002. *Global Cinderellas: Migrant Domestics and Newly Rich Employers in Taiwan.* Durham, NC: Duke University Press.

Liang, Li-Fang. 2014. "Live-in Migrant Care Workers in Taiwan: The Debate on the Household Service Act." *Asian and Pacific Migration Journal* 23: 229–241.

Lin, Stephen, and Danièle Bélanger. 2012. "Negotiating the Social Family: Migrant Live-in Elder-Care Workers in Taiwan." *Asian Journal of Social Science* 40: 295–320.

Lowther, William. 2015. "US Rights Report Shows Weaknesses in Taiwan." *Taipei Times* (27 June), 3.

Pan, Shu-Man, and Jung-Tsung Yang. 2012. "Sexual Abuse of Live-In Care Workers in Taiwan." *Sexual Abuse - Breaking the Silence*, Dr. Ersi Abaci Kalfoğlu (Ed.). Rijeka, Coatia: InTech, DOI: 10.5772/26754. URL: http://www.intechopen.com/books/sexual-abuse-breaking-the-silence/sexual-abuse-of-live-in-care-workers-in-taiwan

Qiu, Zitong. 2013. "Maid in China: Media, Morality, and the Cultural Politics of Boundaries." *Asian Studies Review* 37: 274–276.

Shen, Yang. 2015. "Why Does the Government Fail to Improve the Living Conditions of Migrant Workers in Shanghai? Reflections on the Policies and the Implementations of Public Rental Housing under Neoliberalism." *Asia and the Pacific Policy Studies* 2, 1: 58–74.

Tseng, Yen-Fen and Wang, Hong-Zhen. 2013. "Governing Migrant Workers at a Distance: Managing the Temporary Status of Guestworkers in Taiwan." *International Migration* 51, 4: 1–19.

André Laliberté, professor of political studies at the University of Ottawa, looks into the intersection of the political and the religious in China and Taiwan, in the context of democratic transition, authoritarian resilience, and the implementation of social policy. He has recently been studying the impact of cultural values on the political economy of care in East Asia. He has been a research fellow at the Groupe Sociétés, Religions et Laïcité in Paris, the Woodrow Wilson International Center for Scholars, and the Institute of Humanities and Social Sciences at the University of Hong Kong, among others.

CHAPTER 7

Out of Kilter: Changing Care, Migration and Employment Regimes in Australia

Deborah Brennan, Sara Charlesworth, Elizabeth Adamson and Natasha Cortis

In societies where care provision depends on migrant workers, we might expect a reasonable level of alignment between care and migration regimes. In Australia, care migration and employment regulation have all been in flux since the mid-1990s, but there is little sign of alignment. This chapter examines the changes that have occurred in each of these domains, analyzing changes in migration policy alongside new approaches to organizing, financing and delivering aged-care and child-care. We explore variations between the aged-care and child-care sectors and locate both within the broader context of changing gender relations. Our analysis is at the meso level, focusing on Australia's national policy and regulatory framework. We build on Fiona Williams's insight that care and migration regimes – that is, "clusters of policies, practices, legacies, discourses, social

D. Brennan (✉) · E. Adamson · N. Cortis
Social Policy Research Centre, UNSW, Sydney, Australia

S. Charlesworth
School of Management Centre for People Organisation, RMIT University, Melbourne, Australia

© The Author(s) 2017   143
S. Michel, I. Peng (eds.), *Gender, Migration, and the Work of Care*,
DOI 10.1007/978-3-319-55086-2_7

relations and forms of contestation" – are not necessarily coordinated and that the tensions between them may have profound impacts on care workers, employers, countries of origin and destination countries (Williams 2012, 371–373). Official migration policies may favor the recruitment of skilled workers, for example, offering relative protection and a visible gateway to permanent residence, while less formal pathways channel other migrants (Simonazzi 2009) into jobs that are relatively poorly paid and less likely to be subject to equal protection under employment regulation. The focus on Australia represents a novel contribution, since studies of care and migration focus overwhelmingly on movements from Eastern to Western Europe, from South and Central America to North America, and from Asia to North America, Europe and the Gulf states.

Less than a decade ago, migration analyst Graeme Hugo observed that it was "virtually impossible" for unskilled or semi-skilled workers to enter Australia on a permanent basis except through family reunion or refugee-humanitarian migration (2009, 190). Since then, there have been significant changes not only in migration policy but also in aged care and child care and in the regulatory environment that governs the employment of care workers. Official pronouncements about Australia's migration policy emphasize the global competition for skilled labor, while behind the scenes non-labor market visa categories, such as those provided to working holiday makers and international students, have rapidly expanded the pool of relatively vulnerable, low-skilled migrants who are not always well versed in their rights, and who may be willing, or feel compelled, to work for wages below the legal minimum. Further, the World Bank is actively promoting temporary migration to Australia and New Zealand in order to boost the incomes and skills of the Pacific Island micro-states such as Tuvalu, Nauru, Kiribati, Samoa and Tonga. Care workers are among the groups that are being considered in this context (Curtain et al. 2016).

The distinctive features of the Australian welfare state provide the context for our analysis. Scholars classify Australia as a liberal welfare regime due to its low social expenditure, reliance on means-tested benefits and absence of social insurance (Esping-Andersen 1990). However, Australia also has the highest family payments in the OECD (Whiteford 2010), a universal public health scheme and generous (if poorly targeted) child-care funding – features that differentiate it strongly from the United States, the emblematic "liberal" regime. Social policy historian Frank Castles coined the term "wage earners welfare state" to capture the role that labor market institutions played in social protection in Australia and New Zealand throughout much of the twentieth century (Castles 1985). Centralized wage setting, high tariffs on imported goods and restrictive immigration policies protected male workers until the last quarter of the twentieth century, when a combination of global forces and domestic pressures made this compact untenable. The wage-earners' welfare state was built around the ideal of the male earner/female caregiver household even though large sections of the population did not fit this mold. This, too, began to unravel in the 1970s and has been replaced by a "male earner/female earner + carer" model (Pocock 2014, 67). Around 60 percent of Australian women now participate in the labor force, although almost half are employed part-time (ABS 2016, 10). Women are now far less available to provide unpaid care for children, the elderly, the frail and the chronically ill, resulting in a widespread "work/life collision" (Pocock 2003). Although Australian women's labor force participation has risen, it remains below that of some comparable countries. Widely cited modeling by the Grattan Institute, a center-right think tank, shows the Australian economy would benefit by up to AUD$25 billion in increased taxes and reduced social transfers if Australian women's labor force participation matched that of Canadian women (Daley 2012).

Labor governments have held power at the national level during critical periods of economic and social transformation. Under the Hawke and Keating governments (1983–1996) the welfare state was reconfigured, at least partially, to recognize the challenges of globalization and neoliberalism (Spies-Butcher 2014, 84). Although wage inequalities widened, there was considerable "renovation and refurbishment" of the welfare state and social expenditure grew throughout the 1980s and 1990s (Fenna and Tapper 2012). In office again from 2007 to 2013, Labor introduced a massive, Keynesian style stimulus based on capital infrastructure programs, and this (together with a booming resource trade with China) protected Australia to a large extent from the global economic downturn in 2008–09. In 2016, Australia experienced its 25th year of uninterrupted economic growth and has an unemployment rate below 6 percent. However, the picture is not one of equally shared prosperity. The aggregate level of unemployment masks considerable variation by region, gender, age and birthplace. Inequality has widened, driven by greater dispersion of employment earnings, substantial capital income growth in higher income households and reduction in the progressive impact of taxes and transfers (Greenville et al. 2013).

Australian women's move into paid work has not been matched either by changes in men's involvement in unpaid work or by expanded provision of state-funded services and supports. Australia is one of the world's most unequal countries with respect to the sharing of domestic and caring work, and the disparity between men and women is sharpest for parents (Craig et al. 2010). Work, care and family concerns have been major electoral issues since the mid-1990s and all parties have put forward policies to address concerns such as paid parental leave (finally introduced in 2011) and increased demand for child-care and aged-care services.

The intersections between care and migration and their impacts on gender relations in Australia have similarities to, and differences from, those that prevail in other parts of the world. Australia's political and business leaders emphasize the benefits of skilled migration while barely acknowledging the fact that hundreds of thousands of overseas-born workers compete with local workers for jobs in low-skill, low-wage occupations, including care. This approach is similar to the US strategy of "demand and denial" identified by Michel and Peng. While the United States lacks a "coherent policy for recruiting care workers," it allows "a steady stream of unauthorized migrants willing to take low-paid jobs that [local workers] largely eschew" (Michel and Peng 2012, 415). Australia does not encourage "unauthorized migrants" – quite the reverse – but its migration and employment policies effectively create a large pool of poorly protected workers who are willing to work for low pay and thus, unwittingly, blunt the campaigns of local workers (including established migrants) for improved wages and conditions. We argue that making the connections between care, migration and employment regulation more visible is an important first step toward informed debate and improved policymaking in this area in Australia.

The chapter begins with an overview of shifts in Australia's migration policy since the mid-1990s, especially the transition from permanent to temporary migration and the growth of visas for working holiday makers, international students and others who are accorded work rights even though their primary reason for being in Australia is not employment. The next section explains the restructuring of aged care and child care, focusing on successive governments' increasing promotion of consumer-oriented care policies, underpinned by individualized payments, subsidies or vouchers. We argue that the employment arrangements generated by these market-oriented policies are likely to stimulate demand for workers prepared to work for low wages. The prospect of care migration has begun to enter Australian public debate, largely in the context of formal inquiries into the aged-care and child-care sectors. In the final section, we draw on submissions to two of these inquiries to examine some of the major lines of debate emerging in relation to care migration (see also Adamson et al. 2017).

Reshaping Migration Pathways

Australia is one of the major migration countries of the world. Half the population was born in another country or has at least one parent born overseas. Historically, migration to Australia emphasized settlement and citizenship, with successive governments in the postwar period explicitly eschewing the type of guest worker programs adopted by some European countries (Mares 2012, 25). From the mid-1940s to the mid-1990s, successive governments emphasized permanent residence, with "new Australians" encouraged to bring their families under relatively generous family reunion provisions. In the wake of the early 1990s recession, migration underwent two profound shifts, both designed to give Australia an edge in the global race for skills and talent. First, the Keating Labor government tilted the balance of permanent migration away from family reunion and toward skilled migration. Then the Howard Coalition government introduced a measure for "long-stay" temporary migration, the 457 visa program, enabling businesses to bring workers and their families to Australia for periods of up to four years to address identified skills shortages. Entrants under the 457 program are required to hold a vocational diploma or higher qualification and must have a job paying a minimum of AUD$53,900 per annum arranged before their arrival.

Although the recruitment of highly skilled workers remains the major focus of the migration program, there are a growing number of pathways for migrants who do not meet the criteria typically used to assess skilled work – receipt of wages above a specified level or the requirement for qualifications at a particular standard. A special "labor agreements" stream within the 457 program allows employers to sponsor workers who do not have the skills or English-language ability required for a standard 457 visa. "Working holiday makers" provide another large source of casual labor to Australian employers (Clibborn 2015). The working holiday maker program[1] enables young people aged 18–30 from a range of countries to holiday in Australia for up to a year. Working holiday makers can work in any job for the duration of their stay, but, with some exceptions, cannot remain with any one employer for more than six months. Depending on their visas, those who work as au pairs, anywhere in Australia or in disability or aged care in Northern Australia, are eligible to apply for permission to work with the same employer for the full twelve months. Holders of a Work and Holiday visa 417 may be eligible for a second visa by working a minimum number of days in agriculture, mining or construction in a rural or regional area. The number of working holiday makers in Australia increased sharply following the global downturn of 2008; only 2,690 visas were issued in 2005–06, compared to 226,812 in 2014–15 (DIBP 2015a). There are approximately half a million international students with work rights in Australia (DET 2016b), though most are limited to forty hours' work per fortnight. Recent graduates are also able to work in Australia for a specified period after their studies. Legal analysts Joanna Howe and Alexander Reilly argue that the participation of international students and working holiday makers in the Australian labor market has obviated the need for governments to introduce a dedicated low-skill work visa. In this way, they have been able to avoid political debate about the possible role of migrant labor in suppressing local wages (Howe and Reilly 2015, 260).

In addition, Australia operates an uncapped Seasonal Worker Scheme, allowing workers from the Pacific[2] to work in horticultural industries. In 2015, Australia agreed to issue visas to a small number of citizens from Kiribati, Nauru and Tuvalu, enabling them to work in Northern Australia in a range of occupations including aged care (DIBP 2015b). The World Bank has recently issued a discussion paper canvassing the introduction of a live-in caregiver scheme in which workers from the Pacific Islands could provide care for elderly Australian and New Zealand residents (Curtain et al. 2016). The report notes that "the advanced economies around the Pacific Rim will need migrants in the coming years to fill gaps in their domestic labor markets," especially in sectors that "struggle to attract domestic workers, such as aged care." Canada's program for in-home caregivers for people with high medical needs is suggested as a model for Australia and New Zealand (Curtain 2016).

Although both the Liberal-National Coalition and the Labor Party have adopted extremely harsh approaches to unauthorized boat arrivals by asylum seekers, both support large-scale, planned immigration to meet skills gaps identified by employers and also to a lesser extent for family reunion. Australians are generally positive about immigration, too. In a nationally representative poll conducted in 2016, 73 percent of respondents agreed that "overall, immigration has a positive impact on the economy of Australia." A similar proportion (72 percent) agreed that "accepting immigrants from many different countries makes Australia stronger" and that "immigrants strengthen our country because of their hard work and talents" (Oliver 2016). Migration was not a significant issue in the 2016 federal election campaign, probably due to the bipartisan approach of the major parties. Policies to discourage the tiny number of people who arrive by boat to seek asylum in Australia were, however, a sharp point of contestation, with Labor promoting a doubling of Australia's refugee intake and various measures of regional cooperation. However, tensions around migration are never far away. In the lead-up to the 2013 election, Prime Minister Julia Gillard announced that Labor had a plan to "stop foreign workers being put at the front of the queue with Australian workers at the back" (Hurst 2013). Two years later, there was intense debate about the labor mobility provisions of the China-Australia Free Trade Agreement (Kelly 2015).

In theory, both permanent and temporary migrant workers enjoy the same employment conditions and protections as Australian workers, including payment of the applicable minimum wage. In practice, many temporary visa holders have diminished rights compared to Australian citizens or permanent residents precisely because of their migrant status. Any breach of visa conditions, as would occur, for example, if an international student worked more than forty hours per fortnight, is considered a breach of the Migration Act 1958 and renders the visa holder's employment contract "invalid and unenforceable," meaning that the worker is not entitled to the protections and conditions of the Fair Work Act (Clibborn 2015; Tham et al. 2017, 191.). Further, while 457 visa holders are permitted to change jobs, it is not easy to do so. Being without an employer sponsor for more than three months puts temporary visa holders in breach of their visa conditions and can result in deportation (Mares 2012, 39). Recent media reports have exposed serious exploitation of temporary migrant workers, and the Department of Immigration and Border Protection (DIBP) has acknowledged that migrants are more vulnerable to underpayment and other violations of the Act "because they are more likely to be unaware of their workplace rights, have limited English language skills, and lack support networks" (DIBP 2015a, 741).

Reshaping Care: Markets and Individualization

Care policies in Australia have been radically reshaped since the 1990s, as governments have grappled with the challenges of rising demand, population aging, and heightened expectations about service quality. Public funding of nonprofit, community-based care services such as child care and aged care grew in the 1970s and 1980s, but governments have since retreated from supporting supply and now opt instead to put cash into the hands of consumers, encouraging private businesses to enter the market in the name of choice and competition (Meagher and Goodwin 2015). These shifts have led to the demand for new types of employees such as nannies for child care and home-based carers for the elderly (Brennan 2015). In Europe, policy developments of this type have been linked to the recruitment of low-wage, migrant care workers. It is too early to say how these developments will play out in Australia, but in this section, we outline some of the ways in which new forms of aged-care and child-care funding could potentially be linked to care migration.

Aging and Aged Care

How do migration and care intersect in Australia? Compared with many European nations, Australia has a young population and is well-placed to deal with demographic changes. Public expenditure on long-term care, including aged care, is around 0.8 percent of GDP, while the average for the OECD is 1.2 percent (OECD 2011, 46). Over the next four decades, the proportion of elderly people as a share of the population is expected to increase. The number of people aged seventy or over, for example, is expected to rise by four million, an increase from 9.4 to 17.4 percent of the population (Productivity Commission 2011, 39). Since the structural aging of the population will be accompanied by declining cohorts of younger workers entering the labor market, the provision of adequate services, including respite and residential care, support for paid employment and measures to help elderly people remain in their own homes and communities, will present substantial challenges.

In 2011, the Gillard Labor government commissioned the Productivity Commission to conduct an inquiry into aged care (Productivity Commission 2011). Established in 1991 to guide the federal government on micro-economic reform, the Commission has been called on by both Labor and Coalition governments to provide advice on social policy.

Commission reports draw heavily on neoclassical economics, and their recommendations typically support the promotion of free market principles including consumer choice and competition. Inquiries into both aged care and child care have followed this pattern. The 2011 inquiry into aged care found that many older Australians faced a limited choice of services, variable quality, gaps in provision and inconsistent pricing. In response to Inquiry recommendations, the government introduced a package of reforms known as *Living Longer, Living Better*. The intent of the package was to "build a responsive, integrated consumer-centred and sustainable aged-care system, designed to meet the challenges of population ageing and ensure ongoing innovation and improvement" (DoHA 2012). Its centerpiece was a ten-year plan to reshape the aged-care system by putting cash into the hands of consumers through "consumer-directed funding" (CDC). As a result, from 2015, CDC started to be phased into community-based aged care, with aged-care "budgets" paid to providers to manage on behalf of individual recipients. Eligible people are able to choose their providers and the services they wish to "purchase" with the funds allocated to them (Belardi 2015). CDC will be extended into residential aged care from the beginning of 2017.

The sustainability of aged-care services in this new context will depend greatly on the sector's ability to attract and retain workers. The Productivity Commission discussed labor supply problems in the aged-care system, noting that these would intensify as the labor market tightened in response to population aging. As part of *Living Longer, Living Better*, the Labor government introduced an AUD$1.2 billion "workforce compact" to increase the low wages of aged-care workers. The aim of this compact was to improve worker recruitment and retention through additional payments to employers who agreed to provide wages above the legal minimum. One of the first actions of the Abbott Liberal-National Coalition government elected in 2013 was to revoke this additional funding for workers' wages. According to a spokesperson, Labor's workforce compact was "more about boosting union membership than improving aged care" (Heath and Anderson 2013). Despite promises that the funding would be retained in the aged-care sector, it remains unclear whether or how the funds put aside for the workforce compact have been spent. Further, while it had promised to deliver a workforce development strategy, the federal government has now delegated this process to aged-care providers (Belardi 2016).

CHILD CARE

Early childhood services grew out of the philanthropic tradition in Australia (Brennan 1998). The Child Care Act introduced in 1972 reinforced the principle of public (or at least nonprofit) provision by restricting subsidies to users of nonprofit services. In the early 1990s, however, the Hawke Labor government introduced market forces into the sector on the grounds that competition and private sector involvement would lead to greater choice and lower fees. Subsequent initiatives have intensified the marketization of child care, resulting in the closure of many community-based child-care services (Adamson and Brennan 2014).

Child care was a key issue in the 2007 election. Following Labor's election, Prime Minister Kevin Rudd used social investment arguments to push for the establishment of "a world class system of integrated early childhood learning and child care." The system was to "boost national productivity," lift labor force participation, contribute to social inclusion and be the first step toward an "education revolution." A reform program was devised, and the Council of Australian Governments (COAG), a forum for the representation of all governments in Australia (Commonwealth, States, Territories and local government), endorsed a strategy encompassing children from birth to eight years. *Investing in the Early Years: A National Childhood Development Strategy* set out a "comprehensive response to evidence about the importance of early childhood development and the benefits – and cost-effectiveness – of ensuring all children experience a positive early childhood" (COAG 2009).

The reform agenda included a range of regulatory measures aimed at improving the quality of early childhood education and care. In addition to enhanced accreditation, a new National Quality Framework now requires every service to employ a university-qualified teacher. All other direct service workers (including home-based family day care) are required to hold, or be working toward, an entry-level qualification or certificate in early childhood. The reform agenda has been a very positive development for the sector; however, given the low pay and lack of opportunities for career advancement, the requirement to obtain formal qualifications has resulted in some attrition – particularly among older women. In addition, the reforms led to a backlash from some for-profit providers who regard the new standards and qualifications as excessive.

Child care was a major issue in the 2013 election that ousted the Gillard Labor government and returned the Coalition to office. The Coalition parties did not have a policy on child care, although Prime Minister Tony Abbott had frequently expressed his support for providing subsidies to nannies. Abbott promised to set up an inquiry to fix "Labor's child care mess" (generally assumed to mean high fees and ongoing shortages of places, especially for infants and toddlers) and Coalition candidates referred to the perceived lack of fit between the contemporary labor market and what they saw as Labor's "one-size-fits-all" approach to child-care provision – with its emphasis on centers and regulated family day care, rather than on nannies. The extension of subsidies to nannies was supported by groups representing corporate and professional women. However, most child-care advocacy groups took a cautious approach, supporting some assistance in return for regulation and oversight. The Labor government's Education Minister at the time, Kate Ellis, acknowledged the challenges faced by families needing flexible child care and said the Labor government "would work to clean up the nanny industry" by introducing minimum standards, but that it "is a long road to regulate nannies" (cited in Karvelas 2012).

In what seems to have become an Australian tradition, the new government initiated an inquiry by the Productivity Commission, requesting it to develop options to improve the "accessibility, flexibility and affordability of child care for families with diverse circumstances" (Productivity Commission 2015). The focus of the Commission's inquiry was the design of a new subsidy system, but its lengthy inquiry process and call for public submissions (a regular feature of such inquiries) ignited debate about the role of unregulated forms of child care including nannies and au pairs.

There are no firm data about the employment of nannies or au pairs. Approximately 6,500 individuals identified as being employed as nannies in the 2011 Census, but three years later the Australian Nanny Association estimated that 30,000 nannies were employed, either through private family arrangements or nanny agencies. Nannies employed through agencies receive between AUD$20 and $30 per hour (Howe 2016). As with nannies, there is no formal au pair program and no agreed standards. Conditions and pay vary considerably. Au pairs in Australia have been described as "hiding in plain sight" (Berg 2015) because, although their numbers seem to be growing, there is almost no formal recognition of their existence and thus no standards or regulation of their employment. Agencies recommend that families pay between AUD$150 and $250 per week as well as providing room and board. This level of remuneration is well below the wage payable to a nanny. AuPair World, an international agency that connects au pairs and host families, estimates that there are ten thousand au pairs working in Australia, mostly young working holiday makers (AuPair World 2014). Like nannies, their numbers are thought to have increased dramatically in recent years but, in the absence of regulatory oversight, dedicated visas or public subsidies, there are no official data.

While the Productivity Commission did not recommend extending subsidies to au pairs, it endorsed them as "a low cost care [child care] option for some families" and recommended regulatory changes that would enable working holiday makers to remain with a family for the full twelve months of their visa. The Department of Immigration and Border Protection has since amended its policy in line with the Commission's recommendation. As expected, the Commission recommended that subsidies be extended to nannies and the government has since allocated approximately AUD$70 million to a Nanny Pilot enabling approved service providers to place nannies with about five hundred families between 2016 and 2018. Nannies employed as part of the Pilot must have a visa that permits twelve months or more of continuous employment; this effectively excludes working holiday makers. In a significant departure from the National Quality Standard introduced by Labor, the Coalition-initiated Pilot does not require nannies to hold any type of qualification other than a first aid certificate. Take-up of the pilot has been extremely low; however, since even with an hourly subsidy similar to that available for the users of centers, fees for a nanny are beyond the reach of most families (DET 2016a).

The Care Workforce

Debate about the role of migrant care workers in Australia takes place in the context of a rapidly growing, highly feminized, poorly paid workforce in which foreign-born workers already play a significant part. The community services workforce sustained a 54 percent increase in the decade to 2014, compared with a 21 percent increase in the number of people employed in all industries (AIHW 2015, 46). Community services occupations are dominated by women: 96 percent of child-care workers, 87 percent of personal care assistants, who work mainly in residential aged care, and 82 percent of aged- and disabled-care workers, who work mainly in community-based aged care, are female (Baldwin et al. 2014). Many migrants are employed in care work, despite the lack of dedicated visa pathways. As with gender, the proportion of frontline care workers born overseas varies by sector: 44 percent of personal care assistants and over one-third of aged and disability care workers are migrants, compared with 29 percent of the Australian workforce. In child care, by contrast, only 27 percent of the direct care and education workforce was born outside Australia, similar to the total workforce.

The Department of Immigration and Border Protection is exploring the possibility of a new temporary visa category that would include semi-skilled work in sectors such as child care and aged care. An extension of the 457 visa along these lines was rejected in 2009 because of the potential for exploitation of migrant workers. Low rates of unionization in all of the major care sectors (aged care, child care and disability services) mean that there is limited ability to enforce labor standards. This factor, together with the relatively poor labor minima that apply to work that is classified as non-skilled or semi-skilled in these industries (Charlesworth and Heron 2012), provides a platform for the non-compliance of employers (Tham et al. 2017, 190–191).

Many of the calls for the reconfiguration of the skilled temporary visa to bring in low-skilled child-care and aged-care workers are based on assertions not only of a burgeoning demand for such workers, but also of acute labor shortages. However, the existence of chronic labor shortages, especially in aged care, is contested. Shortages appear to exist in some rural and remote areas, but there is little evidence of a clear labor deficit in care work in general – and some evidence to the contrary. According to the Department of Employment, which is responsible for identifying employer demand in certain occupations, there is little difficulty in recruiting personal care workers. The personal care workforce is projected to grow far more quickly than the workforce overall, but there is little evidence of persistent shortages (DoE 2014b), and most vacancies are filled within four weeks (King et al. 2013, 94). In child care, there is a shortage of center managers and university-qualified teachers (many of whom prefer to work in school settings, where pay and conditions are far more favorable than in child-care centers) but not of frontline child-care workers (DoE 2014a). There are, however, major issues with staff turnover. This is attributed to the poor wages in the sector – a situation only likely to be exacerbated by bringing in more workers.

Public Discourses around Migration and Care

Inquiries into aged care and child care have proved to be important forums for public debate about gender, migration and care. Although migration was not included in the terms of reference for either of the Productivity

Commission inquiries mentioned here, on each occasion some organizations and individuals have explored the issue in their submissions and some have made recommendations either for or against care migration. The submissions point to intriguing differences in attitudes toward migrant care workers in child care and aged care.

Child Care

The inquiry into child care attracted 468 submissions, of which 108 (23 percent) supported expanded in-home child-care provision and eighteen (4 percent) specifically noted the potential role of migration to boost in-home care provision. Support for care migration was most frequently expressed by business groups, employer organizations, nanny and au pair agencies, and parents. They argued that migrant child-care workers would provide a low-cost way of supporting parental labor-force participation of Australia parents, thus boosting the local economy while benefiting source countries through employment and remittances. Many of the submissions echoed the "triple win" thesis propounded by international organizations such as the World Bank (Curtain 2016).

The Australian Chamber of Commerce and Industry (ACCI), the peak body for the business sector, called for a "significant increase in access to au pairs" in its submission to the inquiry. The Chamber argued that migration with "suitable regulatory oversight" could help resolve the time pressures experienced by busy households, thus freeing up labor supply to boost the economy. While noting that "issues of concern" regarding the employment of migrant care workers had arisen overseas, the Chamber was of the view that "in a country such as Australia suitable regulatory oversight should provide a win-win outcome for the workers and the stressed household" (ACCI 2014, Submission 324). Organizations promoting the employment of au pairs and nannies generally shared this view. The Cultural Au Pair Association of Australia (CAPAA), a peak body that seeks to set standards for the industry, called for a change to working holiday visa rules so that au pairs could remain with a family for the full twelve months of their visa. The Association emphasized the low cost of au pairs compared to formal child care, stating that the cost of an au pair to a family would be less than half the fee payable for two children in child care, while the service offered is more convenient and flexible (CAPAA 2014, Submission 238).

Some parents made personal submissions to the Commission, arguing that home-based migrant carers would support their workforce participation by offering a low-cost, flexible service. Such submissions showed little or no awareness of potential negative impacts for migrant caregivers. One mother, for example, proposed the introduction of "special visas for home-based child care workers from developing countries" on the grounds that "we need to ensure young women such as myself remain in the workforce" (Submission 265). It was not only parents who raised the possibility that employing migrants at low wages could lower the child-care costs of Australian families. The Indonesia Institute (a forum for promoting trade with Australia) proposed, "immigration and labor regulations should be liberalized to allow carers from Indonesia (and other Asian countries) to work as nannies in Australia." The Institute suggested that AUD$200 per week (less than one-third of the national minimum wage) would be "acceptable to both nannies and the majority of Australian families" (Indonesia Institute 2014, Submission 219).

As well as being of benefit to themselves, some parents framed care migration as a form of foreign aid: "Employing nannies from third world countries is a great way to assist developing nations as the monies go directly to the nationals involved" (Parent, Submission 443). Another suggested that the wages paid to "domestic helpers" should be "well below the Australian minimum wage, perhaps as little as one third the norm." Such an outcome would be "a win-win situation," according to this submission, because "Australian families would have a low-cost solution to free them to do high value work and the wages that the helpers remitted to their homes would have a beneficial effect both on the situation of their own families and on the countries from which they come" (Unidentified, Submission 463). In these submissions, the perceived benefits to Australian families eclipsed any problems that might faced by migrant workers, and discussion of access to a safety net of awards and conditions for migrant care workers employed in the home was relatively weak. The possibility that migrant care workers might have children and elderly relatives of their own was never mentioned.

Aged Care

While submissions to the child care inquiry rarely mentioned that overseas workers would bring particular benefits to children beyond addressing child care shortages, those to the aged care inquiry, by contrast, frequently couched support for migration in terms of ensuring a diverse workforce that would benefit clients. Submissions in this vein came from migrant community organizations and service users as well as from employers concerned to meet their clients' needs. The Federation of Ethnic Communities Councils of Australia (FECCA), for example, noted that the greatest shortages were of staff who were competent in European languages, particularly Italian and Greek (reflecting Australia's postwar immigration patterns). FECCA recommended remedying this shortage by recruiting trained foreign aged-care workers with relevant language competency and training non-working migrant women already in the country.

As with child care, only a small number of submissions to the aged care inquiry (21 out of 441) discussed migration. Some, however, addressed the importance of a culturally and linguistically diverse workforce – a closely related issue. Service providers and peak bodies were the most likely to point out that ethnic and linguistic diversity would help meet the needs of elderly migrant Australians. This concern is in sharp contrast to the child care submissions, which presented care migration almost entirely as a convenient and cost-saving measure for parents rather than as being of benefit to children.

Another theme in the aged care submissions was the need to resolve labor shortages, although, as noted above, the existence, nature and causes of labor shortages are hotly disputed. Health and aged-care sector peak organizations expressed significant concerns about the impact of existing migration restrictions on their capacity to recruit staff from overseas. Several called for the relaxation of migration controls as a way to address the perceived under-supply of labor. Some industry organizations and service providers called for aged care to become a priority in the skilled migration program, while also recommending that temporary migration be used to attract lower skilled workers in critical areas. A few called for improved access to labor agreements – special arrangements that allow employers to negotiate the entry of overseas workers with defined skill levels and pay rates on the basis of an acute labor market need and a lack of appropriately qualified Australian workers (Uniting Care Ageing NSW, Submission 360; Fronditha Care, Submission 436).

Many of the submissions that focused on labor shortages noted the need for more systematic planning to address workforce needs. One major provider called for "a frank discussion about how...needs for less skilled and unskilled staff will be met in the future, including the role of the immigration program" (Uniting Care Ageing NSW). Another suggested that "consideration...be given to augmenting the local workforce by sourcing suitable staff from overseas, including staff who could receive further training in Australia" (Catholic Health Australia). Some employers referred to the difficulty they experienced in recruiting lower skilled workers and called for more low-skilled occupations to be included in the migration program.

In almost all aged care submissions, support for migration was tempered by recognition of the need to maintain workforce quality, wages and labor standards. Some submissions expressed concern about the skills base of foreign-born workers. One provider noted that a growing proportion of entry-level staff were students who lacked the English-language skills needed for "the exhaustive documentation requirements associated with providing residential aged care" (Manningham Centre Association, Submission 325). Another submission noted "carers...on holiday visas...had no experience in caring for older people [and] were quite unprepared for changing pads and administering medication to dementia patients" (Country Women's Association of NSW). At the same time, some employers expressed the need for cultural awareness training on the part of clients, noting, for example the tendency for staff from Asian and African backgrounds to experience racial discrimination from care recipients. Thus, migration was considered a challenge for employers, employees and service users, and not necessarily a straightforward solution to the needs of the aged-care workforce.

The main trade unions covering aged care workers challenged the presumption of an acute labor shortage, arguing that higher pay and better conditions would attract local workers into aged care, obviating the need to rely on migration. One union argued that "attracting migrant workers is not a panacea for workforce issues in the industry," suggesting that the federal government and aged care providers should "improve the quality and status of jobs within the industry" (LHMU, Submission 335).

CONCLUSION

The rules governing migration, the subsidies and structures underlying the provision of child care and aged care, and the nature and impacts of employment regulation are all in flux in contemporary Australia. Our aim in this chapter has been to review the changing landscape of care and migration, to consider how the two domains intersect and to assess the impacts of this intersection. As we have shown, aged-care policy is increasingly focused on individual payments and home-based care and there is potential for pressure to grow around the recruitment of low-wage workers, including migrants, to meet growing demand. Pressures of this kind are much less evident in child care, which has much stronger industry standards underpinned by the national quality framework and requirements for all direct-care workers to hold a qualification. In this context, the Nanny Pilot, with no requirement for nannies to have early childhood qualifications, is of concern even though it is a very small initiative.

Australian migration policy is increasingly preoccupied with supporting employers to meet their immediate (and self-identified) needs for skilled labor. The main measure in this area, the 457 visa program, has limited direct impact on aged care or child care because the skills list from which entrants under this program are drawn includes only a very limited number of relevant jobs. Further, the minimum wage for 457 visa holders, the Temporary Skilled Migration Income Threshold, is well above the wage received by frontline care workers, making this an unlikely pathway into either aged care or child care.

Despite the official emphasis on skilled migration, a large and uncapped number of international students, graduates and working holiday makers participate in the Australian labor market. While the visas that apply to these categories are not regarded as employment programs, members of these groups provide an important source of low-paid, casual labor, especially in residential aged care, precluding the need for the dedicated visa pathways into care that have been in place in other countries. A small number of Pacific workers are recruited annually through a seasonal workers' program, and there has been a recent expansion of this program into aged care in Northern Australia. The numbers are very small, but the World Bank has recently recommended that Australia and New Zealand consider live-in caregiver programs for Pacific Islanders, based on Canada's program for people with high medical needs (Curtain et al. 2016). The potential impact of such initiatives on the local aged-care and child-care workforces – both of which are struggling to improve their own wages and conditions – has barely been acknowledged by policy makers.

At the beginning of this chapter, we cited Fiona Williams's (2010) observation that lack of co-ordination between care and migration, whether it occurs by default or by design, can have profound impacts on care workers, employers, countries of origin and destination countries. While Australia's care and migration policies appear to be out of step with one another, it seems that despite the historical lack of a low-skill caregiver migration stream there is a growing prospect of recruiting migrant caregivers, both through less formal labor market channels such as the working holiday maker visa program or via specific programs aimed at bringing in temporary workers from Australia's Pacific neighbors. As consumer-directed care policies take effect in coming years, household demand for migrant care workers appears likely to increase.

NOTES

1. The Working Holiday Maker program comprises visa subclass 417 and visa subclass 462. The appropriate visa is determined by country of residence.
2. Seasonal workers from Papua New Guinea, Fiji, Samoa, Solomon Islands, Timor-Leste, Vanuatu and Tonga can be employed for a maximum period of six consecutive months. Seasonal workers from Kiribati, Tuvalu and Nauru can be employed for a maximum period of nine consecutive months.

REFERENCES

ABS [Australian Bureau of Statistics]. 2016. *Labor Force, Australia, Jan 2016*, cat. no. 6202.0.

ACCI (Australian Chamber of Commerce and Industry). 2014. Submission to Productivity Inquiry into Childhood and Early Childhood Learning. Sydney: Australian Chamber of Commerce and Industry.

Adamson, Elizabeth and Deborah Brennan. 2014. "Social Investment or Private Profit? Diverging Notions of 'Investment' in Early Childhood Education and Care." *International Journal of Early Childhood* 46, 1: 47–61.

Adamson, Elizabeth et al. 2017. "Social Care and Migration Policy in Australia: Emerging Intersections?" *Australian Journal of Social Issues* 52, 1: 78–94.

AIHW (Australian Institute of Health and Welfare). 2015. *Australia's Welfare*. Canberra: AIHW.

AuPairWorld. 2014. Submission to Productivity Inquiry into Childhood and Early Childhood Learning. Kassel, Germany: Au Pair World.

Baldwin, Richard et al. 2014. *The Aged Care Workforce in Australia: White Paper*. Canberra: Aged and Community Services Australia.

Belardi, Linda. 2015. "Budget: ACAR to End in Move to Market System in Home Care." *Australian Aging Agenda*, May 13. http://www.australianageinga

genda.com.au/2015/05/13/budget-2015-acar-to-end-in-move-to-market-system-in-home-care/

Belardi, Linda. 2016. "Industry Expected to Take Lead on Workforce Strategy, says Government." *Australian Aging Agenda*, February 11. http://www.aus tralianageingagenda.com.au/2016/02/11/industry-expected-to-take-lead-on-workforce-strategy-says-govt

Berg, Lauri. 2015. "Hiding in Plain Sight–Au Pairs in Australia." In *Au Pairs' Lives: Sisters or Servants?* edited by Rosie Cox, 187–202. London: Palgrave Macmillan.

Brennan, Deborah, 1998. *The Politics of Australian Child Care. Philanthropy to Feminism and Beyond*, rev. ed. Cambridge, UK: Cambridge University Press.

Brennan, Deborah. 2015. "Community Services, Individualism and Markets." In *Social Policy in Australia*, edited by Alison McClelland and Paul Smyth, 3rd ed., 220–29. Melbourne: Oxford University Press.

CAPAA [Cultural Au Pair Association of Australia]. 2014. *Future Demand for Au Pairs*, Submission to Productivity Commission Inquiry into Child Care and Early Learning. Sydney: Cultural Au Pair Association of Australia.

Castles, Frank. 1985. *The Working Class and Welfare: Reflections on the Political Development of the Welfare State in Australia and New Zealand, 1890–1980*. Sydney: Allen & Unwin.

Charlesworth, Sara and Alex Heron. 2012. "New Australian Working Time Minimum Standards: Reproducing the Same Old Gendered Architecture?" *Journal of Industrial Relations* 54, 2: 164–181.

Clibborn, Stephen. 2015. Submission to the Productivity Commission Inquiry into the Workplace Relations Framework.

COAG [Council of Australian Governments]. 2009. *Investing in the Early Years: A National Childhood Development Strategy.* Canberra: Commonwealth of Australia.

Craig, Lyn et al. 2010. "Parenthood, Gender and Work-Family Time in the United States, Australia, Italy, France, and Denmark." *Journal of Marriage and Family* 72: 1344–61.

Curtain, Richard et al. 2016. *Pacific Possible. Labor Mobility: The Ten Billion Dollar Prize*. Sydney: Australian National University and the World Bank.

Daley, J. 2012. *Game-Changers: Economic Reform Priorities for Australia*. Melbourne: Grattan Institute.

DET [Department of Education and Training]. 2016a. *Nanny Pilot Programme*. Canberra: DET.

DET [Department of Education and Training]. 2016b. *International Student Numbers*. Research Snapshot. Canberra: *DET*.

DIBP [Department of Immigration and Border Protection]. 2015a. *Working Holiday Maker Visa Programme Report*, Canberra: DIBP.

DIBP [Department of Immigration and Border Protection]. 2015b. *Special Program Visa (Subclass 416) for the Seasonal Worker Programme*, Canberra: DIBP.

DoE [Department of Employment]. 2014a. *Child Care Workers, Australia*. Canberra: Labor Market Research and Analysis Branch. http://docs.employ ment.gov.au/system/files/doc/other/auschildcareoccupations.pdf

DoE [Department of Employment]. 2014b. *Personal Care Workers, Australia*. Canberra: Labor Market Research and Analysis Branch, October.

DoHA [Department of Health and Ageing]. 2012. *Living Longer, Living Better*, Canberra: DoHA.

Esping-Andersen, Gøsta. 1990. *The Three Worlds of Welfare Capitalism*, Princeton, NJ: Princeton University Press.

Fenna, Alan and Alan Tapper. 2012. "The Australian Welfare State and the Neoliberalism Thesis." *Australian Journal of Political Science* 47, 2: 155–172.

Greenville, Jared et al. 2013. *Trends in the Distribution of Income in Australia*. Canberra: Productivity Commission Staff Working Paper.

Heath, Joanna and Fleur Anderson. 2013. "Abbott's Attack on Unions." *Australian Financial Review*, September 13.

Howe, Joanna and Alexander Reilly. 2015. "Meeting Australia's Labor Needs: The Case for a New Low-Skill Visa." *Federal Law Review* 43: 259–287.

Howe, Joanna. 2016. "Federal Election 2016: Di Natale's Use of Au Pairs Causes Stir." *The Australian*, May 24.

Hugo, Graeme. 2009. "Care Worker Migration, Australia and Development." *Population, Space and Place* 15: 189–203.

Hurst, Daniel. 2013. "Labor's Talk Against 457 Visa Scheme 'Disgraceful and Racist': Murdoch." *Sydney Morning Herald*, 2 April.

Indonesia Institute. 2014. "Submission to Productivity Inquiry into Childhood and Early Childhood Learning" (Submission 219). Subiaco: Indonesia Institute. http://www.pc.gov.au/inquiries/completed/childcare/submis sions/initial/submission-counter/sub219-childcare.pdf

Karvelas, Patricia. 2012. "Regulation to Allow Subsidies for Nannies a Long Way Off, says Child Care Minister Kate Ellis." *The Australian*, 9 August.

Kelly, Paul. 2015. "China Free Trade Deal: The Political Battle Deepens." *The Australian*, 1 August.

King, Debra, et al. 2013. *The Aged Care Workforce 2012: Final Report*. Canberra: Department of Health and Ageing.

Mares, Peter. 2012. *Temporary Migration and its Implications for Australia*. Papers on Parliament, No 57. Canberra: Parliament of Australia.

Meagher, Gabrielle and Sue Goodwin. 2015. *Markets, Rights and Power in Australian Social Policy*. Sydney: Sydney University Press.

Michel, Sonya and Ito Peng. 2012. "All in the Family? Migrants, Nationhood, and Care Regimes in Asia and North America," *Journal of European Social Policy* 22: 406–18.

OECD. 2011. *Help Wanted? Providing and Paying for Long-Term Care*. Paris: OECD Publishing.

Oliver, Alex. 2016. *Understanding Australian Attitudes to the World*, Sydney: Lowy Institute.

Pocock, Barbara. 2003. *The Work/Life Collision*. Sydney: Federation Press.

Pocock, Barbara et al. 2014. "Putting Together Work and Care in Australia: Time for a New Settlement?" In *Australian Public Policy: Progressive Ideas in the Neoliberal Ascendancy*, edited by Chris Miller and Lionel Orchard, 63–80. Bristol: Policy Press.

Productivity Commission. 2011. *Caring for Older Australians*. Canberra: Commonwealth of Australia.

Productivity Commission. 2015. *Inquiry into Child Care and Early Childhood Learning*. Canberra: Commonwealth of Australia.

Simonazzi, Annamaria. 2009. "Care Regimes and National Employment Models." *Cambridge Journal of Economics* 33: 211–232.

Spies-Butcher, Ben. 2014. "Welfare Reform." In *Australian Public Policy: Progressive Ideas in the Neoliberal Ascendancy*, edited by Chris Miller and Lionel Orchard, 81–96. Bristol: Policy Press.

Tham, Joo-Cheong et al. 2017. "Why is Labor Protection for Temporary Migrant Workers So Fraught?" In *Temporary Labor Migration in the Global Era: The Regulatory Challenges*, edited by Joanna Howe and Rosemary Owens. Oxford: Hart Publishing.

Whiteford, Peter. 2010. "The Australian Tax-Transfer System: Architecture and Outcomes." *Economic Record* 86 (275): 528–544.

Williams, Fiona. 2012. "Converging Variations in Migrant Care Work in Europe." *Journal of European Social Policy*, 22, 4: 363–376.

Williams, Fiona. 2010. "Review Article: Migration and Care: Themes, Concepts and Challenges." *Social Policy & Society* 9, 3: 385–396.

Deborah Brennan is a professor at the Social Policy Research Centre, University of New South Wales (UNSW), Australia. Her research focuses on gender and public policy, especially child care and parental leave and the role of private markets in human services. Brennan is investigating the links between care marketization and reliance of low-paid migrant labor in the Oceania region – especially Australia and New Zealand. Her research is funded by the Australian Research Council and the Social Sciences and Humanities Council of Canada.

Sara Charlesworth is a professor at the School of Management and the Centre for People Organisation and Work at RMIT University, Melbourne, Australia. Her research centers on gender inequality in employment at the labor market, industry and workplace levels. Charlesworth's current research is on regulatory responses to gender inequality in frontline care work in the Australian and international contexts, with key projects investigating interactions between markets, migration and the work of care and links between worker job quality and service quality.

Elizabeth Adamson, is a research fellow at the Social Policy Research Centre, UNSW. Her research interests are early childhood education and care policy; the intersection of gender, migration and care work; and comparative care and family policy more broadly. She is the author of *Nannies, Migration and Early Childhood Education and Care: An International Comparison of In-Home Childcare Policy and Practice* (Policy Press).

Natasha Cortis, is a senior research fellow at the Social Policy Research Centre, UNSW. Her research explores issues of industry structure, organizational sustainability and service quality in community services. Her particular interests relate to funding arrangements and relationships between the community sector and government; workforce quality and sustainability in non-profit organizations; and women's employment and economic security.

CHAPTER 8

Closing the Open Door? Canada's Changing Policy for Migrant Caregivers

Monica Boyd

Like many post-industrial nations, Canada's demand for paid care work is increasing as a result of ongoing demographic, social and political transformations. Although Canada has the second lowest proportion of seniors among the G7 countries, with 16 percent of the 2015 population age 65 and older (Statistics Canada 2015), the percentage is expected to double in the near future: 23–25 percent in 2036 and 24–28 percent in 2061 (Statistics Canada 2010). The historically low female labor force participation has changed, from less than 25 percent in the early 1950s to 82 percent of all Canadian women 25–54 percent in 2014 (Statistics Canada 2016). Both trends indicate the need for care services, but in Canada, publicly funded child care and elder care are limited and not universal. Because care workers other than health workers risk bad working conditions and low pay, migrant workers are disproportionately employed in such jobs (Boyd and Lightman 2016; Hondagneu-Sotelo 2007; van Hooren 2012).

The author thanks Joanne Nowak and Alice Hoe for their contributions to this chapter.

M. Boyd (✉)
Department of Sociology, University of Toronto, Toronto, Canada

© The Author(s) 2017
S. Michel, I. Peng (eds.), *Gender, Migration, and the Work of Care*,
DOI 10.1007/978-3-319-55086-2_8

How Canada admits migrant caregivers is a legacy of historical immigration policies whereby foreign-born domestic servants were recruited for housework and child care. Initially the preferred migrant was from Britain and as such the mother of future Canadians (Arat-Koc 1997; Barber 1991). But by the early twentieth century, recruitment spread to other European countries, to Guadeloupe in 1910 and to Caribbean Commonwealth countries in the 1950s (Barber 1991; Macklin 1992). In the last quarter of the twentieth century and at the start of the twenty-first, migrant care workers were predominantly women from less developed economies, often persons of color, attracted to Canada by three consecutive immigration programs: (1) the (non-immigrant) Employment Authorization Program in the 1970s; (2) the Foreign Domestic Worker Movement (FDM), 1981–1992; and (3) the Live-In Caregiver Program (LCP), April 27, 1992 to November 30, 2014. The latter two admitted temporary legal migrants for work in private households, requiring them to live in the homes of their employers. Significantly, these policies deviated from most policies of other countries by permitting the transition to permanent residency after two years of care work

The most recent and longest lasting program, the LCP, epitomized two features noted in other studies of care work and domestic labor: racial distinctions between employer and employee, and the multi-scalar nature of migration regulation, with federal policy setting the conditions of admission and provincial policies governing conditions of employment. At the macro level, immigration policy served as a mechanism for the recruitment of care labor; at the same time, it determined the rights of care workers, including the right of permanent residency. As the policies governing the admission of migrant caregivers created asymmetrical power relations between employer and employee (Anderson 2010; Boyd 1997; Shutes 2014), the micro level contained the potential for employee abuse, "hidden in the household."

Marked shifts in Canada politics and policy formulations recently ended the Live-In Caregiver Program. Following the 2006 and 2008 federal minority governments, both headed by Stephen Harper's Conservatives, and the 2011 Conservative majority government, substantial changes occurred in immigration policy, including ministerial directives that could be implemented by the Minister of Citizenship and Immigration with no Parliamentary oversight or debate (Boyd and Alboim 2012). The existing emphasis on admitting permanent residents for economic purposes was enhanced (Boyd 2014). Another important development during the first millennium decade was the increasing admission of temporary workers alongside permanent residents.

The LCP was affected by these changes. The initial pattern, evident as early as 2010, took the form of heightened control over the program, with changes aimed at preventing egregious abuses associated with the multi-scalar nature of the program, that is, the vulnerability of migrant care workers to unscrupulous employers and recruiting agencies. However, consistent with the "law and order" approach adopted in migration policy domains targeting refugee claimants, marriage fraud and trafficking, the LCP came to be viewed by the Minister as a fraudulent "backdoor" into Canada. It was replaced in December 2014 by a new Caregiver program, firmly part of the temporary worker program and governed by market-based assessments of labor needs.

Within these multifaceted contexts of immigration policies, this chapter surveys recent and current Canadian immigration policy covering women recruited for care work in private households. It begins with Canada's globally unique Live-In Caregiver Program, in operation between 1992 and 2014, highlighting the size of the program and noting the origins of the workers. It then inventories LCP's problems and policy responses to those problems throughout its history. It concludes by noting the major policy changes, effective December 1, 2014, and assessing how these changes will transform the migration-for-care opportunities of migrant women.

CANADA'S LIVE-IN CAREGIVER POLICY

Building on the previous Foreign Domestic Worker Movement (FDM) and earlier policies (see Daenzer 1997; Macklin 1992; Schecter 1998), the LCP admitted temporary foreign workers as live-in employees to work without supervision in private households to care for children, seniors or people with disabilities. However, compared to the FDM, it increased the education and training requirements, stipulating the following criteria needed to hire a LCP temporary worker:

(1) A positive Labour Market Opinion (LMO) from an employer in Canada.
(2) A written contract with the future employer signed by the worker and the employer.

(3) Successful completion of the equivalent of a Canadian secondary school education.
(4) At least six months training or one year of full-time work experience as a caregiver or in a related field or occupation (including six months with one employer) in the past three years.
(5) Good knowledge of English or French.
(6) A work permit issued by Citizenship and Immigration Canada before entering Canada.

The Labor Market Opinion, later re-labeled a Labour Market Impact Assessment (LMIA), required would-be employers to apply to Human Resources and Skills Development Canada/Service Canada (HRSDC/SC), currently called Economic and Social Development Canada (ESDC). A review was undertaken of the employer's job offer and the employment contract to ensure that it met the requirements for wages and working conditions as well as provincial labor and employment standards and that no Canadian resident was available for the job.

To date, the Live-In Caregiver Program has been Canada's longest-lasting policy, in effect for over two decades; as with the FDM, it was globally unique because temporary care workers were permitted to transition to permanent resident status. (Although new visas are no longer given out, the LCP remains in effect for those entering as temporary LCP migrants before December 2014, whose permits were issued before December 2014, and/or who are awaiting application processing for permanent admission to Canada.) Because the admission of live-in care-givers was determined by demand in the form of would-be employers seeking live-in caregivers, numbers of migrants remained low until the first decade of the twenty-first century. In the mid-1990s, the annual flow of temporary admissions (i.e., visas issued) under the LCP was less than 3,000 and remained slightly above 2,000 until 2004 (Citizenship and Immigration Canada 2005). Deriving a consistent trend-line for all LCP years is not possible because of variations in the public reporting of temporary worker data, but by the early twenty-first century, increasing numbers of temporary workers permits were issued, peaking at nearly 30,000 in 2007 (Fig. 8.1).

Nearly 90 percent of arrivals over this time were women from the Philippines (Citizenship and Immigration Canada 2005; Kelly et al. 2011). There are many reasons for the predominance of Filipinas in the LCP. For one thing, with the inception of the Foreign Domestic Worker

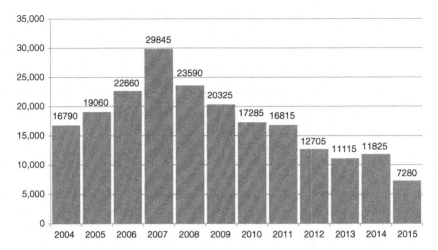

Fig. 8.1 Number of temporary worker permits in the Live-in Care Program, by the year in which the permits became effective, Canada (excluding the Yukon), 2004–2015

Source: Immigration, Refugees and Citizenship Canada, Temporary Residents as of March 31, 2016. http://open.canada.ca/data/en/dataset/67fd1fae-4950-4018-a491-62e60cbd697

Movement in 1982, Canada became a sought-after destination for migrant care workers because it allowed transitioning to permanent resident status. Policies of the Philippine government also played a key role. States can stimulate (or discourage) the migration of their peoples. Scholars frequently point to the culture of migration, which reflects the impacts of structural adjustment policies, in this case the efforts of the Philippine government to foster emigration to generate remittance behaviors (Barber 2000, 2008; Rodriguez 2010). Personal remittances represent a significant share of the Philippine GNP, rising from 3.3 percent in 1990 to 13.3 percent 2005, dropping slightly in 2013 and 2014 to approximately 10 percent (World Bank 2015).

Other reasons for the predominance of women from the Philippines include recruitment agencies and consumer preferences for Filipinas, possibly reflecting a racist desire for lighter-skinned nannies or a perception of these women as compliant, dutiful and nurturing workers (Bakan and Stasiulis 1995; Guevarra 2014). The more demanding entrance criteria associated with LCP also are factors. Filipina domestic worker and care-giver applicants tend to have higher education levels than their counter-parts from other countries as a result of the system of education in the Philippines formed during US military rule and under later influences, giving them a better chance of meeting selection criteria. Further, the system of training nurses in the Philippines means they more easily meet the LCP criterion of six months of training or twelve months' employment in a caregiving capacity (Stasiulis and Bakan 2003).

The LCP in principle allowed all caregivers in the program to apply for permanent residence visas after working as live-in caregivers for 24 months. How many women entered Canada as temporary LCP work-ers and subsequently became permanent residents cannot be determined from publicly available statistics. However, the rate appears low, keeping in mind that several years must pass from the temporary permit issue to the completion of 24 months as a live-in caregiver, and that processing delays can occur. Certainly, the numbers of LCP workers who become perma-nent residents in any given year are much lower than the numbers of permits issued a few years earlier (Fig. 8.2. versus Fig. 8.1). The 2014 and 2015 numbers reflect enhanced processing of applications towards the end of the LCP and are discussed later

Problems and Processes of Change: A Brief Moment in Time

Extensive critiques of the Canadian Live-In Caregiver Program exist, both from the general context of women migrating for care and from the specific requirements of the program that shaped both employment experiences and processes of transitioning to permanent resident status. At the macro level, the migration of low-wage care workers reinforces global structures of inequality between more advanced receiving countries and developing send-ing countries. Further, the migration of workers, particularly those in health-care occupations such as nursing, long-term care and others requiring a high level of education, results in "brain drain" and creates health-care shortages in the sending country (Altman and Pannell 2012; Lindio-McGovern 2012, chap. 2). At the meso level, care migration erodes social relationships and communities in sending countries, fragmenting relationships within families and communities and creating transnational mothering and globalized care chains (Hochschild 2000; Isaksen et al. 2008). In addition, in countries such as the Philippines, where a large proportion of the population are emigrants, temporary migrant worker programs such as the LCP aggravate income

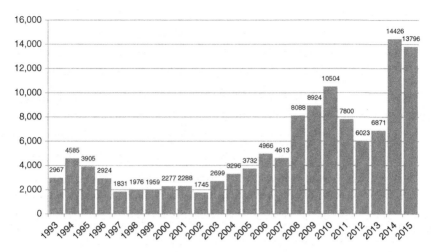

Fig. 8.2 Number of Annual Permanent Resident Admissions from the LCP, Principal Applicants, Canada 1993–2015

Source: Immigration, Refugee and Citizenship Canada. Permanent Residents as of March 31, 2016. http://open.canada.ca/data/en/dataset/ad975a26-df23-456a-8ada-756191a23695-en/dataset/67fd1fae-4950-4018-a491-62e60cbd6974

inequality between households. Studies find that, because of remittances, families with a migrant abroad tend to have higher income than families that do not (Gorodzeisky and Semyonov 2014).

Migration regimes fostering the emigration of women for care work also reinforce gendered and racialized ideologies about care and work (Altman and Pannell 2012; Guevarra 2014; Liang 2011). A gender-specific supply of care workers rests on cultural norms and stereotypes of women as "natural caregivers" [women in destination countries are able to escape these gender restrictions by transferring them to migrant women (Altman and Pannell 2012)]. By the same token, migration policies aimed at the admittance of care workers reflect stereotypes of race, class, and nationality, with a racialized ideology used to legitimate the suitability of particular groups to work as caregivers (Browne and Braun 2008; Guevarra 2014; Liang 2011). Finally, such policies may render care work a private household problem, masking the critical need for universal health and child care in post-industrial societies and minimizing governmental responsibility (Walia 2010).

In addition to these general considerations, as noted in the introduction, the Canadian LCP generated tensions between caregivers and employers and between caregivers and the state. These multi-scalar sites of asymmetrical dependency rested on the live-in requirement, the power of employers alongside reduced mobility opportunities for migrants, and the liminality associated with transitioning from temporary to permanent resident status.

Requirements to Live with the Employer
The LCP continued the FDM requirement that the migrant caregiver live with the employer, as the federal government argued that those positions were unlikely to be filled by local Canadian residents. But as Rollins (1985) and others note, these employment relations are those of middle- and upper-class, often white, women governing low-waged, predominantly women of color employed in the context of entrenched race relations or under migration regimes that give them temporary and precarious legal status. A large literature highlights the negative consequences of employer–employee relations in the private setting of the home. For one thing, invisible working conditions make in-home work difficult to regulate (Mantouvalou 2013). Studies report that caregivers are constantly on-call, forced to work overtime without pay, denied sick leave, assigned to tasks not contractually covered, paid in cash with no report of employer benefits, and lacking recourse to bureaucratic rules and regulations governing disputes. They also note the dearth of record-keeping to prove to immigration authorities that migrants have worked for the required 24 months of work (Atanackovic and Bourgeault 2014; Canada 2009; Labadie-Jackson 2008; Straehle 2012; Tungohan et al. 2015; Walia 2010). Through curfews, banned telephone use and visitor restrictions, caregivers can be isolated; they have also reported physical, mental, and sexual abuse, often used by employers to exert control (Hodge 2006; Lindio-McGovern 2012, Chap. 2; Silvera 1989).

Centrality of Employer
Because employers provide employment opportunities and their homes are designated as work sites, they assume a state-mandated importance in shaping work conditions and in enabling (or not) migrant caregivers to apply for permanent residency status. Employers and employees are ostensibly governed by a contract stipulating the level of payment

(which must be at the minimum wage), hours worked, job tasks, and living arrangements. As the previous section indicates, however, such contracts may be violated by employers, creating two additional problems for the caregiver.

First, the need to accumulate 24 months of work to satisfy permanent resident visa requirements means that many migrant women in bad situations are reluctant to leave the employer. They fear that a record of frequent job changes will be viewed negatively by the authorities who approve permanent residence visas or by potential employers, and new job searches will create delays in meeting the 24-month requirement. Second, immigration jurisdiction falls under federal policy, but labor standards are the responsibility of the provinces. The federal government cannot enforce provincial labor standards, and many domestic workers are unaware of the level of government they should access if they face exploitation (Bakan and Stasiulis 1995; Daenzer 1997).

Following consultations in 2008–2009, a number of administrative changes were announced by the Minister of Citizenship and Immigration Canada (CIC) in December 2009 and in August 2010 (CIC 2009, 2010) to alleviate the problems. One change extended the period for accumulating the mandatory 24 months of care employment from three to four years and provided the option of counting weeks or hours. Three additional changes addressed employment relations. One was the mandatory inclusion of clauses in the employment contract on employer-paid benefits, accommodations, duties, hours of work including overtime hours, level of wages, holiday and sick leave entitlements, and terms of termination or resignation. New employer-paid benefits were also mandated for employers wishing to hire migrant women through the LCP. Employers were required to pay for the following: (1) transportation to the place of work in Canada from the LCP migrant's country of residence; (2) private medical insurance prior to activation of provincial health coverage; (3) workplace safety insurance or the equivalent if former was not available; (4) all recruitment fees associated with hiring an LCP migrant. Employers were forbidden to recoup these expenditures from employees, though de facto such actions could still occur since detection requires reporting the violation.

Two additional initiatives were targeted at the problems faced by Live-In Caregivers: (1) establishing emergency processing of labor market opinions (the employer's authorization to hire) and of new work permits for caregivers already in Canada who faced abuse, intimidation or threats in their current jobs; and (2) offering a new caregiver telephone service through the CIC Call Centre, designed to better inform caregivers and employers of their rights and responsibilities under the program. A final change announced on December 15, 2011 (CIC 2011) provided open work permits to LCP workers who had met the working conditions for becoming permanent residents but were waiting for review of their completed applications. These permits allowed women to move out of their employers' homes and seek other employment, mitigating the lengthy waiting time for the issuing of permanent residency visas.

At the time, these changes appeared to signal a greater involvement by the federal government in management practices that could alleviate the migrant caregivers' dependency on and vulnerability to their employers. However, they also included actions against "fraudulent" employers and immigration consultants, indicating a changed tone and foreshadowing a new direction for Canada's migration regime governing migrant care workers. Eventually the requirement for live-in employment would disappear, but so too would the near-automatic right of permanent residency heretofore extended to all LCP caregivers who had met specified conditions, most notably 24 months of service.

Temporary Legal Status, Precarity and Challenges of Liminality
The breaching of employment contracts and abuse often went unreported because of the LCP caregivers' temporary legal status. Caregivers were reluctant to report abuse out of fear of deportation or delays in obtaining permanent residency (Atanackovic and Bourgeault 2014; Tungohan et al. 2015). Some employers even illegally withheld legal documents to restrict the mobility of the caregivers (Canada House of Commons 2009). For critics of the program, temporary status limited the workers' ability to assert their labor rights and negotiate their conditions of work, placing them in exploitative situations (Khan 2009; Streahle 2012; Walia 2010). Caregiver vulnerability and long-term separation from their families underpinned the argument that the program and others like it violated fundamental human rights, such as the right to family life and exclusion of social benefits; nor did it correspond to the norms of the ILO and UN treaties (Khan 2009; Kontos 2013).

As noted previously, Live-In Caregivers were required to put in 24 months of full-time domestic work within a three-year period. This requirement meant that migrant women were reluctant to take vacations, visit family elsewhere or change jobs near the end of their employment, as such behaviors could affect the three-year minimum. Further, if employers did not document overtime or long days, the additional hours could not be used to fulfill the 24–month requirement. Following the 2008–2009 consultations, on April 14, 2010, the federal government changed the counting protocol. Caregivers could now meet requirements either by using months as the unit or by using hours. They had the option of becoming eligible after 3,900 hours over a minimum of 22 months, in which a maximum of 390 overtime hours could be counted. Additionally, instead of the three-year period in which months or hours in domestic work must be accrued, a four-year limit was allowed.

State-mandated health care checks also affected the potential to transition to permanent residence status. As part of the LCP application process, medical examinations were required to ensure applicants were in good health. However, upon applying for permanent residency status, a second medical examination was required to meet the general requirements for all would-be permanent residents. The consequences are evident in the case of Juana Tejada, a Filipina worker in the LCP program. As a result of a cancer diagnosis (and its predicted costs to the Canadian health care system), Ms. Tejada was found ineligible for permanent residence status. Ms. Tejada's case highlights the vulnerable period between being a temporary worker at the end of a working contract and applying for and achieving permanent status (Keung 2008, 2009). Media attention and pressure from advocacy groups forced the federal government to remove the requirement for a second medical examination for LCP workers in December 2009, but the revisions retained problematic elements. For one, in the operational guidelines, frontline immigration officers were advised that they retained "the discretion to request a medical examination." For another, the new regulations only applied to those entering Canada after the regulations came into effect on April 1, 2010. In all, some 40,000 workers who arrived before the regulatory change were still required to have the second medical exam (Keung 2010).

A final challenge associated with becoming a permanent resident stems from the state-mandated higher entrance requirements of the LCP and the shift to recruitment from the Philippines. At first glance, this does not seem to be a problem. An exceptionally well-educated LCP workforce evolved for three reasons: the education system in the Philippines, the level of training of nurses, and the Philippines' state-sponsored export of people as sources of remittances. As shown

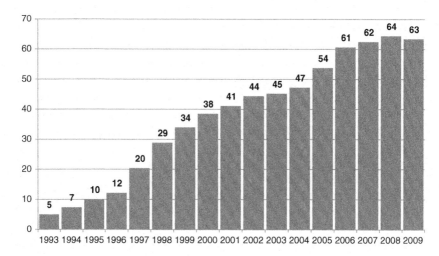

Fig. 8.3 Percentages with University Degrees or Higher, Principal Applicants Admitted as Permanent Residents from the Live-In Caregiver Program, by Year of Admission, Canada 1993-2009

Source: Kelly, Park, de Leon and Priest 2011

in Fig. 8.3, educational levels steadily rose for those admitted into Canada as permanent residents under the LCP, primarily as a result of the preponderance of Filipina applicants. Between 2005 and 2009, over half were university graduates (more recent data are not publicly available).

However, research finds that relative to their degrees and training, Canada's LCP workers become deskilled during their employment as caregivers, and most are not working in occupations for which they were trained (Torres et al. 2012). In addition, although LCP workers came to Canada with the intention of returning to their careers after completing the program, pressures to remit money and financially support family reunification caused many to put such initiatives on hold. Equally problematic is the fact that their previous skills and credentials are not always recognized in the labor market; nor does their LCP experience match the "Canadian experience" required by many employers. Many have remained in related occupations, not enjoying upward mobility after becoming permanent residents (Atanackovic and Bourgeault 2014; Pratt 2008, Appendix 1; Spitzer, Torres and Hanley 2008; Tungohan et al. 2015).

Back to the Past?

Despite criticism of the vulnerability and exploitation of foreign female caregivers, the Live-in Care Program continued the policy of the earlier Foreign Domestic Worker program, which permitted transitioning from temporary to permanent resident status for those workers. As such, the migration regime adopted by Canada with respect to the explicit recruitment of temporary domestic female workers was unique among the migration regulations and practices of other advanced welfare states.

Between 2009 and 2011, the federal government began to make changes to the program, ostensibly targeting some of the abuses in the employer-employee relationships, in part by regulating employers in conditions of work, pay, and benefits. More quietly, regulations enacted from 2012 on applied greater sanctions to fraudulent employers or employers violating the terms of reference. The LMO/LMIA assessments became more stringent to ensure that live-in care workers really were in short supply and Canadian-born workers were unavailable. These changes occurred alongside efforts to tighten immigration regulations in other areas, including reducing fraudulent marriage migration and barring trafficking, which entailed denying visas to dancers. Changes also included June 2012 amendments to the *Immigration and Refugee Protection Act* requiring the automatic detention of incoming refugee claimants arriving in large groups. For critics, the latter three (fraudulent marriage, trafficking and refugee detention) revealed the Harper government's fondness for distinguishing between the "good" and the "undeserving"; they also signaled the adoption of criminal justice measures in recent immigration legislation, a process commonly called "crimmigration" (Stumpf 2013).

The LCP was not immune to the shifting orientation in immigration policy. Applying for a LMO/LMIA became more expensive for would-be employers, rising from $275 to $1000 in June 2014. Now fees are not returned if the petition fails, and twitter threads suggest that the high cost deters applications. The same month, the Minister for Employment and Multiculturalism, Jason Kenney, criticized the LCP for being "out of control" and having "mutated into a program of family reunification whereby migrants were coming to work for their own relatives in jobs that might not otherwise exist" (Hough 2014; Keung 2014). Kenney is quoted as follows:

"I was in Manila a few years ago to give a seminar on nannies' rights.... I was there with 70 caregivers who were coming to Canada. None had questions about rights. All 70 of them were going to work for relatives in Canada and all they wanted to know was: what was the penalty for working outside the home illegally, and how long it would take them to sponsor family members," said Mr. Kenney during an editorial board meeting with the National Post on Tuesday. (Hough 2014)

The federal government had previously voiced concerns that as many as 40 percent of LCP workers were employed by family members, with consular staff in Manila estimating the number as closer to 70 percent (Hough 2014; Robertson 2014).

One reporter noted that the June 2014 allegations about abuse sounded similar to claims made by government spokespersons about other immigration and refugee programs just before the introduction of major overhauls tightening these programs (Keung 2014). The remarks did indeed signal impending alterations in the rules and regulations governing the migration of women into Canada for care. Ongoing consultations, by invitation only, over the Live-In Caregiver Program were initiated in 2014 by the Conservative government's Minister of Citizenship and Immigration (CIC), Chris Alexander. On October 31, 2014, CIC announced sweeping changes to the LCP, effective December 1, 2014. These included:

- Increasing the number of permanent resident visas issued in 2015 from the existing backlog of permanent resident applications, generated by former LCP workers before the announced program changes.
- Removing the requirement that caregivers live in the home of their employer.
- Creating two "pathways" for permanent resident status for migrant care workers to replace the existing LCP

Close scrutiny suggests the changes may not necessarily resolve issues deriving from the living-in requirement. Equally if not more significant, the practices associated with the two pathways (described below) are likely to ensure that most migrants admitted to Canada to provide care will be temporary workers, unable to transition to permanent resident status.

Reducing the Backlog: An important dimension of the liminality facing LCP workers is the time it takes to obtain permanent resident visas once the care work requirements have been met. Although the granting of open permits removed the need to continue to work for a specific employer, family reunification is a lengthy process, and delays in processing completed applications extend absences between Live-In Care workers and their families. Problematically, processing times for the permanent residency of LCP workers increased from eighteen months in 2011 to 47 months in 2015.[1]

As a result, the LCP had a significant backlog of applications for permanent residence, about 60,000 on October 31, 2014 (Mas 2014). In his announcement of pending changes, Minister Alexander noted the doubling of permanent resident admissions levels for caregivers in 2014, with 17,500 admissions planned, including spouse and dependents. Figure 8.2 shows that approximately 14,400 principal applicants from the LCP were admitted in 2014, followed by nearly 13,800 in 2015. Processing the backlog also skyrocketed with the 2015 admission of 13,258 spouses and dependents of LCP caregivers, up from 3,263 in 2014 (Fig. 8.2 source). The Liberal government elected in October 2015 continued to expedite the backlog, targeting 22,000 total admissions in the care stream for 2016; these numbers include those in the new program discussed below, but LCP-derived admissions will dominate (only 75 permanent residents entered through the new care categories in 2015).

Two Pathways

To replace the Live-In Caregiver Program, two "pathways for permanent residency" became effective on December 1, 2014: (1) Caring for Children; (2) Caring for People with High Medical Needs. For both, foreign caregivers must obtain regular temporary worker permits, reaffirming that the pathways are subsets of the larger temporary worker program. The potential for transitioning to permanent resident status remains, with applications for permanent residency processed within six months of the receipt of a completed application. Similar to the earlier LCP, both pathways require applicants to have at least two years of full-time work (a minimum of thirty hours a week or more) in a designated occupation over a four-year period. However, in contrast to the earlier FDWM and LCP programs, the new pathways permit only a limited number of permanent resident applications to be processed annually. The number of applications through each pathway is capped each year at 2,750 principal applicants (PAs), for a total of 5,500 annually, down substantially from earlier years (see Fig. 8.2 for LCP-related admissions in previous years).

The first "pathway" bears some resemblance to the LCP program which ceased processing applications for temporary admission as of November 30, 2014. But it has significant differences as well. As in the final days of the LCP, the Child Minder pathway does not require workers to live in the homes of their employers; a live-in arrangement is permitted if the employer and foreign caregiver in the Child Minder pathway have agreed. However, living in the employer's home may continue to be de facto reality for migrant caregivers in the Child Minder stream, particularly if the required Labour Market Impact Assessments find that local Canadian workers are available to give care only while "living out." In the latter circumstance, the only jobs approved for non-Canadian residents may be those that require living with the employer

To hire a caregiver on a regular temporary permit, employers are told to ensure that the temporary foreign worker has the training, qualifications and experience to do the work. However, for those applying for permanent resident visa, educational requirements in the Child Minder pathway are similar to those in the LCP, with one new stipulation: a Canadian post-secondary education credential of at least one year, or an equivalent foreign credential, supported by an Educational Credential Assessment. This latter requirement is new but can be found in other admissions categories in the economic class; in this requirement, the education of the applicant must be independently assessed, at the applicant's expense, by an arms-length assessment organization that bids with the Canadian government for the contract. If the education received outside Canada is deemed not to be equivalent, the application is returned and no further action is taken or is possible.

Canada's immigration regulations now stipulate that English and French are the only languages that can be identified as a job requirement in LMIA applications and in job advertisements for temporary foreign workers unless employers can demonstrate that another language is essential for the job. And the level of linguistic competency must enable caregivers to communicate effectively and independently in an unsupervised setting. As with education, the requirements become more precise when the temporary caregiver seeks to become a permanent resident. In order to transition from being a temporary foreign worker in the Child Minder pathway to becoming a permanent resident, the caregiver application must meet the requirement of a language test, again at the applicant's expense; the applicant must demonstrate an "initial intermediate" level of language by meeting Canadian Language Benchmark

5 in a designated third-party language test. This reformulation of the earlier language requirements also appears in the requirements of those seeking permanent admission in the skilled worker class, the express entry class and the provincial nominee class.

To be eligible to apply for permanent residency, caregivers in the Caring for People with High Medical Needs pathway must have two years of full-time work experience in Canada (authorized by a work permit) providing in-home care or care in a health facility to the elderly or persons with disabilities or chronic disease. Although these categories are subject to change at any time by the Minister of Citizenship and Immigration, current hires must be for the following occupations: (1) registered nurses or registered psychiatric nurses (NOCS group 3012); (2) licensed practical nurses (NOCS 3233); (3) nurses' aides or patient service associates (NOCS 3413); (4) home support workers (NOCS 4412) (but not housekeepers). Again, applicants must undergo a third-party language test and achieve a Benchmark Level 7 competency score for the first occupation and a Level 5 competency for the other occupations.[2]

To apply for permanent resident status, educational requirements in the High Medical Needs pathway are the same as those for Caring for Children, with one important limiting proviso: workers in this category must meet the employment requirements for the occupation as listed in the National Occupational Classification System. For those seeking work in regulated occupations (such as nursing), requirements include being licensed to practice in Canada and registering with the appropriate regulatory body in the province of residence and work. This licensing and registration also is required of temporary workers recruited in the High Medical Needs pathway.

In practice, these licensing/certification stipulations will depress both temporary and permanent resident visas for migrant caregivers seeking employment as licensed nurses or practical nurses, especially those who trained in countries lacking international equivalency agreements with Canada. Persons trained in regions outside the United States, the United Kingdom, Northern and Western Europe and Australia are likely to be the most negatively affected. Further, the requirement that workers be licensed to practice in Canada suggests that nurses' aides, patient service associates or home support workers will predominate in temporary worker permits, particularly for migrants from countries, including the Philippines, whose nursing degrees are not accepted by Canadian professional or regulatory bodies as equivalent to Canadian degrees. In short, deskilling – working in an occupation with requirements that are lower than one's training – may be likely for highly educated migrant women whose care work training and experience was obtained in the Global South.

CONCLUSION

The recent replacement of the LCP by the two pathways is applicable to successful Labour Market Impact Assessment employer applications submitted on or after December 1, 2014. Caregivers who entered Canadian under the Live-In Caregiver Program now have the option of complying with LCP regulations necessary for permanent resident status or moving to the new care streams. As of 2016, major federal government activities are twofold: processing a large backlog of LCP applications for permanent resident visas and posting detailed web instructions for employers seeking to hire temporary migrant caregivers. The latter stipulate both employment conditions and job advertisement protocols required for the LMIA. Posts also contain instructions for migrant care employees seeking to become permanent residents from the two new care pathways.

It is too early to determine the consequences of the care pathways, but the numbers of temporary migrants for care will surely decline in response to the $1,000 LMIA fees for employers. In addition, the 2,250 annual caps issued for permanent visas in each of the two pathways will reduce transitions from temporary to permanent resident status. Articulated while the Conservative Party was still in power, caps will be filled by applications at the start of each calendar year and closed when the allowable number is reached (Canadian Bar Association-Quebec 2015).

Most assuredly, given the looming gray tsunami and the child care dearth associated with Canada's liberal care regime (van Hooren 2012), migrant caregivers will continue to be admitted as temporary workers as they have in the past. The new pathways do offer the possibility of obtaining permanent resident status. But compared with the past Live-In Caregiver Program, transitioning to permanent residency will be reduced by employer LMIA costs, licensing requirements and numerical caps. Instead, many temporary care workers in the new pathways will be allowed to work in Canada but they may never be able to transition to permanent resident status. In sum, Canada's policy towards migrant care worker recruitment has moved closer to the "forever temporary" care worker policies found elsewhere in the world.

NOTES

1. This can be found at: http://www.cic.gc.ca/english/information/times/perm/skilled-fed.asp.
2. This can be found at: http://www.language.ca/documents/levels_5-10_b.pdf.

REFERENCES

Altman, Meryl and Kerry Pannell. 2012. "Policy Gaps and Theory Gaps: Women and Migrant Domestic Labor." *Feminist Economics* 18: 291–315.

Anderson, Bridget. 2010. "Migration, Immigration Controls and the Fashioning of Precarious Workers." *Work Employment and Society* 24: 300–317.

Arat-Koc, Sedef. 1997. "From 'Mothers of the Nation' to Migrant Workers." In *Not One of the Family: Foreign Domestic Workers in Canada*, edited by Abigail B. Bakan and Daiva Stasiulis, 53–79. Toronto: University of Toronto Press.

Atanackovic, Jelena and Ivy Lynn Bourgeault.2014. "Economic and Social Integration of Immigrant Live-In Caregivers in Canada." *IRPP Study* No. 46. http://irpp.org/wp-content/uploads/assets/research/diversity-immigration-and-integration/atanackovic-bourgeault-no46/study-no46.pdf.

Bakan, Abigail and Daiva Stasiulis. 1995. "Making the Match: Domestic Placement Agencies and the Racialization of Women's Household Work." *SIGNS: Journal of Women in Culture and Society* 20: 303–330.

Barber, Marilyn. 1991. *Immigrant Domestic Servants in Canada*. Canada's Ethnic Groups booklet 16. Ottawa: Canadian Historical Association.

Barber, Pauline Gardiner. 2000. "Agency in Philippine Women's Labour Migration and Provisional Diaspora." *Women's Studies International Forum* 23: 399–411.

Barber, Pauline Gardiner. 2008. "The Ideal Immigrant? Gendered Class Subjects in Philippine-Canada Migration." *Third World Quarterly* 29: 1265–1285.

Boyd, Monica. 1997. "Migration Policy, Family Membership and Female Dependency: Canada and Germany." In *Remaking the Welfare State*, edited by Patricia Evans, Thelma McCormack and Gerda Wekerle, 142–169. Toronto: University of Toronto Press.

Boyd, Monica. 2014. "Recruiting High Skill Labour in North America: Policies, Outcomes and Futures." *International Migration* 52, 3: 40–54.

Boyd, Monica and Naomi Alboim. 2012. "Managing International Migration: The Canadian Case." In *Managing Immigration and Diversity in Canada: A Transatlantic Dialogue in the New Age of Migration*, edited by Dan Rodríguez-García, 123–150. Montreal and Kingston: McGill-Queen's University Press.

Boyd, Monica and Naomi Lightman. 2016. "Gender, Nativity and Race in Care Work." Paper Presented at the annual meeting of the American Sociological Association, Seattle WA, August 19.

Browne, Colette V. and Kathryn Braun. 2008. "Globalization, Women's Migration and the Long-Term-Care Workforce." *The Gerontologist* 48, 1: 16–24.

Canada House of Commons. 2009. *Migrant Workers and Ghost Consultants.* Report of the Standing Committee on Citizenship and Immigration, Chair David Tilson MP. 40th Parliament, 2nd Session, June. http://www.parl.gc.ca/content/hoc/Committee/402/CIMM/Reports/RP3969226/402_CIMM_Rpt08/402_CIMM_Rpt08-e.pdf. Ottawa: House of Parliament.

Canadian Bar Association-Quebec. 2015. "Questions for CIC: Mr. Matthew Graham." http://s3.amazonaws.com/migrants_heroku_production/datas/2040/CIC_written_responses_to_CBA_Quebec_questions_-_Sept_17_2015_original.pdf?1452700906.

Citizenship and Immigration Canada. 2005. "2004 Foreign Worker Overview." *The Monitor* 10 (summer). www.collectionscanada.gc.ca/webarchives/20060205140006/http://www.cic.gc.ca/english/monitor/issue10/05-overview.html.

Citizenship and Immigration Canada. 2009. "Backgrounder: Improvements to Live-in Caregiver Program." www.cic.gc.ca/english/department/media/backgrounders/2010/2010-08-18a.asp.

Citizenship and Immigration Canada. 2010. "Minister Kenney Announces Improvements Affecting Temporary Foreign Workers, Including Live-In Caregivers." News Release, August 19. http://news.gc.ca/web/article-en.do?crtr.sj1D=andcrtr.mnthndVl=12andmthd=advSrchandcrtr.dpt1D=6664andnid=554169andcrtr.lc1D=andcrtr.tp1D=1andcrtr.yrStrtVl=2010andcrtr.kw=andcrtr.dyStrtVl=1andcrtr.aud1D=andcrtr.mnthStrtVl=1andcrtr.page=6andcrtr.yrndVl=2010andcrtr.dyndVl=31.

Citizenship and Immigration Canada. 2011. "Kenney Announces Important Change for Live-in Caregivers." News Release, December 15. http://news.gc.ca/web/article-en.do?crtr.sj1D=andcrtr.mnthndVl=12andmthd=advSrchandcrtr.dpt1D=6664andnid=645909andcrtr.lc1D=andcrtr.tp1D=1andcrtr.yrStrtVl=2011andcrtr.kw=andcrtr.dyStrtVl=1andcrtr.aud1D=andcrtr.mnthStrtVl=1andcrtr.page=1andcrtr.yrndVl=2011andcrtr.dyndVl=31.

Daenzer, Patricia. 1997. "An Affair between Nations: International Relations and the Movement of Household Service Workers." In *Not One of the Family: Foreign Domestic Workers in Canada*, edited by Abigail B, Bakan and Daiva Stasiulis, 81–118. Toronto: University of Toronto Press.

Gorodzeisky, Anastasia and Moshe Semyonov. 2014. "Making a Living in Two Labor Markets: Earnings of Filipinos in the Global and the Domestic Economy." *Research in Social Stratification and Mobility* 37: 77–89.

Guevarra, Anna Romina. 2014. "Supermaids: The Racial Branding of Global Filipino Care Labour." In *Migration and Care Labour: Theory, Policy and Politics*, edited by Bridget Anderson and Isabel Shutes, 130–149. London: Palgrave MacMillan.

Hodge, Jarrah. 2006. "Unskilled Labour: Canada's Live-In Caregiver Program." *Undercurrents* 3, 2: 61–66.

Hochschild, Arlie. 2000. "The Nanny Chain." *The American Prospect* 11, 4: 32–36.

Hough, Jennifer. 2014. "Caregiver Program 'Ran out of Control': Foreign Workers to be Reformed in 'Fairly Near Future.'" *National Post*, June 25 A1.

Hondagneu-Sotelo, Pierrette. 2007. *Doméstica: Immigrant Workers Cleaning and Caring in the Shadows of Affluence*. Berkeley: University of California Press.

Isaksen, Lisa Widding, Sambasivan Uma Devi and Arlie Russell Hochschild. 2008. "Global Care Crisis: A Problem of Capital, Care Chain, or Commons?" *American Behavioral Scientist* 52: 405–425.

Kelly, Philip, Stella Park, Conely de Leon and Jeff Priest. 2011. "Profile of Live-in-caregiver Immigrants to Canada, 1993–2009." TIEDI Report # 18. http://www.yorku.ca/tiedi/pubreports.html.

Keung, Nicholas. 2008. "Dying Nanny Told to Leave County; 'I Paid My Dues Here,' Says Filipina Woman Denied Residency after Diagnosis of Cancer." *Toronto Star*, June 9, A4.

Keung, Nicholas. 2009. "Nanny Back in Hospital as her Cancer Worsens." *Toronto Star*, March 8, A7.

Keung, Nicholas. 2010. "Law's Loophole Leaves Ailing Nannies at Risk: Immigration Officials Still Have the Discretion to Deport Caregivers who Fall Ill in Canada." *Toronto Star*, June 7, GT5.

Keung, Nicholas. 2014. "Filipinos Fear End of Immigrant Dreams for Nannies: Community Alarmed by Ottawa's Claim that Residency Program is Being Abused." *Toronto Star*, July 22.

Khan, Sabba A. 2009. "From Labour of Love to Decent Work: Protecting the Human Rights of Migrant Caregivers in Canada." *Canadian Journal of Law and Society* 24, 1: 23–45.

Kontos, Maria. 2013. "Negotiating the Social Citizenship Rights of Migrant Domestic Workers: The Right to Family Reunification and a Family Life in Policies and Debates." *Journal of Ethnic and Migration Studies* 39: 409–424.

Labadie-Jackson. Glenda. 2008. "Reflections on Domestic Work and the Feminization of Migration." *Campbell Law Review* 31, 1: 67–90.

Liang, Li-Fang. 2011. "The Making of an 'Ideal' Live-in Migrant Care Worker: Recruiting, Training, Matching and Disciplining." *Ethnic and Racial Studies* 34: 1815–1834.

Lindio-McGovern, Ligaya. 2012. *Globalization, Labor Export and Resistance*. London and New York: Routledge.

Macklin, Audrey. 1992. "Foreign Domestic Worker: Surrogate Housewife or Mail Order Servant?" *McGill Law Journal* 37: 681–760.

Mantouvalou, Virginia. 2013. "Workers without Rights as Citizens at the Margins." *Critical Review of International Social and Political Philosophy* 16: 366–382.

Mas, Susana. 2014. "Foreign Caregiver Reforms Impose Cap, Make Live-in Requirement Optional." *Canada Broadcast Corporation (CBC) News*, October 31. http://www.cbc.ca/news/politics/foreign-caregiver-reforms-impose-cap-make-live-in-requirement-optional-1.2819800.

Pratt, Geraldine. 2008. "Deskilling across the Generations: Reunification among Transnational Filipino Families in Vancouver." Philippine Women Centre of BC [*Ugnayan ng Kabataang Pilipino sa Canada*] Working Paper 08-06. Vancouver: Metropolis British Columbia. mbc.metropolis.net/assets/uploads/files/wp/2008/WP08-06.pdf.

Robertson, Dylan. 2014. "Planned Changes to Nanny Program Spark Alarm." *Calgary Herald* June 25, A6.

Rodriguez, Robyn Magalit. 2010. *Migrants for Export: How the Philippine State Brokers Labor to the World*. Minneapolis: University of Minnesota Press.

Rollins, Judith. 1985. *Between Women: Domestics and their Employers*. Philadelphia: Temple University Press.

Schecter, Tanya. 1998. *Race, Class, Women and the State: The Case of Domestic Labour*. Montreal: Black Rose Books.

Shutes, Isabel. 2014. "A Right to Care? Immigration Controls and the Care Labour of Non-Citizens." In *Migration and Care Labour: Theory, Policy and Politics*, edited by Bridget Anderson and Isabel Shutes, 87–109. London: Palgrave Macmillan.

Silvera, Makeda. 1989. *Silenced: Talks with Working Class Caribbean Women about their Lives and Struggles as Domestic Workers in Canada*, 2nd ed. Toronto: Sister Vision Press.

Spitzer, Denise L. and Sara Torres. 2008. "Gender-based Barriers to Settlement and Integration for Live-In Caregivers." CERIS Working Paper No 71. Toronto: CERIS - The Ontario Metropolis Centre.

Stasiulis, Daiva and Abigail B. Bakan. 2003. *Negotiating Citizenship: Migrant Women in Canada and the Global System*. New York: Palgrave Macmillan.

Statistics Canada, Demography Division. 2010. *Population Projections for Canada, Provinces and Territories 2009 to 2036*. Catalogue no. 91-520-X (June). Ottawa: Minister of Industry.

Statistics Canada. 2015. "Canada's Population Estimates: Age and Sex, July 1, 2015." *The Daily*, September 29. http://www.statcan.gc.ca/daily-quotidien/150929/dq150929b-eng.htm.

Statistics Canada. 2016. "The Surge of Women in the Workforce." *The Daily*, March 31. http://www.statcan.gc.ca/pub/11-630-x/11-630-x2015009-eng.htm.

Strumpf, Juliet P. 2013. "The Process is the Punishment in Crimmigration Law." In *Borders of Punishment: Migration, Citizenship, and Social Exclusion*, edited by Katja Franko Aas and Mary Bosworth, 58–75. Oxford: Oxford University Press.

Straehle, Christine. 2012. "Global Justice, Temporary Migration and Vulnerability." *Global Justice: Theory Practice Rhetoric* 5: 71–81.

Torres, Sara, Denise L. Spitzer, Karen D. Hughes, Jacqueline Oxman-Martinez and Jill Hanley. 2012. "From Temporary Worker to Resident: The LCP and Its Impact through an Intersectional Lens." In *Legislated Inequality: Temporary Labour Migration in Canada*, edited by Patti T. Lenard and Christine Straehle, 227–319. Montreal and Kingston: McGill-Queen's University Press.

Tungohan, Ethel et al. 2015. "After the Live-In Caregiver Program: Filipina Caregivers' Experiences of Graduated and Uneven Citizenship." *Canadian Ethnic Studies* 47, 1: 87–105.

van Hooren, Franca J. 2012. "Varieties of Migrant Care Work: Comparing Patterns of Migrant Labour in Social Care." *Journal of European Social Policy* 22, 2: 133–147.

Walia, Harsha. 2010. "Transient Servitude: Migrant Labour in Canada and the Apartheid of Citizenship." *Race and Class* 52, 1: 71–84.

World Bank. 2015. "Personal Remittances, Received (% of GDP)." http://data.worldbank.org/indicator/BX.TRF.PWKR.DT.GD.ZS.

Monica Boyd is a professor of sociology and held the Canada Research Chair in Immigration, Inequality and Public Policy from 2001 to 2015 at the University of Toronto. She has been active in United Nations activities focusing on Beijing+10 and the 2006 High-Level Dialogue on Migration, preparing invited reports for UNIRSD, UN-DAW, UNFPA, the UN Commission of Women, and the UN Population Division. In 2015 she won the Outstanding Contribution Award from the Canadian Sociological Association honoring her exceptional scholarly merit and impact on Canadian sociology.

CHAPTER 9

Explaining Exceptionality: Care and Migration Policies in Japan and South Korea

Ito Peng

The worldwide flow of female migrants from poorer to richer countries to perform care work is now a global reality, and East Asia is absolutely part of this trend (Anderson and Shutes 2014; Asis and Piper 2008; Michel and Peng 2012; Oishi 2005; Peng 2017; Raghuram 2012; Yeoh and Huang 2010). Within East Asia, Japan, South Korea (Korea), Taiwan, Hong Kong and Singapore are the top destination countries/regions for female migrant care workers. Like other rich Organization for Economic Co-operation and Development (OECD) countries, these East Asian societies are all experiencing huge demands for care and serious shortages of care workers. Yet among these migrant-worker receiving countries, Japan and Korea stand out as exceptions to the general global trend. Although the two countries share many social, demographic and economic characteristics in common with Taiwan, Hong Kong and Singapore, they differ markedly from them in terms of their approaches to and use of foreign care workers. What explains their differences?

First, all the five East Asian destination societies have been experiencing rapid population aging, very low fertility, and increased married women's labor market participation. These changes have all contributed to a huge demand for care. Further, because of their high educational level and the availability of other employment options, most native-born

I. Peng (✉)
Department of Sociology, University of Toronto, Toronto, ON, Canada

© The Author(s) 2017   191
S. Michel, I. Peng (eds.), *Gender, Migration, and the Work of Care*,
DOI 10.1007/978-3-319-55086-2_9

women (and men) in these societies are unwilling to accept care work jobs, which tend to be low-wage and low-status. This has exacerbated the labor shortage in the care sector. Consequently, all these societies have become increasingly reliant on foreign migrant care workers to fill the care demand. Yet, whereas foreign domestic and care workers are widely employed by families to provide child care and elder care in private homes in Taiwan, Hong Kong and Singapore, in Japan and Korea the use of foreign domestic or care workers in private homes is very low or almost non-existent. Rather, in recent years, small channels have opened for migrant care workers to work in institutional settings in these two countries.

Broadly, then, there is a spectrum of approaches to foreign care workers among the five richer East Asian societies, ranging from widespread use of foreign domestic workers within private homes, as in Singapore and Hong Kong, to almost no use of foreign domestic or care workers within private homes or institutions in Japan. Within this spectrum, two broad types of care migration regimes can be observed: (1) countries/regions that actively use foreign domestic and care workers to satisfy their care demands – Singapore, Hong Kong and Taiwan; and (2) countries that have limited and/or restrictive use of foreign domestic and care workers – Japan and Korea. In all cases, foreign domestic and care workers fall under the category of temporary migrant workers and are not considered potential candidates for naturalization. As well, in all these countries acceptance and use of these workers are shaped by family and care policies and regulated by immigration policies.

In Singapore, Hong Kong and Taiwan, most families must seek private market solutions to their care needs because their governments provide very little public child care or elder care. Instead, these governments have liberalized immigration policies to facilitate the entry of domestic and care workers into their countries and introduced direct and indirect financial and tax incentives for families to access foreign domestic and care workers. By contrast, in Japan and Korea, despite recent attempts to broaden the intake of foreign workers, the entry of foreign domestic and care workers into the countries is highly restricted; rather, both governments have increased social care programs and government subsidies to compensate families to care or to help families purchase care. In many ways, Singapore, Hong Kong and Taiwan's policy approaches to domestic and care workers are more in line with the general trend observed among OECD countries of a shift toward increased financialization and marketization of care, and a rollback in public care provisions.

In this chapter I focus on Japan and Korea, two East Asian countries that seem to be impervious to the prevailing trend by remaining resistant to taking in foreign care workers. Why are they so reluctant to accept foreign care workers, particularly given the fact that they face huge care worker shortages and their governments, under tight fiscal constraints like those in other countries, should find the use of foreign care workers an attractive option? I show that these countries' reluctance to open up their borders to foreign care workers can be explained by the combination of prevailing notions about how care should be provided, a pervasive and persistent negative public sentiment toward immigration (a reflection of their collective imaginaries and narratives about national identity and nationhood), and the restrictive employment regimes associated with their long-term care insurance systems. In short, their approaches to migrant care workers can be explained by a cultural and institutional understanding and framing of care and national identity, and by their institutionalized employment regimes. An analysis of care and migration policies in Japan and Korea is interesting and important because, first, they serve as the exception to the global trend toward increased use of foreign care workers, and second, because the two cases highlight how local contexts can influence approaches to care and immigration policies. Finally, Japanese and Korean exceptionality also underscores the importance of cultural and institutional factors in determining national policies toward care and migration.

The next section provides a brief background to the transnational migration of care workers in East Asia. I compare the two dominant approaches to migrant care workers that are evident: the *liberal private market approach* employed by Taiwan, Hong Kong and Singapore, and the *regulated institutional approach* found in Japan and Korea. The third section focuses on Japan and Korea. Here I discuss how cultural and institutional factors in these countries have helped shape their national policies toward care and immigration. I also point out some differences between Japan and Korea in order to avoid a binary typology framework that fixes Japan and Korea as one cluster against Taiwan, Hong Kong and Singapore cluster; rather, I emphasize the broader range of approaches to care and migration that are evident within East Asia. The final section points to the importance of looking at intersections of care, immigration and employment regimes in the analysis of transnational care migration, and the implications of the Japanese and Korean cases for the comparative analysis of transnational migration of care workers.

BACKGROUND: ASIA-PACIFIC INTRA-REGIONAL CARE MIGRATION

Today, Asia is the second largest and the fastest-growing global migration epicenter in the world, with 75 million international migrants living and working in the region, only one million fewer than Europe (UN-DESA 2016). Much of the international migration in Asia, as in Europe, is intra-regional: of the 75 million migrants in 2015, 62 million were born in the region (UN-DESA 2016). Unlike the earlier history, when most of the migrants were men, today just as many Asian women as men are migrating for work, and many of them become domestic and care workers. Statistics on migrant domestic and care workers are difficult to find. However, of the estimated 67 million *domestic workers* worldwide in 2013, nearly 24 million (35.4 percent) were reported working in Asia and Pacific regions, and within that group, 3.34 million (14.1 percent) were *migrant domestic workers* and over 80 percent were women (ILO 2015; Peng 2017).[1]

The combination of rapid population aging, low fertility, increased employment on the part of native-born women and a growing tension between, on the one hand, the decline in male-breadwinner households, and on the other, persistent gendered and familialistic attitudes toward care in the richer East Asian countries have led to a surge in demand for care. At the same time, women's high educational levels and the expansion of non-manual and service-sector employment (other than domestic and care work) in all areas in these countries make care work unattractive to native-born women. This is further exacerbated by the low wages, low status and poor working conditions associated with domestic and care work. In all these countries, the turnover rates of native-born female care workers are extremely high, and there are serious shortages of care workers. To address this problem, all five countries have considered foreign domestic and care workers as a solution, although some countries have been much more intense in using them than others.

Singapore, Hong Kong and Taiwan have adopted what may be called a *liberal private market approach* to care and migration. In general, these governments have actively promoted the private use of domestic and care workers by making it easier for families to hire them and offering direct and indirect support for families that do so. For example, both the Singaporean and Hong Kong governments offer direct and indirect financial incentives to private households to employ migrant domestic workers.[2] The Singaporean government has liberalized regulations on hiring foreign domestic workers since the 1990s, including tax reductions for families with elderly members employing foreign domestic workers (Yeoh and Huang 2010). It has also introduced a Foreign Domestic Worker Grant in 2012 providing SG\$120 monthly stipend to middle and low-income elderly households to help offset the cost of hiring foreign domestic workers (Singapore-Agency for Integrated Care 2012). In Hong Kong, the government suspended the Employees' Retraining Levy (also called "Maids' Levy") in 2008 and then abolished it in 2013.[3] The number of registered foreign domestic workers in Singapore increased from 140,000 in 2002 to 231, 5000 in 2015 (TWC2 2011; Singapore-Ministry of Manpower 2015), while in Hong Kong, the number rose from 179,000 in 2000 to 320,000 in 2015 (Hong Kong-Census and Statistics Department 2015). Today, the use of foreign domestic and care workers is so prevalent in these countries that in Singapore nearly one in every five households employs a foreign domestic (see Table 9.1), and approximately 50 percent of Singaporeans aged 75 and over are dependent on foreign care workers for their daily care (Ostbye et al. 2013).

In 1992 Taiwan introduced a Foreign Live-in-Caregiver program that gave families with frail elderly members access to live-in foreign care workers and fast-tracked the immigration process for these migrants. Moreover, the government introduced a number of universal and income-tested old-age support programs to middle- and low-income elderly families to supplement their incomes. While these financial

Table 9.1 Ratio of foreign domestic/care workers to households

Country	Tot # Foreign domestic/care workers	Tot # of households (million)	Total population (million)	Ratio of foreign Domestics/care workers to households
Singapore	220,000	1.17	5.47	1/5.3
Hong Kong	320,000	2.4	7.19	1/7.5
Taiwan	240,000	8.19	23.4	1/34.1
Japan	2,377	51.84	126.95	1/21,809
South Korea	70,000*	18.5	50.5	1/264.3
Canada	8,000	13.3	35.7	1/1,662.5

supports are an important source of income for elderly families, they are not enough for them to pay for private home or institutional care services at the going rate for native-born workers. Instead, these programs have encouraged the use of foreign live-in-caregivers. Today, there are about 225,000 registered foreign live-in-caregivers in Taiwan, the vast majority of whom are caring for the elderly in private homes and earning sub-par wages.

While all three countries prefer private, home-based care arrangements, they differ amongst themselves in terms of how they use foreign migrant care workers. In Singapore, most foreign domestic workers are employed to care for the elderly, while in Hong Kong foreign domestic workers are more likely to work as nannies for children, although in recent years the number of domestic workers caring for the elderly has increased noticeably. In Taiwan, immigration law limits the use of foreign live-in caregivers to care for the frail elderly within private homes, but in reality many of these workers do the double duty of caring for both the elderly and children. In all three countries, the majority of foreign domestic and care workers traditionally came from the Philippines and Indonesia; recently, however, Vietnamese have increasingly begun to fill the ranks.

In contrast to these three countries, Japan and Korea have adopted a more *regulated and institutional* approach to care and immigration, although there are some differences between the two countries in the use of foreign care workers. Both governments have significantly expanded public and/or publicly funded or subsidized child care and introduced Long-Term Care Insurance (LTCI) to meet the elderly care needs. Most child care in Japan and Korea is center-based,[4] and LTCI provides non-live-in domiciliary (e.g. home helper) and community and institutional-based care services, delivered by public and/or private for- and not-for-profit service providers. Both countries have resisted the intake of private foreign live-in domestic and/or care workers and instead have adopted selective temporary foreign worker policies to recruit foreign nurses and care workers for institutional care for the elderly (but not for child care).

In Korea, H2 visas grant Joseonjok migrants (ethnic Koreans from China) long-term stays, multiple entries, access to some jobs that are denied to other non-Koreans (such as care work in the informal sector), and the right to change jobs. However, formal care work – such as employment as certified care workers for LTCI (*Yoyongbahosa*) – is still legally closed to foreign workers, including Joseonjok.[5] While most Joseonjok work in low-wage manufacturing and service-sector occupations, a growing number, particularly older women, are being recruited into elder care (Um 2012), and the foreign wives of Korean nationals are also increasingly found in low-wage service-sector work, including care (Yang 2016). In all cases, foreign care workers in Korea are employed privately by care institutions or individuals, and therefore they work *outside* of the LTCI system.

A similar use of co-ethnic migrant workers is also evident in Japan. As in Korea, the foreign wives of Japanese nationals and resident Brazilian and Peruvian Japanese, who came to Japan under a special foreign workers program for co-ethnics in the 1990s, are now being recruited to elder care work. In addition, since 2008 the Japanese government has been accepting up to one thousand nurses and care workers per year from the Philippines, Indonesia and Vietnam through bilateral economic partnership agreements (EPA). These nurses and care workers are only allowed to work in elder care institutions *within* the LTCI system. The number of these EPA nurses and care workers remains low, however, because of language tests and licensing requirements needed for long-term stay.

Japan and Korea thus contrast sharply with Taiwan, Hong Kong and Singapore in their more *regulated institutional approaches* to care workers. As well, in both Japan and Korea, foreign care workers are employed almost entirely in elder care services and in institutional settings. The use of foreign domestic and care workers in private family homes is almost non-existent.

Explaining Care and Migration Policies in Japan and South Korea

The reason for Japan and Korea's resistance to opening immigration to foreign care workers may be explained by the combination of the prevailing notions about how care should be provided, a pervasive anti-immigration public sentiment, and the employment regime associated with the LTCI.

Prevailing Notions About Care

Although Japan, Korea, Taiwan, Hong Kong and Singapore share in common the Confucian axiom about filial piety and familial obligations to care, the forms of familial care practices vary from one another. In all cases, families have outsourced their familial care responsibilities to non-familial caregivers in one form or another. In Taiwan, Hong Kong and Singapore, however, families are more likely to do so by employing foreign domestic workers and caregivers within the home ("like one of the family"), as filial piety is widely understood in these countries to mean that care should be provided *within* home, though not necessarily by family members. In Japan and Korea, it is more common and acceptable to outsource care to publicly or privately provided care services at home (but not live-in) and in community or institutional settings. For more than two decades, the governments in the two countries have been promoting public and private child care and elder care services through regulation and funding. Starting with the Angel Plan in 1994, the Japanese government steadily expanded its public child care system by activating and regulating the care market in an effort to encourage a higher birthrate and higher maternal employment. In 2014, the average enrollment rate of children aged three to five in formal early childhood education and care (ECEC) was 91.0 percent, well above the OECD29 average of 83.8 percent. In 2014, the proportion of children aged zero to two in formal child care in Japan was noticeably lower, at 30.6 percent, but nevertheless nearly treble the 1998 figure of 11.1 percent (OECD n.d.). Similarly, the Korean government has hugely strengthened its support for child care since 2003, particularly by extending and increasing child care subsidies for families to purchase services in the market (Peng 2011, 2012; An and Peng 2015). In Korea, the average enrollment rate of children aged three to five in formal ECEC in 2014 reached 92.2 percent, while that of the zero to two group soared from 3.0 percent in 2001 to 35.7 percent in 2014 (OECD n.d.).

Both countries also have instituted Long-Term Care Insurance programs (LTCI) – in 2000 in Japan and 2008 in Korea – thereby socializing the cost of elder care through mandatory social insurance systems. Although the family continues to be the main care provider for the elderly in both countries, much of the non-familial elder care is now provided through services paid for by LTCI. Few elderly people in these countries employ live-in caregivers at home, let alone *foreign* live-in caregivers. In Japan, the number of people certified to receive LTCI care rose from 2.18 million (9.9 percent of the 65+ population) in 2000 to 6.03 million (17.9 percent) in 2013 (Japan-MOHLW 2015). Although the majority of elderly people needing care receive it from both family members and LTCI services, 64 percent of these people were receiving care *primarily* from their co-residing family members, and less than 15 percent were dependent *primarily* on the LTCI services (Japan-Cabinet Office 2014).

As public opinion surveys show, most Japanese people prefer to receive old-age care from their spouses and children first and then from home helpers (i.e., LTCI services) (Japan-Cabinet Office 2012).

In Korea, the total number of LTCI service recipients quickly rose from 146,543 in 2008 to 445,779 in 2015 (KNHIS 2015). Recent surveys show a significant increase in public expectations that the elderly be cared for by family members *and* the state (i.e., LTCI services) since the introduction of LTCI. Public opinion surveys of the elderly and their family caregivers show a support and satisfaction rate for LTCI of 74.9 percent in 2009 and 86.9 percent in 2011 (Rhee et al. 2015). As in Japan, the proportion of elderly people receiving care from non-familial caregivers outside of LTCI in Korea is small.

In both countries, approaches to child and elder care differ from those of Taiwan, Hong Kong and Singapore in that the use of non-familial caregivers within the home is neither common nor preferred; rather the existence of well-established social care systems for children and the elderly deter the use and the development of a market for live-in caregivers in private homes. To be sure, in Japan and Korea the outsourcing of care has been carried out largely through social care systems, in the form of center-based care for children and home care, community care or institutional care for the elderly, offered by public and/or private market care providers employing almost entirely native-born care workers.

The extensive use of, and preference for, social care in Japan and Korea are partly a historical legacy of the two countries' early economic and industrial policies. In the early twentieth century, the Japanese government adopted industrialization strategies that involved active social investment in human capital and social infrastructures. The government built schools and hospitals and established universal public education, transportation, communication and public health care systems in an effort to modernize the nation and raise an educated industrial labor force (Johnson 1995; Peng 2015; Peng and Tiessen 2015). In the post-war era, early child care and education became a national priority. Public and private kindergartens and public child care facilities expanded rapidly across the country, the former offering early childhood education for the growing number of middle-class families, and the latter, subsidized or free child care for children of single mothers and other poor families (Peng 2002b; Shimoebisu 1994). Similar economic and industrial strategies were also pursued in Korea during the post-war era. For example, President Park Chun-Hee, who was educated in Japan during the colonial period, adopted very similar economic and industrial policies to Japan during his authoritarian rule between 1961 and 1979 (Kim and Vogel 2011). In Korea, child care institutions developed rapidly after the Korean War to accommodate orphans and children from poor families. This in turn established an institutional framework that led to the subsequent expansion of public child care institutions, albeit the main target of public child care centers remained the children of poor working mothers. During the 1960s and 1970s, child care centers continued to grow as the government's industrialization plans drew more mothers into the labor market (Song et al. 2009).

State investments in human capital (including ECEC) and public institutions (kindergartens and child care centers) also created a strong path-dependent development pattern that favored the socialization of care. In Japan, for example, the urgent push to expand public child care immediately after the war set the subsequent path for the institutionalized public child care system. As a part of the postwar economic reconstruction effort, the government rushed to construct child care centers to support working mothers.[6] Between 1946 and 1950 the number of public child care centers more than quadrupled, from 827 to 3,684, as did the number of children being cared for, from 67,000 to over 292,000, respectively (Matsumoto 2009). With this policy in place, the number of children cared for in centers grew, along with public expectations of and demand for more public child care. Indeed, in the mid-1970s when the government tried to roll back state support for such services, it faced one of the largest protest movements in the country's postwar history, organized under the slogan "As Many Child Care Centers as Postboxes" (*Posuto no aru dake Hoikusho*) and spearheaded by women's organizations (Matsumoto 2009; Peng 2002b). By 2016, there were 30,859 centers, caring for more than 2.46 million children, across the country (Japan-MOHLW 2016b).

One reason why nearly half of Japan's child care centers are still *publicly* run, that is, operated directly by local and/or national governments, despite constant government attempts to privatize them since the mid-1990s, is that child care workers constitute one of the largest public employee groups in Japan, and as such they have the backing of powerful public-sector workers' unions. Nevertheless, most certified "private" child care centers are also regulated by the government: their fees are set by the state and paid to the centers on a per-capita basis directly from the local government. By the time the issue of elder care became a national policy priority in the 1990s, the precedent for socializing care was already in place, and government bureaucrats and policymakers saw LTCI as a natural and acceptable option to address the elder care issue, a position that was also supported by grassroots movements led by women's groups and senior citizens groups (Peng 2002a).

Korea's LTCI is also not a historical accident. There is a significant amount of cross-national "policy learning" between Japan and Korea, not only because of their historical connections, but also because of their similar policy and institutional frameworks. After observing Germany and Japan implement their LTCI systems, Korea introduced its own in 2008. Unlike Japan, however, the Korean government had to rely much more on private-sector care providers to deliver LTCI services because of its less developed elder care infrastructure. Japan had been developing public elder care services since the 1980s, whereas when Korea introduced its LTCI system, the proportion of the population over the age of 65 was barely 10 percent.

Opening Korea's LTCI service provisions to the private-for-profit sector has contributed to a less regulated LTC market compared to Japan's. Nevertheless, their similar history of economic development strategies, characterized by state investments in human capital and public institutions, has shaped national preferences for social care and set a template for its state-led expansion in the two countries. In short, in both Japan and Korea, the historical legacy of state-led economic development involving public investments in care institutions has helped shape popular understandings about care and how it should be provided, leading to a national consensus about the "norm" of socializing care and the unacceptability of using private live-in-caregivers.

Pervasive Negative Public Sentiment Toward Immigration

Collective public imaginaries about ethnic and cultural homogeneity in Japan and Korea also contribute to pervasive negative public sentiment toward foreigners and immigration (Peng 2016). Both countries identify themselves as ethnically and culturally homogeneous with such commonly used identifiers as *tan'itsu minzoku* (unitary nation) in Japan and *danil minjok* (unitary nation) and *Han minjok* (Korean nation) in Korea. In Japan, the "myth of Japanese homogeneity" emerged during Japan's nation-building period at the end of the nineteenth century (Howell 1996; Siddle 2011, 151; Tegtmeyer-Pak 2004). Oguma (1995) claims that in its attempt to remake Japan as a modern nation and an emerging

Asian colonial power during the Meiji period (1868–1912), the Japanese government deliberately created the narrative of the Japanese nation and its people as the direct descendants of the Emperor, who, in turn, was thought to have descended from the Sun Goddess. This collective imaginary allowed the Japanese to distinguish themselves from other less developed Asian countries and provided a rationale for its Asian colonization.

Eckert et al. (1990) attribute modern Korean nationalism to the country's reaction against foreign imperialism, particularly Japanese colonialism. After World War II, successive political regimes sought to reclaim and reshape Korean identity through national cultural policy, including reaffirming the ideas of Korean ethnic and cultural purity and homogeneity and enforcing the use of *Hangru* (the original Korean characters) as opposed to Chinese characters in writing (Yim 2002). As in Japan, this discourse of "ethnic homogeneity based on the 'one ancestor myth'" (Kim 2005, 5) contributes to Korean people's low cultural receptivity toward foreigners. Kim notes:

> Legally, their [foreign migrant workers'] stay in Korea can in no circumstance exceed three years; geographically, their workplace concentration in small towns segregates them from main urban centers; and socially and culturally, they are isolated and disdained by mainstream society, as Koreans extend no welcome. In short, Koreans shun foreigners, especially transnational migrant workers, primarily from poor Asian countries. (Kim 2005, 4)

Studies of public opinion in Japan show pervasive ideas about Japanese homogeneity and uniqueness. A 2013 national opinion survey found that 68 percent of Japanese adults agreed with the statement "Japanese people have significantly better qualities compared to people from other countries," and 54 percent agreed that "Japan is a first-class nation" (NHK 2013). Public opinion polls also consistently show strong public aversion to foreigners. For example, one conducted in 2004 found that people opposed accepting foreign unskilled/semi-skilled workers at a ratio of nearly 2:1 (25.9 percent vs. 16.7 percent), and a majority were ambivalent about foreign care workers (Cabinet Office 2004).

The World Value Surveys also found that Japan and Korea share similar value orientations. The 2010–2014 World Value Survey shows 44.2 percent of Koreans and 36.3 percent of Japanese claiming that they *would not* like to have immigrants/foreign workers as neighbors, compared to 35.8 percent of Singaporeans, 21.1 percent of Hong Kongers, and 20.2 percent of Taiwanese. Similarly, 34.1 percent of Koreans and 22.3 percent of Japanese claimed that they *would not* like to have people of different race as neighbors, whereas only 18.8 percent, 12.6 percent and 8.4 percent of Hong Kongers, Singaporeans, and Taiwanese, respectively, thought so (World Value Survey 2015). These findings suggest qualitatively different attitudes toward foreigners in Japan and Korea as compared to Taiwan, Hong Kong and Singapore. Such pervasive negative public sentiments toward foreigners thus go some way to explaining why immigration policies in Japan and Korea remain highly restrictive, despite serious shortages of care workers.

The Employment Regime and Current Social Care Systems

Finally, the employment regime associated with the current social care systems in Japan and Korea creates huge barriers to employing foreign care workers, although differences in the regulation of LTCI and the availability of co-ethnics willing to work in the elder care sector in the two countries also influence the extent to which foreign care workers are used in these places. First, the LTCI system in Japan is highly institutionalized and regulated, whereas in Korea the regulation of elder care market is less stringent because of the system's reliance on private for-profit care providers.[7] In both countries, the LTCI laws stipulate that only publicly certified home helpers and care workers can provide care *within* the LTCI system (i.e., their services being paid by the LTCI). In Japan, all fees for LTCI services are set by the government, and only local governments, quasi-public welfare corporations, non-profit organizations, hospitals and for-profit companies licensed and supervised by prefectural government are allowed to provide care (Shimizutani 2013, 14). The market competition is therefore highly restricted.

Unlike the German, Austrian and Korean LTCI systems, Japanese LTCI provides only services and not cash allowances – a condition that Japanese feminist groups lobbied hard for during its policy development, for they feared that cash allowances would result in families using money for non-care related uses, leaving women with the continuing burden of unpaid family care (Peng 2002a). Japan's service-only care regime and regulated quasi-market system therefore created a formal market for care and a strong institutional mechanism that regulates training requirements for care workers and determines who can provide care, where care should be provided, and under what conditions. Certification training in Japan is significantly lengthier and more difficult than in Korea, but it assures the quality of care. The requirements discourage the use of uncertified care workers but also foreign care workers. Wages for Japanese care workers are low compared to average industrial wages, but not absolutely low. Institutions hoping to hire foreign care workers, such as in the case of EPA nurses and care workers, must register and satisfy the government requirements. Once institutions employ EPA nurses and care workers, they must pay wages equivalent to their domestic counterparts. EPA nurses and care workers are obliged to write and pass the Japanese certification examination after three to four years of employment in order to qualify for long-term stay. Nevertheless, the combination of tightly regulated care market and the training and qualification requirements for care workers in Japan creates high barriers to employing foreign care workers.

Although primarily service-based, the Korean LTCI also allows cash provision to families, particularly those in regions where services are not readily available (Rhee et al. 2015). Approximately 35 percent of LTCI recipients receive a cash allowance (family care allowance) rather than services. The limited supply of long-term care institutions and care providers, along with political concerns over the huge expenditure involved in developing a public elder care system infrastructure, has prompted the Korean government to open up the LTCI service delivery system to private-sector care providers by relaxing regulations for LTC service provisions (Rhee et al. 2015). This has led to a rapid expansion of care services and compromised the quality assurance of the LTCI system in Korea. Within three years, from 2006 to 2009, the number of institutional facilities increased nearly three-fold from 815 to 2,016, while in-home service provider organizations grew more than twelvefold, from 1,045 to 12,935 (Rhee et al. 2015).

Though they must be certified to work within the LTCI system, the certification requirement for care workers (*yoyangbahosa*) in Korea is less strict than that of Japan (*kaigofukushi-shi* or *kaigoshi*). Private for-profit LTC institutions also often employ low-wage nursing aides (*gambyoin*) to provide supplementary elder care outside the LTCI system. The cash allowance permits families to employ foreign care workers at a lower wage, thus creating a dual care market whereby formal LTCI provides standard elder care services according to the system, while in the secondary care market, care services can be purchased at a lower price. It is here that an increasing number of female migrant Joseonjok care workers are being employed (Um 2012). Furthermore, as pointed out earlier, the availability of co-ethnic workers willing to provide care services at a low wage in Korea also supports the secondary care market. Based on the institutional arrangements and financing structures, the Korean care regime therefore looks more like those of Germany and Austria, where the combination of a regulated qualification system (though not very strict in Korea), a cash allowance option, and the prominent role played by private-for-profit sector, has resulted in what Simonazzi (2009) refers to as a "dualistic market." In Korea this combination of formal and informal market in turn creates both incentives and pressures to use migrant care workers, a demand that Joseonjok conveniently fulfill.

Recent Immigration Policy Changes in Japan and Korea

Both Japanese and Korean governments have recently made some changes in their immigration policies to allow limited intake of foreign workers. The Japanese government has committed to accepting up to one thousand EPA nurses and care workers per year from the Philippines, Indonesia and Vietnam. But because of the high barrier to entry, the number of Filipina and Indonesian care workers entering Japan has in fact declined since 2010 (Onuki 2011; Michel and Peng 2012; Ohno 2012). As of October 2015, there were a total of only 1121 EPA care workers in Japan, 872 of whom were working as elder care worker trainees and 249 as certified elder care workers (MHLW, 2016). Despite a strong lobby to increase immigration from the Japan Business Association (*Keidanren*), the country's largest employers' association and a powerful policy voice within and outside the government, the Japanese government has been hesitant to move forward on substantial immigration policy reform in fear of public backlash. The public reception of EPA nurses and care workers remains ambivalent. While key institutional actors such as the Ministry of Health, Labor and Welfare, Japan Medical Association, Japan Nurses Association, and Japanese Trade Union Confederation (*Rengo*) have expressed conditional support for opening immigration to foreign care workers, the Japan Medical Service Employees Union (*Irouren*) has been dead set against the immigration policy reform (Yamasaki 2006). As illustrated by the *3rd Basic Plan on Immigration Control* issued by the Ministry of Justice in 2005, a tentative idea to open immigration to foreign nurses and care workers has been put forward, but with much caution and ambiguity:

> The nation's productive population, which already peaked at 87.17 million in 1995 and turned down, is predicted to decline to 53.89 million in 2050.... [T]o make up for the decline and to maintain a productive population at that peak, the nation would have to accept some 650,000 foreign nationals annually. It is, however, not appropriate to simply supplement the decline by accepting foreign nationals alone.
>
> ...However, the time has also come for the immigration control administration to consider what the acceptance of foreign workers should be in a population-declining age....
>
> As for nursing-care workers who will be in growing demand due to the ageing of the population, consideration will be given to whether and how to accept foreign workers in the field.... (Japan MOJ 2005)

As in Japan, the Korean government also has been adjusting its immigration policies to allow the selective importation of foreign workers. Korea began to experience shortages of labor in "3D" jobs (those that are dirty, dangerous, and demeaning) in the late 1980s. To address this problem, the government reformed immigration policies in 1990, including the introduction of the Industrial and Technical Trainees Program (ITTP) (modeled after Japan) in 1991 to import a limited number of foreign workers, most of whom were Joseonjok. The number of foreign workers more than doubled within a year, from 21,235 in 1990 to 45,449 in 1991, with over 90 percent of them undocumented workers who had been already in the country (Kim and Kwon 2012; Lee 2009). However, with growing domestic and international criticisms over the lack of labor standards and employer exploitation of foreign workers, the ITTP was replaced by the Employment Permit System in 2003. Korea now uses EPA agreements with signatory countries to import semi- and low-skilled workers. By 2012, 791,000 documented foreign workers were working in Korea, over 500,000 of whom were low-skilled workers (Statistics Korea 2012).

In addition to having a poorly regulated care market that encourages the use of co-ethnic care workers, Korea also faces some significant challenges in maintaining its strict immigration policies. First, Korea has large Korean diasporic populations (*Joseonjok*) in the immediate neighboring countries of North Korea and China. The existence of this population and their eagerness to "return" to South Korea – as many of them are second- and third-generation offspring of those who originally migrated out of Korea – creates both economic incentives and moral pressure on South Korea to absorb them. The prospect of Joseonjok return does not provoke strong public opposition based on the national rhetoric of ethnic and cultural homogeneity because they are co-ethnics. Indeed, unlike the case of *Nikkeijin* in Japan, whom Japanese people can dismiss as being more Latin American than Japanese, not only do Joseonjok look like Koreans, but they also speak Korean (albeit with some accent) and understand Korean culture. It is therefore hard for the Korean government to resist their return, particularly in light of the huge labor shortage.[8] Indeed, the relaxation of residency and mobility regulations for H2 visa holders in the 2007 immigration reform (primarily affecting Joseonjok) was followed by a sharp increase in the foreign worker population, particularly low-skilled workers.

Second, partly because of the relatively lax immigration controls and proximity to North Korea and China, there is also a huge undocumented migrant population in Korea. According to a government report, there were nearly 600,000 illegal migrants in the country in 2011 (Kim and Kwon 2012). This situation is further sustained by Korea's large informal economic sector, including care work, and small and medium enterprises that are dependent on the low-wage labor of these people. Moreover, government crackdowns on undocumented migrant workers are made difficult by an active civil society movement that support migrants' rights (on role of civil society groups in China and Taiwan, see also Laliberté's chapter in this book).

Third, Korea also has a large and growing population of marriage migrants, who are entitled to live and work in the country. Between 2002 and 2010, a total of about 787,000 people migrated to Korea through international marriages, most of them women, with the largest proportion being Joseonjok (32 percent), followed by ethnic Chinese (23 percent), and Vietnamese (18 percent) (Oh et al. 2012). International marriages now represent approximately 15 percent of all new marriages in Korea, and many of these foreign wives provide significant amounts of unpaid care work for their aging Korean parents-in-law (Michel and Peng 2010; Lee 2013). For example, international marriage couples are more likely to co-reside with husbands' elderly parents than non-international marriage couples in Korea (Lee 2013). As the number of such marriages continues to rise, it will be increasingly difficult for the government to sustain its non-immigration policy for long.

Finally, it is important to underscore that although Korea's immigration policy is more open than Japan's, its *formal* care sector nevertheless remains firmly closed to foreign workers. Korean employers are prohibited from hiring foreign care workers within the LTCI system. In fact, until very recently, foreigners, even long-term residents, were excluded from writing the care-worker certificate examination (*yoyobahosa*). This strict regulation, which is partly a result of an immigration legacy that does not acknowledge low-skilled occupations such as care work as legitimate categories for foreign workers, is becoming increasingly contradicted by the practice of informal employment of foreign nursing aides in private care institutions outside of the LTCI (Um 2012).

CONCLUSION

Against the global trend toward increased use of foreign migrant care workers, Japan and Korea stand out as two East Asian countries stubbornly resisting the formal intake of such workers. Despite serious shortages of care workers, the two governments have not adopted more open immigration policies to address this demand. Unlike Taiwan, Hong Kong and Singapore, Japan and Korea have maintained highly regulated and institutional approaches to foreign care workers because of the national social, cultural and institutional factors that are shaping their care, migration and employment regimes. Despite their shared familialistic values, Japan and Korea have developed public institutions based on social care regime principles that were partly shaped by the two countries' early economic and industrial policy strategies, and partly by their postwar social and economic imperatives. As part of nation-building processes, these two East Asian countries also created similar collective imaginaries focused on the idea of national ethnic-cultural homogeneity. While these imaginaries were important in helping the two countries develop national solidarity – and foster more collectivist solutions to care – the sentiments they engender have also created barriers for more open immigration and multicultural environments. Finally, the existing social care systems in the two countries, particularly their LTCI systems, have been configured to prohibit the use of foreign care workers. Thus the combination of care, migration and employment regimes in the two countries discourage the private use of foreign care workers in the first place, and in the second, create strong political and institutional barriers to importing migrant care workers.

Building on current scholarship about understanding local and national specificities in determining transnational care migration, this comparative analysis of Japanese and Korean policies underscores the importance of examining the intersection of care, migration and employment regimes in conjunction with cultural contexts. In Japan and Korea, the use of live-in-foreign domestic or care worker is very rare or almost non-existent, not simply because of practical problems such as small living spaces or difficulties associated with hiring foreign domestic or care workers. Rather, it is because the idea of having personal live-in migrant domestic or care workers is quite foreign in these two countries, as the current social and cultural norms preclude the use of such workers in private homes. This cultural assumption – that families do not use live-in migrant domestic or care workers – is in part informed by policies and institutions and at the same time, contributes to the formation and practices of policies and institutions. An implicit comparison of Japan and Korea with Taiwan, Hong Kong and Singapore thus highlights noticeable diversities amongst East Asian and familialistic welfare states because of the differences in social, cultural and institutional contexts.

Finally, the basic conceptual premise of focusing an analytical lens on care, migration and employment regimes also offers insight and currency beyond Asia. For example, as shown above, the market dualism created by the cash allowance option and the opening of the LTCI market to for-profit care providers in Korea renders it more similar to Germany and Austria than to Japan. The tightly regulated care market and emphasis on non-cash service provisions in Japan also suggest some commonalities with Scandinavian welfare states, although the higher wages for care workers in Scandinavia compared to those for their counterparts in Japan probably reduces the demand for foreign care workers in Scandinavia. It would be well worth extending the comparisons of care and migration policies to Europe and East Asia.

NOTES

1. The ILO defines "domestic work" as "work performed in or for a household or households" (ILO 2012, 24). It is widely acknowledged that much of the domestic work involves reproductive work, and a significant amount of that relates to direct or indirect "care." In this chapter, I use care work to include domestic work as well as direct personal care work performed within households and work in community and institutional settings.
2. In Hong Kong and Singapore most family-based care workers are classified as "domestic workers" or "domestic helpers." These workers are employed in private homes, live with their employers, and perform, in addition to care work, other household and other domestic chores.
3. The levy was re-introduced under different format in late 2013.
4. By center-based care I mean not home-based child care in individual private homes.

5. In both Japan and Korea, there is no formal immigration employment category for "care work". In the case of Japan, nurses and care workers enter the country through the EPA category, which is not a formal immigration category. In the case of Korea, there is a more informal care market outside of LTCI within private and semi-public institutions such as hospitals for the elderly where Joseonjok women are being employed.

6. In Japan, orphanages were separated from public child care centers under a different policy stream within child welfare.

7. They are institutionalized in terms of the way in which services are organized (e.g. the use of care assessments and care managers, the standard fee schedule for care services set by the government, etc.), not in terms of the form of care. In fact, much of the LTCI services in both countries are in the form of domiciliary care provided by home-helpers and visiting nurses.

8. The pressure to accept Joseonjok was particularly great under the more pro-reunification oriented political regimes, such as those of Kim Dae-Jung (1998–2003) and Roh Moo-hyun (2003–2008). Under the conservative and pro-business presidents, Lee Myung-Bak (2008–2013) and Park Geun-hye (2013–current), the government has been actively recruiting high-skilled workers while trying to manage entry of low-skill workers and crackdown on illegal immigration.

References

An, Mi Young and Ito Peng. 2015. "Diverging Paths? A Comparative Look at Child Care Policies in Japan, South Korea and Taiwan." *Social Policy & Administration Journal* 50: 540–58.

Anderson, Bridget and Isabel Shutes, eds. 2014. *Migration and Care Labour: Theory, Policy and Politics.* London: Palgrave.

Asis, Maruja M.B. and Nicola Piper. 2008. "Researching International Labor Migration in Asia." *Sociological Quarterly* 49: 423–444.

Eckert, C.J., Ki-Baik Lee et al. 1990. *Korea Old and New: A History.* Seoul: Ilchokak

Howell, David L. 1996. "Ethnicity and Culture in Contemporary Japan." *Journal of Contemporary History* 31, 1: 171–190.

Hong Kong Census and Statistics Department. 2015. *General Household Survey.* http://www.censtatd.gov.hk/hkstat/sub/sp200.jsp?productCode=D5250023

International Labour Organization (ILO). 2015. *ILO Global Estimates on Migrant Workers: Results and Methodology - Special focus on migrant domestic workers,* Geneva: ILO.

International Labour Organization (ILO). 2012. *Decent Work for Domestic Workers in Asia and the Pacific: Manual for Trainers.* http://www.ilo.org/wcmsp5/

groups/public/—asia/—ro-bangkok/—sro-bangkok/documents/publica
tion/wcms_184194.pdf
Japan Cabinet Office. 2014. *Annual Report on the Aging Society: 2014.* http://
www8.cao.go.jp/kourei/english/annualreport/index-wh.html
Japan Cabinet Office. 2012. *Heisei-24-nendo Koreisha no Kenko ni Kansuru
Yoronchosa (2012 Public Opinion Survey on Elderly Health).* http://www8.
cao.go.jp/kourei/ishiki/h24/sougou/gaiyo/
Japan Cabinet Office. 2004. *Koreisha Kaigo ni Kansuru Yoronchosa – Heisei 15-
nen (Public Opinion Survey on Elder Care).* http://survey.gov-online.go.jp/
h15/h15-kourei/index.html
Japan Ministry of Health, Labor and Welfare (MHLW). 2016. *EPA niyoru gaiko-
kujin kaigofukushishi kouhosha tou ukeire no saranaru katsuyousaku (Further Use
of EPA Foreign Care Worker Candidates).* http://www.mhlw.go.jp/file/05-
Shingikai-12201000-Shakaiengokyokushougaihokenfukushibu-Kikakuka/shir
you1.pdf
Japan Ministry of Health, Labor and Welfare (MHLW). 2016b. *Hoikusho-to
Kanren Jokyo torimatome (Situations of Daycare and Related Issues).* http://
www.mhlw.go.jp/stf/houdou/0000135392.html
Japan Ministry of Health, Labor and Welfare (MHLW). MOHLW. 2015.
Heisei 27-nen Kaigohoken-Jigyo Jokyo Hokoku (2015 *Report on LTCI).*
http://www.mhlw.go.jp/topics/kaigo/osirase/jigyo/m15/1502.html
Japan MOJ. 2005. *Basic Plan for Immigration Control,* 3rd ed. http://www.moj.go.
jp/ENGLISH/information/bpic3rd.html (accessed 12/04/2015).
Johnson, Chalmers. 1995. *Japan, Who Governs? The Rise of the Developmental
State.* New York: Norton.
Kim, Byung-Kook and Ezra F. Vogel, eds. 2011. *Park Chun Hee Era: The
Transformation of South Korea.* Cambridge, MA: Harvard University
Press.
Kim, Eungi A. 2005. "Low Cultural Receptivity towards Foreigners in Korea: Kim,
The Case of Transnational Migrant Workers." *Korea Observer* 36 (1): 1–20.
Kim, Junmo and Yong-Soo Kwon. 2012. "Economic Development, the Evolution
of Foreign Labor and Immigration Policy, and the Shift to Multiculturalism in
South Korea." *Philippine Political Science Journal* 33, 2: 178–201.
KNHIS (Korea National Health Insurance Service) 2015. *National Health
Insurance System of Korea.* http://www.nhis.or.kr/static/html/wbd/g/a/
wbdga0704.html
Lee, Beyong Ha. 2009. "The Development of Korea's Immigration Policies:
Security, Accumulation, Fairness and Institutional Legitimacy." *Korea
Observer* 40: 763–799.
Lee, Hye-Kyung. 2013. "Employment and Life Satisfaction among Female Marriage
Migrants in South Korea." *Asia Pacific Migration Journal* 22, 2: 199–230.

Matsumoto, Narumi. 2009. "*Sengo Sogoki no Hoikusho: Gen-hoikusho Hobo no Katari wo Tegakari ni*" (*Child care Centers in the Early Postwar Years*), *Bunkyogakuin University Anthropological Research Journal* 11, 1: 197–212.

Michel, Sonya and Ito Peng. 2012. "All in the Family? Migrants, Nationhood, and Care Regimes in Asia and North America." *Journal of European Social Policy*, 22: 406–418.

NHK (Nihon Hoso Kyoku). 2013. *Dai 9-kai Nihonjin no Ishiki-Chosa (9th Survey of Japanese Identity)*. https://www.nhk.or.jp/bunken/summary/yoron/social/pdf/140520.pdf

OECD. n.d.. *Family Database*. http://www.oecd.org/els/family/database.htm (accessed 20/04/2017).

Oguma, Eiji. 1995. *Tan'itsu Minzoku Shinwa no Kigen: "Nihojin" no Jieizo no Keifu.* (*The Limits of Single-Ethnicity Myths: The Genealogy of the Japanese Self-Image*). Tokyo: Shinyo Sha.

Oh, Jung-Eun, Dong Kwan Kang, et al. 2012. *Migration Profile of the Republic of Korea*. Korea: IOM Migration Research & Training Centre.

Ohno, Shun. 2012. "International Migration of Southeast Asian Nurses and Care Workers to Japan under Economic Partnership Agreements." *Southeast Asian Studies* 49: 541–569.

Oishi, Nana. 2005. *Women in Motion: Globalization, State Policies and Labor Migration in Asia*. Stanford, CA: Stanford University Press.

Onuki, Hironori. 2011. "The Global Migration of Care Labour: Filipino Workers in Japan." In *Feminist Ethics and Social Policy: Towards a New Global Political Economy of Care*, edited by Rianne Mahon and Fiona Robinson, 60–77. Vancouver: UBC Press.

Ostbye, Truls, Rahul Malhotra, Chadima Arambepola and Angelique Chan. 2013. "Does Support From Foreign Domestic Workers Decrease the Negative Impact of Informal Caregiving? Results from Singapore Survey on Informal Caregiving." *The Journals of Gerontology*, Series B, 68: 609–21.

Peng, Ito. 2017. *Transnational Migration of Domestic and Care Workers in Asia Pacific*, ILO Working Paper, Geneva: ILO. http://www.ilo.org/wcmsp5/groups/public/—ed_protect/—protrav/—migrant/documents/publication/wcms_547228.pdf

Peng, Ito. 2016. "Testing the Limits of Welfare State Change: Immigration Policy Reforms in Japan." *Social Policy & Administration* 50: 278–296.

Peng, Ito. 2015. "The 'New' Social Investment Policies in Japan and South Korea." In *Inclusive Growth, Development and Welfare Policy: A Critical Assessment*, edited by Reza Hasmath, 142–60. New York and Oxford, UK: Routledge.

Peng, Ito. 2012. "Social and Political Economy of Care in Japan and South Korea." *International Journal of Sociology and Social Policy* 32: 636–649.

Peng, Ito. 2011. "The Good, the Bad, and the Confused: Political Economy of Social Care in South Korea." *Development and Change* 42: 905–23.

Peng, Ito. 2010. "Social Care Expansion Reforms and their Implications for Care Workers in South Korea." *International Labour Review* 149: 461–476.

Peng, Ito. 2002a. "Social Care in Crisis: Gender, Demography and Welfare State Restructuring in Japan." *Social Politics* 9: 411–43

Peng, Ito. 2002b. "Japan: The Interaction of Gender and Demography in a Low-Birth Rate and Aging Society." In *Child Care at the Crossroads: Gender, Entitlements, and Welfare State Restructuring*, edited by Rianne Mahon and Sonya Michel, 31–56. New York: Routledge.

Peng, Ito and James Tiessen. 2015. *An Asian Flavour for Medicare: Learning from Experiments* in Japan, Korea *and Taiwan*. Ottawa: Laurier-MacDonald Institute. www.macdonaldlaurier.ca/files/pdf/MLICanadasHealthcareCrisisSeries5_r4.pdf

Raghuram, Parvati. 2012. "Global Care, Local Configurations – Challenges to Conceptualizations of Care." *Global Networks* 12: 155–74.

Rhee, Jong Chul, Nicolae Done, and Gerard F. Anderson. 2015. "Considering Long-Term Care Insurance for Middle-Income Countries: Comparing South Korea with Japan and Germany," *Health Policy* 119: 1319–29. http://www.sciencedirect.com/science/article/pii/S016885101500161X

Shimizutani, Satoshi. 2013. *The Future of Long-Term Care in Japan*. Tokyo: Research Institute of Economy, Trade and Industry. http://www.rieti.go.jp/en/

Shimoebisu, Miyuki. 1994. "Kazokuseisaku no Rekishiteki tenkai" (*The Historical Development of Family Policy*). In *Gendai Kazoku no Shakai Hosho (The Modern Family and Social Security)*, edited by Shakai Hosho Kenkyujo, 251–272. Tokyo: University of Tokyo Press.

Siddle, Richard. 2011. "Race, Ethnicity and Minorities in Modern Japan." In *Routledge Handbook of Japanese Culture and Society*, edited by Victoria Lyon Bestor and Theodore C. Bestor with Akiko Yamagata, 163–171. New York: Routledge.

Simonazzi, Annamaria. 2009. "Care Regimes and National Employment Models." *Cambridge Journal of Economics* 33: 211–232.

Singapore Agency for Integrated Care. 2012. *Foreign Domestic Worker Grant*. http://www.aic.sg/FDWGrant/

Singapore Ministry of Manpower. 2015. *Foreign Workforce Numbers*. http://www.mom.gov.sg/documents-and-publications/foreign-workforce-numbers

Song, Sookhyun, Yunjin Song and Misuk Kim. 2009. "The Historical Analysis of Day-Care Policy in Korea." Available at: http://www.welfareasia.org/5thconference/papers/Song%20S_day-care%20policy%20in%20Korea.pdf (accessed 12/06/2015)

Statistics Korea. 2012. *2012 Foreigner Labor Force Survey*. http://kostat.go.kr/portal/english/news/1/8/index.board?bmode=read&aSeq=269160

TWC2. 2011. *Fact Sheet: Foreign Domestic Workers in Singapore (Basic Statistics).* http://twc2.org.sg/2011/11/16/fact-sheet-foreign-domestic-workers-in-singapore-basic-statistics/

Tegtmeyer-Pak, Katherine. 2004. *Development of National Migration Regimes: Japan in Comparative Perspective.* San Diego, CA: Center for Comparative Immigration Studies, University of San Diego, Working Paper#110.

Um, Seong-gee. 2012. *At the Bottom: Migrant Workers at South Korean Long-term Care Market.* PhD thesis, University of Toronto.

UN Department of Economic and Social Affairs, Population Division (UN-DESA). 2016. *International Migration Report 2015: Highlights* (ST/ESA/SER.A/375).

World Value Survey. 2015. http://www.worldvaluessurvey.org/WVSOnline.jsp

Yang, Kyung-Eun. 2016. *Economic Integration or Segregation? Immigrant Women's Labor Market Entrance and Their Support Service Utilization in South Korea,* PhD thesis, University of Toronto.

Yeoh, Brenda S. A. and Shirlena Huang. 2010. "Foreign domestic workers and home-based care for elders in Singapore." *Journal of Aging and Social Policy* 22, 1: 69–88.

Yamasaki, Takashi. 2006. *"Kango-Kaigo'bunya ni okeru Gaikokujin Rodosha no Ukeire Mondai"* (*Issues of Foreign Worker Acceptance in Nursing/Care Fields*), *Refarensu* 2: 4–34.

Yim, Haksoon. 2002. "Cultural Identity and Cultural Policy in South Korea." *International Journal of Cultural Policy* 8, 1: 37–48.

Ito Peng is a professor of sociology and public policy, and Canada Research Chair in Global Social Policy at the Department of Sociology, and the School of Public Policy and Governance, University of Toronto. She has written extensively on family, gender and social policies in East Asia. She is currently principal investigator of a large international partnership research project entitled *Gender, Migration, and the Work of Care,* funded by a major Partnership Grant from the Social Sciences and Humanities Research Council of Canada.

PART IV

From the Global to the Local, and Back Again

The Grassroots-Global Dialectic: International Policy as an Anchor for Domestic Worker Organizing

Jennifer N. Fish and Moriah Shumpert

When I see, like this, people from different parts, there is a hope that we will win one day, the domestic workers and the migrant workers, especially if we have a real law so that domestic work will be work that gives dignity, and the work will get dignity and the workers also will be treated as a human being, and a human life, a better life, and this work will come to be like any other work. This gives us hope that in any other country they will join together and stitch the apron, that means that we are all locked together. (Sister Escaline Miranda, National Domestic Workers Movement, India)

In 2010–2011, the International Labor Organization (ILO) anchored the widest mobilization ever of grassroots domestic worker movements when it became the venue for negotiations on the first global policy for paid household labor. As this largest house of international labor policy considered the potential to adopt a pathbreaking convention on "Decent Work for Domestic Workers," established national domestic worker organizations across the world came together through the International Domestic Workers Network (IDWN) to play a pivotal role in the discussions.[1] Alongside civil society organizations and global union allies, this representation of "actual workers" sat at the ILO table to demand that

J.N. Fish (✉) · M. Shumpert
Department of Women's Studies, Old Dominion University, VA, USA

© The Author(s) 2017
S. Michel, I. Peng (eds.), *Gender, Migration, and the Work of Care*,
DOI 10.1007/978-3-319-55086-2_10

policy makers consider the impact of a convention on "those who toil everyday" as central "cogs in the wheel" of the global economy.[2] In this way, a formerly excluded occupational sector pushed the ILO to consider both the informal economy and transnational migrants – hallmarks of globalization's economic restructuring and tangible evidence of its social, legal and political exclusions.

The ILO is the United Nations' only tripartite organization, with each member nation having worker and employer delegates from "peak" national associations as well as government representatives. All of the parties gather annually in Geneva to formulate and review policy at the International Labor Conference (ILC). In these formal meetings, a commitment to balanced social dialogue among the parties undergirds the organization's general ethos and practice of policy making. When the IDWN and its NGO and union allies took over the civil society observer section of the deliberations, the ILO shifted to a "tripartite-plus" model so as to be more inclusive. ILO Director-General Juan Somavia told official delegates that the participation of domestic workers required the "capacity to come down to the reality of what you are discussing today."[3] By confronting decision makers with the lives of "actual workers," the IDWN challenged the ILO to expand its purview in order to include those workers who fall into the web produced by the overlap between the informal economy, migration and care work in private homes.[4]

Domestic workers bolstered their stance by bringing aligned NGOs with symbolic histories of collective activism to this global policy forum to demand that domestic worker rights be recognized as human rights.[5] As Somavía contended in his personal meeting with IDWN leaders:

> [A]ll over the world, different ways of organizing of domestic workers have taken place. I think that what has happened in terms of global consciousness on the issue is the result of organization, as always. You never have social progress unless you have an organized vision, and people saying, look, we have to move in this direction.[6]

After two years of tripartite negotiations, the ILO's government, labor and employer delegates voted on the world's first Decent Work for Domestic Workers Convention on June 16, 2011.[7] The workers who had guided their national movements to this international stage watched from the third floor of the Palais des Nations, one the largest venues on the United Nations campus in Geneva. The results were read out: "Votes in Favor – 434; Votes Opposed – 8; Abstentions 42; The Majority – [gavel strike] *Approved*."[8] With these words, the formal ILO rules of order vaporized as the gallery exploded in cheers, activist songs and tears. From their position high above the proceedings, activists dropped an enormous banner reading, "C189 CONGRATULATIONS, NOW THE DOMESTIC WORK FOR GOVERNMENTS, RATIFY, IMPLEMENT." The entire hall applauded as they sang, "Up, up domestic workers, down, down with slavery!" in celebration of this symbolic victory.

Adoption of the convention brought domestic workers into the international spotlight and made their plight tangible.[9] IDWN president Myrtle Witbooi claimed the moment on behalf of its worldwide membership:

> Today we celebrate a great victory for domestic workers. Until now we have been treated as "invisible," not respected for the huge contribution we make in society and the economy and denied our rights as workers. It is an injustice that has lasted too long. After three years of organizing domestic workers throughout the world, the International Domestic Workers Network became the driving force behind this massive campaign to finally recognize domestic work as real work, worthy of the recognition and protection of all other sectors.[10]

Not only did domestic workers celebrate the rights and protections embedded within the convention, they saw themselves as central to its attainment. Ernestina Ochoa, leader of the Peruvian domestic workers' movement, boldly claimed to the international press, "This is not free, this is what society owes us."[11]

With the ILO standards in place, domestic worker organizations have gone on to build transnational alliances that engage both labor and gender interests. At the same time, the attainment of a global policy has allowed them to exercise power at the national level by drawing on the convention to demand that their states assure protections. As they did so, the IDWN's common appeal for the "same rights to 'decent work' as any other workers" at the ILO radiated across the globe. Through connections made at the ILO, domestic workers brought their demands with the backing of several international NGOs, policy research institutes and global unions. With their respective foci on migrant rights, the elimination of child labor and trafficking, informal labor and human rights, these organizations solidified a wider commitment to promote the ratification of Convention 189 as a critical step in making decent work a reality for workers around the world.[12]

The ILO victory catapulted the movement far beyond the UN halls in Geneva. With protections on paper, a labor-gender activist alliance began to focus on assuring that these rights "have teeth."[13] Four years after its passage, twenty-two countries have ratified the convention, and domestic worker activists and their allies are now assessing its impact on state support for its protections and their effect on the livelihoods of domestic workers on the ground – measures arguably more meaningful than global policy as a rhetorical nod to human rights.

This chapter explores how C189 has supported domestic workers as well as the national and transnational mobilization of their occupational sector, since its passage. We analyze the dialectical relationship between domestic worker organizing around the ILO and its impact among domestic workers at the local level. Drawing on six years of ethnographic research with the IDWN, we explore how activists have used the global policy arena to gain recognition and push their demands.[14] Next we turn to how the ILO's focus on domestic work has stretched the institution to take into account migration and the informal economy – two terrains formerly under-addressed by this institution. We then turn to the national scale to examine how C189 has helped shape national domestic worker efforts on the ground.

GETTING TO RIGHTS: DOMESTIC WORKER ORGANIZING THROUGH INTERNATIONAL INSTITUTIONS

Discursive Strategies

Domestic Workers, need a Convention.
Are you listening, employers?
Are you listening, governments?
Domestic workers, in the ILO.[15]

Immediately after the end of most of the formal tripartite discussions on domestic work policy at the ILO, union-inspired IDWN songs like this rang from the deliberation halls as activists sought to infuse their histories into the proceedings. Although domestic workers and their NGO allies were barred from speaking during the official sessions, they utilized a variety of activist techniques to make their voices heard. According to the ILO's structure, only one representative from each country's worker and employer groups can speak at the official negotiations. Because most domestic worker representatives joined the ILO as NGO observers, they could influence the system only by making their presence known in the larger negotiation arena and persuading those who did have access to the floor – government delegates and workers' spokespersons – to make public statements on their behalf. Although mediated in this way, "actual workers" could be particularly persuasive because of the level of authenticity stemming from the range of lived experiences they brought into the room. With this advantage, domestic workers took every opportunity to be seen as central to the policy dialogue.

As they engaged directly with the ILO process, domestic workers could hold the institution accountable from both a discursive and a moral perspective. Throughout the negotiations, domestic workers continually infused direct emotional appeals to the decision makers, personalizing the sector by drawing vivid pictures of the women who suffer most dramatically under a global economic system without standards or protections. Halimah Yacob, vice chair for the Committee on Domestic Workers and a member of the Singaporean Parliament, served as the spokesperson for the workers group. Speaking to her counterpart employer and government representatives, she continually described domestic workers as "someone's mother, daughter, wife, sister." When IDWN members gained access to the few available spaces for formal commentary from NGO observers, they also painted highly personalized images of domestic workers while using the language of the ILO to elevate their effectiveness. For example, Fish Ip Pui-Yu, leader of the Hong Kong domestic workers' delegation, reminded delegates of the overarching global economy that motivates migrant domestic workers to leave their home countries:

In today's world, vast numbers of women are migrating. They leave their own children and elders behind, in the care of others. They do it precisely because of their love for their families so that the money they earn can pay for education, health care and so on. Off they go, most of them to work as domestic workers and caring for others.[16]

In many instances, activists sought to humanize domestic workers and migrants by referring to their own motherhood. Marissa Begonia, a United Kingdom-based domestic worker from Hong Kong, used this strategy in a public demonstration outside of the famous three-legged chair monument at the UN's main entrance:

> Years ago I took a decision to leave my children behind. It is my responsibility to keep my children alive. Through domestic work, that is how my children grew up, it is how I educated my children. This has made me strong. It has given me the courage to continue.[17]

Begonia later demanded, "We are human beings and should not be treated like caged animals."[18]

The IDWN used the ILO venue to portray domestic workers as human beings worthy of respect and rights, emphasizing their suffering under conditions that subjected them to substantial human rights violations and abuses. Narbada Chhetri, a Nepali domestic worker rights activist based in New York, described her satisfaction in being able to describe these conditions in such a venue:

> I am very excited here, because, our sisters they did not get their wages and their recognition — four years, seven years, twelve years, eighteen years — no raise, no proper food. Now we have one sister, she is working twenty-three years as a domestic worker, now she is homeless, and she was raped. She did not get her wages, so I now I think they are recognized as a worker.[19]

As they made their collective appeal, domestic workers turned to delegates themselves and asked them to look at their own reliance on household labor to reproduce their daily lives and assure their privileged place in their respective countries. This strategy capitalized on the distinctive relationship between the delegates and this occupational sector, as it uniquely touched on their own lives and private households. The workers appealed to the delegates to "look deep in your hearts"[20] and "value the daily fabric of our lives"[21] by assuring protections for those "who make all other work possible."[22]

As the presence of domestic workers implicitly emphasized this distinctive moral perspective, it simultaneously interrogated the historic exclusion of the "most vulnerable," namely women, migrants and people of color, from international law. Domestic worker delegates framed the policy discussions as part of a much larger ethical obligation to redress severe historic injustices and become "custodians of a legacy"[23] that would define a new global consciousness for marginalized – mainly women and migrant – workers. Drawing from the language of the ILO, they reiterated that the treatment of domestic workers serves as a measure of our "floor values" as a global society. Thus, the domestic worker convention became not only a pivotal policy but also a statement on the shift to a global ethos that echoed the ILO's overarching vision of decent work as a pillar of Somavía's focus on fair globalization and human rights.

Domestic Worker Alliances

Domestic workers' capacities to take part in these policy discussions stem directly from the support of two major organizations with the longest-standing investment in domestic worker organizing: on the labor side, the International Union of Food Workers (IUF), based in Geneva; and on the gender front, Women in Informal Employment: Globalizing and Organizing (WEIGO), a research policy network based at Harvard University. Over two decades prior to the first ILC meetings on domestic work in 2010, these organizations provided resources that allowed domestic workers from around the world to align in person. Their combined efforts provided a physical and organizational space for domestic workers to meet and establish a series of original and effective strategies that would bring their voices into ILO deliberations in distinct and defining ways. For example, these organizations enabled domestic workers to meet face-to-face in Amsterdam to determine the priorities of a global movement and subsequently provided the vital resources necessary to bring domestic worker representatives to the ILO meetings for the discussions that led to passage of C189.

Although domestic work formed the center of the policy deliberations, INGOs (international non-governmental organizations) and NGOs representing a range of civil society interests joined the policy-making process to demonstrate solidarity and articulate the links between their concerns and those of the migrant domestic work sector. The IDWN drew strength and capacity from the backing of these organizations. At the same time, domestic work became the "cause of the day," as NGOs used the case of domestic work to emphasize a range of social injustices – from human trafficking to child labor to unregulated migration. As the Migrant Forum Asia group interjected in the opening of the 2010 debate session:

> We recognize domestic workers who are with us today, who will be directly affected by what is done or not done in their name in the 99th session of the ILC. We stand in solidarity with the domestic workers who cannot be physically present here, but who engage in the various national and regional partnerships. We assure their voices are heard and their demands for rights and recognitions are considered, recognized, respected and protected.[24]

Alongside NGOs, the physical presence of domestic workers within the negotiations allowed feminist government delegates ("femocrat" partners), who were empowered through their official capacity to speak from the floor, to position themselves as allies. UN Women director Michelle Bachelet, for example, reinforced the vital role of domestic workers in her public statement at the close of the 2011 ILC.

> ... [D]omestic work renews and sustains society; it keeps the economic engine and social wheels of society moving. If all those persons who today work in domestic work were to cease doing so one day, society will grind to a halt.

Here, Bachelet backed domestic workers using her own femocrat capital as well as her institutional tie to UN Women as a vested agency.

As the femocrat allies advocated for domestic worker rights, they also took the opportunity to point to the workings of more general transnational gender inequality in the systematic exploitation of women. As an affiliated gender expert attested in one of the many organizational meetings for NGO and worker representatives:

> The Convention is part of a much larger struggle in history ... that has to do with recognizing the value of reproduction.... [T]he work that was done in homes, the work of reproduction, the care work that today domestic workers are doing, got devalued, and people that did that work received no minimum wage, no social security protections, all the things that you are talking about today. There is of course, in these relationships, a deep message of gender. It was women who stayed in the homes to do the work, and it was men who moved outside of the homes to do the other kind of work.[25]

Between the domestic workers and their allies among the delegates, a reciprocal or mutually reinforcing relationship developed. The physical, political and even emotional presence of real workers brought the femocrats' statements into sharp focus, thereby strengthening the rhetorical positions of women in government who could speak on behalf of domestic workers. The histories of social injustice they brought to the table took form in the physical bodies of domestic workers who were sitting alongside the delegates. Thus, allies became ventriloquists for domestic workers' causes, although, ironically, the power that allowed them to speak from the floor perpetuated a particular gender hierarchy.

Framing Human Rights

With the prospect of participating in an international convention that became official in 2008 when the ILO put the Decent Work for Domestic Workers discussions on the 2010 agenda, the IDWN focused its strategy on presenting a united demand for dignity and human rights.[26] While they spoke different languages and represented a wide diversity of national contexts, within the ILO domestic workers contended that their work carried the "same face" and therefore deserved universal basic protections. As Narbada Chhetri proclaimed, "[A]ll over the world, it is the same. Only faces change, the doors [of the houses] change, but the treatment is mostly similar."[27] She called for universal protection that would assure domestic workers' rights across diverse contexts. In her leading role as the workers' spokesperson in favor of the Convention, Halimah Yacob asserted, "We all have a vision, and we will achieve that vision. We lead in solidarity together, in one heart, in one direction."[28]

This rights-centered framework allowed domestic workers to demand moral and ethical protections, "just like any other worker."[29] By repeatedly claiming that "domestic worker rights are human rights," the IDWN could bring the larger UN discourse of universal protections into the discussion. These standards became ethical touchstones for those left out of the global economy. In other words, if those considered furthest from protections could be woven into the umbrella of protections, the international standardization system would prove its worth in its ability to reach those widely considered the "poorest of the poor." Thus, by using domestic work to establish what the ILO negotiations called a "floor" of social protections, the process not only set labor standards, but also created the moral fabric of an imagined and applied global community of rights.

The strength of collective organizing around a human rights framework extended far beyond the ILO. While domestic workers aligned at the ILO, they also took their activism to the surrounding streets of Geneva through downtown demonstrations with local union leaders, public art performances of song and dance, poetry and a major march across the city. Domestic workers from Latin America and Africa joined in dance, while Chinese, Filipina and Korean domestic workers performed their adaptation of traditional Korean labor songs:

> We get up to work before sunrise.
> Work in home at the doors behind.
> We've made the comfort in your home.
> Why our work's never recognized?[30]

Elsewhere, Hong Kong domestic worker leaders unfurled a quilt with "over 3,500 patches, which each represent a domestic worker from Asia with her demands."[31] When IDWN advocates and allies grasped this quilt, they presented a united front conjoining activist demonstrations to the demands for solidarity within the policy negotiations. These events built familiar activist practices into a strong aligned claim and helped sustain solidarity within the very long hours of the ILO deliberations. Within the ILO process, the IDWN developed a "Platform of Demands" that outlined their common quest for dignity and included a plea to be treated as "real workers."[32] Through these strategies, domestic workers gained a global activist identity as they worked on the fringes of the ILO's formal deliberations – a maneuver that became one of the most powerful defining dimensions of the IDWN's role.

This alignment of domestic workers experienced a "dream-come-true" moment when the ILC passed Convention 189. As Narbada Chhetri exclaimed,

> I'm very very happy, I'm very excited because this convention is for our sisters, and those who are voiceless and those who are suffering from years and years. Now this convention shows their value of their work contribution. This is the rights and recognition for our sisters.[33]

Like Chhetri, many representatives saw this victory as a symbol of a much larger struggle for justice and rights. Halimah Yacob reflected on this moment as she ended her term as vice chair of the Committee on Domestic Work:

> You have proved that it is important for the trade union movement all over the world. This is an historical effort. You are emancipating a group of 100 million people all over the world.[34]

Yet even with this wide recognition of formerly "invisible" sectors of the working population, the activist representatives immediately understood that the victory marked the beginning of "a much longer battle" to assure that domestic workers themselves would be able to access their rights. With this monumental achievement, Fish Ip Pui-Yu contended "[We] have got a little bit of liberation, but I am sure that in our lives, with all the sisters, we will get liberated, somewhere, sometime."[35]

ACTIVIST-INSTITUTION-POLICY DIALECTICS

This reflection takes us to a discussion of how C189 demanded that the ILO look not only at the specific sector of domestic work and its role in the global service economy,[36] but also at the formerly uncharted terrains (for the ILO) of migration and the informal economy. In a speech to the 2010 ILC, Vicky Kanyoka, then IDWN Africa Regional Coordinator, observed:

> We often migrate from our own families and homes to work in homes that are very far away, isolated from the support of our own communities. Many domestic workers see their own families not even once a year, especially those who work outside their own countries.[37]

To write protections into public policy, C189 had to deal with the global state of migration. At the time of these negotiations, ILO experts estimated that 232 million migrants were living outside their home countries, 50 percent of whom were women.[38] In the domestic work sector, women constituted over 90 percent of transnational migrants.[39] Thus, while migrants today are generally equally divided between the sexes, domestic work remains one of the most heavily feminized sectors of export labor. As they leave their own countries to pursue work in other households, "women migrants are doubly vulnerable to this lack of legal protection for domestic work, because of their gender and their status as migrants," one union official noted.[40] Peruvian domestic worker activist Ernestina Ochoa contended, "Our migrant sisters are the most exploited; they are the ones who live in the shadows. Their paperwork is withheld, and for them, there are no rights."[41] This staggering "multiplier effect" motivated domestic workers and their allies to bring migrants into the realm of convention protections. As the debates unfolded, a tension arose between the creation of policy to protect against the interrelated abuses so common to migrant domestic labor and the potential imposition of too many requirements on Member States, who were not fully prepared or willing to reform these transnational labor practices.

The first proposed draft of what would become C189 called for three particular standards in relation to migration: (1) the assurance of a written contract for labor in the household; (2) regulations for the repatriation of migrants under necessary conditions; and (3) cooperation across sending and receiving Member States. The policy discussions addressed migration by dealing with the technicalities of the third-party employment agencies that handled transnational employment and state relations. More complex and far outside the scope of the Convention lurked larger questions about how international governance could regulate the scale of migration, as well as states' ethical responsibilities to marginalized workers who leave their own families in pursuit of opportunities purportedly offered by global cities. As the ILC debated each of the articles dealing with migration, it became clear that ILO policy on domestic work would not be fully adequate to the task of dealing with the larger issues presented by international border-crossings and massive economic inequality. One activist reflected on the most difficult aspects of her life as a live-in domestic worker, recounting, "[T]here is a gap between you and your children."[42] What policy could address this emotional toll, or the lost years of separation from one's children? In many ways, the negotiated terms seemed to treat the symptoms with very particular prescriptions, but without a larger analysis of the source of the global condition. Yet even in their inadequacy, they constituted the most comprehensive attempt to date to deal with the migrant global workforce.

In the end, the tripartite partners agreed to three initial focus areas: contracts, repatriation, and agreements between sending and receiving countries. The final draft of the convention also included a rather banal blanket protection, Article 8(3), which read, "Members shall take measures to cooperate with each other to ensure the effective application of the provisions of this Convention to migrant domestic workers."[43] This article ensured that international migrants would enjoy the same rights as indigenous workers. Yet its placement within the overall document is almost hidden, enfolded within an article listing three other technical protections. Furthermore, without specifying migrants, Article 2(1) states, "The Convention applies to all domestic workers."[44]

By looking at the language, placement and omissions, one can read the sensitivities to (and at times strategic avoidance of) larger questions of migration. With reference to related conventions, the final document links to larger, more comprehensive established agreements that place the protection and regulation of migrants in the realm of global governance – at both applied and ideological levels. The Preamble of the final document notes, "...the particular relevance for domestic workers of the Migration for Employment Convention (Revised), 1949 (No. 97), the Migrant Workers (Supplementary Provisions) Convention, 1975 (No. 143), the Workers with Family Responsibilities Convention, 1981 (No. 156), the Private Employment Agencies Convention, 1997 (No. 181), and the Employment Relationship Recommendation, 2006 (No. 198), as well as of the ILO Multilateral Framework on Labour Migration: Non-binding principles and guidelines for a rights-based approach to labour migration (2006)."[45]

With these references, the final document reinforces the assumption that migrant domestic workers are protected by all of these established instruments which apply to the larger circumstances for migrant workers more generally. Furthermore, the Preamble includes reference to the International Convention on the Protection of the Rights of All Migrant Workers and Members of Their Families, among other related documents that create a protective umbrella for migrants across all sectors. With these matters taken care of in the Preamble, the Convention's treatment of migrant domestic workers focuses on the practicalities of this specific sector – where the particularities of labor in private households evoke larger concerns about responsibility and rights within global transnational flows.

As the debates around migration moved forward, participants became aware of the tension between recognizing the need for "special protections" for migrant workers and assuring the feasibility of implementation. During the 2011 negotiations, the French government representatives underscored the importance of recognizing the distinct needs and vulnerabilities migrants shared. "After all, they live and work in a country that is not their own."[46] The United States backed this position, claiming "...certain classes of migrant domestic workers must receive additional protections," and pointed out the need for "appropriate regulations."[47]

Many countries, however, resisted policy protections that would lock them into offering migrants rights such as social security provisions or citizenship benefits. With their core commitment to social democracy, many European countries offered strong resistance to the notion of extending benefits to outsiders (Kettunen et al. 2015). In their eyes, such assurances would require the redistribution of tax-based resources to the "masses of migrants" who were reaching their borders in search of undocumented work. The United Kingdom, for example, resisted such requirements, stating, "this will only make the Convention non-ratifiable."[48]

The Arab-country bloc also opposed special protections for migrants, contending that workers' treatment as "one of the family" assured their protections. According to the 2010 Arab-Country statement,

> All the domestic workers are migrant workers, temporary or provisional workers that live in the Gulf area and most times we deal with those workers as part of our family. We provide to them decent housing and decent meals. We share a family with them as well, taking into consideration the social conditions prevailing in our countries.[49]

Yet within these Arab countries, the only bodies representing domestic workers are the employment agencies that arrange such trade, mainly with Asia; unionization and collective organization of domestic workers are prohibited. Thus, to date, small faith-based operations, such as Catholic Relief Services, provide the only advocacy for migrants in these countries, some of which must be offered in clandestine forms (for similar advocacy in Hong Kong and Taiwan, see Chapter 6).

Given this circumstance, rather than relying on the variant systems, laws and power structures within countries, the ILO set out to assure a global rights scheme as a means to deliver the special protections migrant domestic workers need. With the prospect of imposing these standards "from above," domestic workers held out hope that the articulation of rights at the international level would shift values and beliefs within the countries that rely on migrant labor. Grace Escaño, a Filipina activist within the Netherlands, expressed this aspiration:

> For us, this Convention is a big tool. We are trying to prove to them that there is a capacity issue. We want to prove that Dutch women can have a career because the domestic workers are taking [over] their [domestic] jobs. We are trying to impose the idea that Dutch children must respect the domestic workers. So, for us, we are really working so hard from the Netherlands. Now, it is so hard because of the criminalization of "illegals." We are always telling to them [government officials] that there is a demand for domestic workers.... Hopefully this Convention will be approved and we will go home with a positive outcome.[50]

The domestic work policy negotiations turned ILO conversations to the notion that "you can have migration with rights."[51] As the hopes of domestic workers like Escaño show, these rights must be translated into effective implementation, in both labor practices as well as altered perceptions that would re-value domestic labor and recognize its central worth in the global economy.

Throughout discussions of C189, the issue of migration prompted expressions of the need for multilateral cooperation in recognizing the mutual dependency on domestic work between the world's sending and receiving regions. As advocates of these policy rights repeatedly contended, domestic workers do not just leave their home countries for the promise of economic gain in more developed countries. Their movement is orchestrated through extensive state relations, co-coordinated structures, and a massive system of interdependency that thrives upon women's care labor as a vital source of national income, on the one hand, and social provision, on the other. Thus, sending and receiving countries build relations around the trade in women's care labor. This globalization of household labor elevates the need for protections to the level of international governance. No longer can national laws assure fair labor standards when so many migrants work in countries where they have no citizenship rights. Thus, in order for C189 to be effective, it needed to spell out the terms of migration as a vital dimension of its umbrella.

The interdependency of states that send and receive domestic workers is carried out through work permit systems and third-party agencies that recruit and place domestic workers in employment sites abroad. Sringatin, chair of the Indonesian Migrant Workers' Union, spoke of the larger realities for migrant domestic workers worldwide: "Every migrant worker leaving the country must go through a labor agency. No-one can organize their own work abroad."[52] Thus, negotiations on the intersection of migration and domestic work pointed out that in the best of circumstances, these agencies provide accurate images of the expectations for domestic work in the destination country, offer extensive training, and take responsibility for the longer-term health of the employment relationship. But at other times, reliance upon a third party allows for some of the most egregious forms of human rights violations through trafficking, misrepresentation of the work and extreme exploitation.

Across this continuum of third-party practices, domestic workers remain completely dependent on two levels. First, their livelihoods are largely determined by their geographic locations as suppliers to the global care chain. Second, as individual workers within these patterned transnational flows, migrants' everyday livelihoods often hinge upon one employer and the fragility of minimal access to rights as non-citizens. This is exacerbated by their isolation – and even incarceration – within private households. When a migrant must depend upon a specific job to retain the right to live in the destination country, the employer holds even greater power. In the most exploitative conditions, the threat of deportation becomes bound up with economic, gender and racial oppression. Thus, systems and people work together to create particular vulnerabilities for migrant domestic workers outside of their own countries of origin. As leader of the Hong Kong and international domestic worker movements Fish Ip Pui-Yu described it,

> Poor work permit systems also lead to abuse. Where a migrant domestic worker has a permit that says she can only work for that employer, or indeed that particular diplomatic mission, in her host country, this keeps her in a situation of dependency. She dare not leave that employer, no matter if someone in the household is being abusive, because, if she does, she is rendered "illegal" because she is not allowed to work anywhere else.[53]

Pui-Yu centered her public statements on governments' responsibility to work together within a regulated global set of standards, so that domestic workers would be protected across borders. In one of the designated public addresses to the ILO's entire tripartite, she contended, "Governments of origin and destination countries need to collaborate better to ensure there will be no abuses in the job referral process.... Member States have obligations to remove all obstacles"[54] to the achievement of decent work for migrant domestic workers.

In the reactions to proposed migrant protections, the ILO debates revealed larger country relations, reinforced particular alliances, and drew lines among countries based upon their positions and practices. Conversations about a global domestic worker policy became occasions for presenting the larger geopolitics surrounding migration. The range and complexity of these positions hobbled the convention's ability to make a difference within the dominant market economy forces. In the final document, countries are obligated to assure that the rights inscribed in the convention are accessible to migrants working within each country. Ultimately, the centrality of migration in domestic work also fortified the case for a global policy as the only potential set of standards that could address the realities of this sector – where protections must travel *with* the human supply chain. Even though the Workers group felt it had compromised in ways that reduced their original hope for protections, the extensive focus on migration, along with its reach to employment agencies and bilateral relations, increased workers' claim to rights while earning a great deal of political support which, in turn, led to increased awareness of the wider conditions of domestic workers' lives.

ILO POLICY ACCOMPLISHMENTS AND THEIR INFLUENCE ON ORGANIZING

Convention 189 established a conversation and set of ideals regarding domestic work that moved beyond the global policy arena to the national sphere. As Manuela Tomei, director of the ILO's Conditions of Work and Employment Programme, pointed out, the relevance of this instrument will depend on states. Accordingly, domestic workers must rely on states to implement changes that will materialize in their daily lives. Otherwise, an international policy is only a paper "without teeth," as domestic workers warned. Halimah Yacob put it this way: "[A] standard is not helpful if it is not linked to national laws and standards." Given this reality, Yacob encouraged domestic workers to think of the implementation of national standards rather than an "international aspiration" alone.[55]

Accordingly, domestic workers and their allies began to focus on workers' capacity to exercise activism at the state level and collaborate with national allies to promote ratification. Sam Gurney, policy officer for the ILO Governing Body and a member of the International Relations Department of the International Trade Union Confederation for the EU, emphasized this vital link at a public demonstration outside of the UN just after adoption of C189:

> Domestic workers have set the agenda, inside, behind us in the UN building, because, an ILO Convention, it can do some things, it is a template, it is something to build on, but to win real rights, to prove that domestic workers are workers, that takes domestic workers to organize, to be in unions, to work with NGOs, to fight for their rights, and so our job in the trade union movement is to make sure that the resources and the support is there for all of you, the domestic workers in Europe, in Asia, in Latin America, all around the world, to fight for your own rights. We will support you in that solidarity. You are workers, we are workers! Let's build for next year.[56]

Thus, one of the first real tests of this global standard fell to union organizers at the national level. Dan Gallin, general secretary of the IUF and lead advocate for domestic worker rights among global union leaders, framed this critical transfer from global policy to national organizing as follows:

> If you don't have a strong trade union movement which is capable of enforcing legislation and conventions, whatever, you're not going to get much effect. But in the first place, the struggle to obtain these conventions is an opportunity for propaganda and agitation, and you can raise consciousness around a certain issue by such campaigns, for one thing. So that in itself is already a gain.[57]

From this perspective, passage of C189 served as a catalyst to invigorate more coordinated national organizing efforts, strengthened by the backing of the global union of domestic workers. Chris Bonner, coordinator of the domestic worker organizing efforts for WIEGO, asserted that the convention victory was "as much about process as it was about the outcome." Soon after, she proclaimed, "Now we can move to building organizations vs. lobbying for rights. That work is nearly over." While acknowledging this as the "hard part" of assuring actual change in domestic workers lives, she also asserted, "I cannot imagine a better position of departure for an organizing campaign than what we have now. And the ILO will help on this one."[58]

With adoption of the convention, domestic workers now held a pivotal position because of the attention they had received at the level of international organizations, INGOs and governments who listened to their claims and witnessed the transnational solidarity of the IDWN within the policy negotiations. Shirley Pryce, head of the Jamaican Domestic Workers Union, proclaimed after the victory, "We are on the map – the other unions and the Government know we are there."[59] Adoption of C189 thus not only strengthened domestic workers' own movement but also afforded them platforms for national organizing by building relationships with governments and engaging individual organizations within the much larger network involving the UN, other unions and invested transnational NGOs.

Even as they were debating the convention, some governments amplified their support by assuring the domestic workers and their allies that they would ratify it. Domestic worker organizations kept them to their word, lobbying governments to hold them accountable to their commitments within the UN arena. Louise McDonough, representative of one of the leading governments in support of the convention, Australia, charged other governments to consider ratification in her closing remarks to the wider 2011 ILC body:

> We appreciate that ratification will often require amendment to national legislation, and Australia is no exception in this regard. However, if national law and practice was already adequate, this house would not have been charged with developing international instruments for domestic workers across the world who largely work in the informal economy. As always, ratification of ILO conventions requires amendments to national law and practice, and this situation is no different — so our approach should not be that we can't ratify, but rather how can we ratify? Because if countries don't amend their laws to meet the international standard, the situation for domestic workers around the world will not change.[60]

Paul MacKay, vice chair of the Employers Group in the 2011 negotiations, underscored this statement by asserting that the real test of an ILO convention lies in its impact on workers at the local level. As he contended at the close of the vote, "The success will be that time in the future when domestic workers themselves say, this was the start. These documents were the start of a change in our lives. That is what success will look like. Not these documents; we have just started the job."[61] MacKay also referred to the vital role NGO organizations and allies played as counterpart negotiators with domestic workers themselves. Robert B. Shepard, lead government representative for the United States, confirmed this opening for government-NGO-domestic worker communication made possible through the ILO when he reported,

> I think we listened to the National Domestic Workers Alliance. We listened to Human Rights Watch, I mean obviously we have to assess their positions and how they might fit in, but we certainly are happy to listen to them. They made some good suggestions, very helpful. We listened all the time to the organizations.[62]

In one case, an employer organization even joined this movement to support domestic workers by showing governments and other employer organizations how improved conditions for domestic workers would benefit all parties. Betsey McGee, leader of the New York branch of Hand in

Hand, The Domestic Employers Network, offered strong public support for the convention, noting that it could be "used to change cultural norms, shape national policies, structure incentives for better care. This is a future we welcome."[63]

The relationships to NGOs formed within the ILO opened the door for domestic worker organizations, who used them as allies in approaching their governments, thereby strengthening their demands for ratification. The ILO victory also enabled domestic workers to engage UN agencies, NGOs and other organizations invested in related claims for migrant worker rights and informal economy workers. After the 2011 ILC, Ai-jen Poo, director of the National Domestic Workers Alliance and co-director of the Caring Across Generations Campaign, both in the United States, framed the transnational activism as part of a larger and growing social movement:

> The entire ILO process was a lesson to me in the importance of movements—movements that create progressive governments, movements of women and workers that demand change, and the great acts of leadership that movements create. Paying tribute to the leadership of women in movements in particular as I leave Geneva today.[64]

Employer advocate McGee saw the movement of domestic workers that emerged from the ILO as part of a much longer historical arc of human rights and social justice struggles:

> There's been a great shift across the world in how we think about women, and about gay people, and about some other issues of the last twenty, thirty, forty years. There's going to be a great shift in how people think about domestic workers and how they think about the employers of people who work in their home. And that shift will be in the direction of understanding the rights and responsibilities much more completely than is the case today.[65]

The alignment of dedicated advocates at the ILO placed domestic work within a much larger human rights struggle that linked national contexts and domestic worker organizations across vast geographical divides. As the IDWN alliance carved out spaces within the tripartite organization and stretched its boundaries, governments listened and workers attained a platform to demand ratification. Working on policy at the global level, the ILO pointed to the vital need for national organizing to ensure that international standards would take hold at the state level, thereby guaranteeing domestic workers the rights outlined in this landmark convention.

At the international level, organizing efforts have focused on C189's application to migrants as one of the ultimate litmus tests of the policy's meaning in practice. In October of 2015, worker delegates from affiliates of the International Domestic Worker Federation (IDWF), the global union launched from the IDWN in 2013, attended a global seminar hosted by the United Nations Office of the High Commissioner of Human Rights (OHCHR) to continue the discussion around the vulnerabilities of migrant domestic workers. This three-day seminar placed special emphasis on developing ways to address and mitigate human rights violations for domestic workers working under irregular migration status. In her address to the seminar's attendees, IDWF president Myrtle Witbooi contended:

> Today we come together to ask what is being done to bring these workers out of the shadows? After a four-year campaign, victory came on June 16th, 2011 in the shape of ILO Convention 189. This convention provided protections for all workers and established grounds to demand recognition of the rights of domestic workers in nations worldwide. However, as an international instrument, Convention 189 has not yet been ratified and absorbed into the labor laws of all countries. The issues of migrant workers are now at the forefront of the conversation.[66]

Here, Witbooi clearly calls attention to the Convention's failures in implementation. She alludes to migrant workers as the exemplar of the complexities of making this instrument meaningful in the lives of all domestic workers.

In some ways, the exclusion of migrant domestic workers from the protections of C189 has undermined the strength of worker organizations on the ground by reinforcing lines of division. Hong Kong, one of the leading receiving countries for migrant domestic workers in the Asia-Pacific region, is also one of the few countries where migrant workers have access to the full realm of protections available to local workers. However, a national call for stricter language regarding employment agencies' treatment of migrant domestic workers drew new divisions around these protections. Since these agencies often facilitate relationships between workers and their employers, their role came under closer scrutiny following C189's adoption. As IDWF organizer Fish Ip Pui-Yu notes:

At that time we have many Filipinos, generally Filipinos and then sometimes some Thai workers, some Sri Lankan. But the majority are Filipino.... We have huge problems especially regarding the Indonesian migrant domestic workers. Almost all of them are underpaid. This is because the agencies are promoting that they are receiving this wage and they also tell the employer. And the Indonesian consulate in Hong Kong was also telling the workers, you should receive less wage because you need to compete with Filipino. So the strategy is really to lower the wage.[67]

In addition to encouraging competition, the differing levels of rights and protections available to migrant and local workers also affect migrants' full claim to protections. Although in Hong Kong migrant workers have the ability to report cases of labor abuses, many are brought to a standstill by the conflict between their rights as workers and their legal limitations based on their migrant status. IDWF general secretary Elizabeth Tang described this complication, saying,

As migrants they are also included in the immigration laws that have other elements which limit their rights. Like the most difficult one, that is the two-weeks rule, they have the right to change employers here unlike some other countries. But if they change employers, they must find a new employer and then submit a new application to change the contract within two weeks, and two-weeks is very short. If they are not able to do it they have to go back to their countries. That poses a lot of limitations to them because even if they don't like their employers for some reason and they want to change but then cannot find a new employer then they'll just stick to their employers even if their employers are abusive. If the abuses are really serious they can still file a case against their employers, but this two-weeks rule is really infamous among migrants.... That scares many domestic workers who rather keep quiet and just forget about the past and try to look for a new job rather than bringing the employer to court and do all these things.[68]

In addition to complications brought on by multiple policies regarding migrant labor, the inability of worker groups to fully realize labor protections for migrants has undermined the ability of domestic worker organizations to build a more secure sector. Witbooi echoed this reality as she described the importance of organizing migrants: "The aim is about mobilizing and not letting workers get exploited. That is the aim. We want to have a strong sector by protecting migrant workers."[69]

For workers, the reasons for cross-border protections are many. Thus, any effort to regulate transnational domestic work relies on C189's relevance as workers cross national borders. As these narratives depict, even though C189 is the only standardized way to ensure protections for the hundreds of thousands of domestic workers in this growing informal economy sector, its relevance to migrants presents one of the most complex challenges of application in real life.

Thus, while this global policy has empowered workers' organizing efforts by bolstering their connection to a global standard and related national efforts, the policy's "teeth" appear most compromised when viewed through the lens of migration. Here, compliance, regulation and employment agency mandates make it very difficult to turn policy into practice. Yet domestic worker activists worldwide have repeatedly claimed how important C189 has been as an anchoring tool, to demand national rights protections, recognition or organizing, and adherence to the standards put forth in the ILO language. With the increased moral weight of human rights woven into this historic victory for labor, domestic workers have acquired new tools in their efforts to continue the struggle for recognition and protections. As South African domestic workers chanted as they crafted the first laws for this sector in the new democracy, "women won't be free until domestic workers are free."

Today, with the acquisition of this first global policy, migrant domestic worker rights are integrally connected to the rights established at both the national and global levels. As the global movement grows, each domestic worker's ability to make human rights relevant to her own daily life reflects this dialectical relationship between the micro household and both national and international standards. As Manuela Tomei proclaimed on the day domestic workers won C189, "This is not the end, it is just the beginning of a very long battle." Six years after the global policy victory, domestic workers' strengthened activism provides a foundation for the widest reach of rights, as C189 offers a gateway to the assurance of care labor protections across the global care chain.

NOTES

1. For an overview of the organizational path to this policy formation, see the ILO's two "Decent Work for Domestic Workers" reports: 2010a and 2010b.

2. The IDWN and its ally representatives used these expressions in their public statements as part of their strategy to demand rights. International Labour Conference, author fieldnotes, 2010.
3. Statement by Juan Somavía to the opening 2010 Domestic Workers Committee, author fieldnotes, ILC, 2010.
4. For a discussion of "siloization" in the ILO, see Mahon and Michel, this volume.
5. For a history of domestic worker activism in the US, see Nadasen 2015.
6. Meeting between Juan Somavía and IDWN leaders, June 4, 2010.
7. This vote also included the accompanying set of Recommendations. For the full policy document see ILO Convention 189 [http://www.ilo.org/dyn/normlex/en/f?p=NORMLEXPUB:12100:0::NO::p12100_instrument_id:2551460] and Recommendation No. 201 9 http://www.ilo.org/dyn/normlex/en/f?p=NORMLEXPUB:12100:0::NO:12100:P12100_INSTRUMENT_ID:2551502:NO].
8. Only Swaziland opposed the Convention vote. Some experts suggest that this may have been an error, given the country's general support for the Convention throughout the process. With the abstentions, the Convention passed with an 83 percent majority.
9. For a range of insider analyses of the domestic work convention, see Blackett 2011, Boris and Fish 2014, Pape 2016, and Tomei 2011.
10. Myrtle Witbooi, statement delivered to the media at the 2011 ILC, June 15, 2011.
11. Statement to the international media, June 16, 2011, United Nations.
12. See the IDWN's "Platform of Demands" for a full list of policy priorities.
13. Domestic workers continually used this expression to point out that policy alone would have little meaning in their lives without changes on the ground.
14. Jennifer Fish worked with the International Domestic Workers Network to document their participation in the 2010 and 2011 International Labor Conferences in Geneva. She has followed the organization through its emergence as the first global union, conducting interviews with several of its key founders and working directly with domestic worker organizations at the national level. Moriah Shumpert conducted scholar-activist fieldwork with the South African Domestic Service and Allied Workers Union and the International Domestic Workers Federation in 2015. She collected a series of interviews on models of organizing and conducted ethnographic research on unionization and transnational movements in South Africa and Thailand. This chapter is based upon our collective data and shared analyses of the relationship among grassroots, national and transnational organizing.
15. Song created by the IDWN and performed throughout the 2010 and 2011 International Labour Conferences.

16. Formal speech to the ILC Plenary, June 9, 2011.
17. Public demonstration speech, June 10, 2010.
18. Ibid.
19. Speech at the closing session of the Workers' Group of the Committee on Domestic Work, June 10, 2011
20. Domestic workers and their ally spokespersons used this term repeatedly to bring an affective appeal into the ILO process.
21. Drawn from the 2010 public statement of Nisha Varia, Senior Researcher, Human Rights Watch at the Committee on Domestic Work discussions, June 12, 2010.
22. This slogan, "the work that makes all other work possible," later became widely used in the National Domestic Workers Alliance's 2014 campaign in the United States.
23. These terms "most vulnerable" and "custodians of a legacy" came up frequently in both years' discussions to refer to domestic workers' marginalized position and their agency to set new policies.
24. International Labour Conference, author fieldnotes, 2010.
25. Elisabeth Prügl, speech at the Poster Exhibit sponsored by the International Working Group of Domestic Workers, Maison des Associations, Geneva, June 9, 2010.
26. For an analysis of human rights in the context of relevant social struggles, see Sen 2012.
27. Interview with Jennifer Fish, conducted on June 8, 2011.
28. Speech at the opening meeting of the Workers Group of the Committee on Domestic Work, June 1, 2010.
29. Domestic workers advocates repeatedly echoed this statement. At the same time, they called for consideration of the "special" nature of this work, thus creating what historian Eileen Boris has called a hybrid construction of domestic work because of their dual plight for recognition as workers and consideration as a special category. For further discussion of this concept, see Boris and Klein 2015 and Smith 2012.
30. Lyrics provided by Ip Fish Pui-Yu, June 2011.
31. As depicted in an event flyer from Asian Domestic Workers for the June 8, 2010 demonstration.
32. International Domestic Workers Network, 2010. *Platform of Demands.* Geneva: International Labour Conference, 99th Session.
33. Interview with Sofia Trevino of WIEGO, conducted June 10, 2011.
34. Halimah Yacob, closing speech to the Workers Group of the Committee on Domestic Work, June 10, 2011.
35. Interview with Jennifer Fish, conducted June 16, 2011.
36. For in-depth analysis of domestic work in the global care economy, see, for example, Lutz 2011, Piper 2010, and Sassen 1991.

37. Vicky Kanyoka, speech to the Tripartite Committee on Domestic Work, ILC, Geneva, 3 June 2010.
38. The ILC discussions used these working figures in the negotiations, recognizing that accurate estimates had not yet been attained. For the most contemporary assessment of domestic work and migration, see ILO 2015.
39. Ibid.
40. Luc Demaret, interview by Natacha David, International Trade Union Confederation, June 4, 2010.
41. Public statement at the opening meeting on gender just prior to the opening of the 2010 ILC discussion on Decent Work for Domestic Workers, June 6, 2010.
42. Hester Stephens, General Secretary, South African Domestic Service and Allied Workers Union, in discussion with the author, June, 2013.
43. See the final Convention articles at: http://www.ilo.org/dyn/normlex/en/f?p=NORMLEXPUB:12100:0::NO::P12100_ILO_CODE:C189.
44. Ibid.
45. Ibid.
46. Public statement of the French government, author fieldnotes, ILC, 2010.
47. Ibid.
48. International Labour Conference, author fieldnotes, 2010.
49. Ibid. The speaker is apparently referring to the "kafala" system through which migrant workers are sponsored in the Gulf States. The system is, however, rife with exploitation, especially of female migrants; see Human Rights Watch 2014.
50. Statement at an NGO domestic worker demonstration, Geneva, author fieldnotes, 2011.
51. Maria Elena Valenzuela, meeting statement at the International Labour Organization Global Action Programme on Migrant Domestic Workers and Their Families Advisory Board Meeting, February 4, 2014; author meeting notes.
52. Sringatin, interview by Celia Mather, WIEGO, June 8, 2010.
53. Ip Pui-Yu, "To the Plenary of the International Labour Conference," speech to the ILC, Geneva, June 9, 2011.
54. Ibid.
55. Statement by Halimah Yacob at the ILC discussions, June 5, 2010; author fieldnotes.
56. Sam Gurney, "Statements on Global Mobilization of Domestic Workers," speech at the domestic worker/NGO demonstration at the Broken Chair monument at UN Headquarters, Geneva, June 10, 2010.
57. Dan Gallin, former IUF General Secretary, in discussion with Jennifer Fish, June 2012.
58. Interview with Jennifer Fish, conducted June 16, 2011.

59. Interview with Celia Mather, conducted June 13, 2010.
60. Closing statement by of the Australian Government to the Domestic Workers Committee, June 15, 2011.
61. Interview with Jennifer Fish, conducted June 16, 2011.
62. Interview with Jennifer Fish, conducted June 15, 2011.
63. Betsey McGee, public statement at the Friedrich Ebert Stiftung panel discussion at the ILC, Tuesday, June 7, 2011.
64. Ai-Jen Poo, letter to the NDWA and its supporters reporting on her observation of the 2011 ILC discussions.
65. Betsey McGee, statement at the IDWN closing meeting at the ILC, June 11, 2011.
66. Myrtle Witbooi, address given during a global seminar hosted by the United Nations Office of the High Commissioner of Human Rights, New York, September 28, 2015.
67. Interview with Moriah Shumpert, conducted September 27, 2015.
68. Interview with Moriah Shumpert, conducted September 25, 2015.
69. Interview with Moriah Shumpert, conducted September 26, 2015.

REFERENCES

Blackett, Adelle. 2011. "Introduction: Regulating Decent Work for Domestic Workers." *Canadian Journal of Women & the Law* 23, 1: 1–46.
Boris, Eileen and Jennifer N. Fish. 2014. "'Slaves No More': Making Global Labor Standards for Domestic Workers." *Feminist Studies* 40: 411–43.
Boris, Eileen and Jennifer Klein. 2015. *Caring for America: Home Health Workers in the Shadow of the Welfare State.* New York: Oxford University Press.
International Domestic Workers Network. 2010. "Platform of Demands." Edited by International Domestic Workers Network. Geneva: WIEGO.
International Labour Organization (ILO). 2010a. "Report IV (1) Decent Work for Domestic Workers." http://www.ilo.org/wcmsp5/groups/public/—ed_norm/—relconf/documents/meetingdocument/wcms_104700.pdf
International Labour Organization (ILO). 2010b "Report IV (2) Decent Work for Domestic Workers." http://www.ilo.org/wcmsp5/groups/public/—ed_norm/—relconf/documents/meetingdocument/wcms_123731.pdf
International Labour Organization (ILO). 2015. *ILO Global Estimates on Migrant Workers: Results and Methodology, Special Focus on Migrant Domestic Workers.* Geneva: ILO.
Kettunen, Pauli, Sonya Michel and Klaus Pedersen, eds. 2015. *Race, Ethnicity and Welfare States: An American Dilemma?* Cheltenham and Camberley, UK and Northampton, MA: Edward Elgar.
Lutz, Helma. 2011. *The New Maids: Transnational Women and the Care Economy.* London: Zed Books.

Nadasen, Premilla. 2015. *Household Workers Unite: The Untold Story of African American Women Who Built a Movement.* Boston: Beacon Press.

Pape, Karin. 2016. "ILO Convention C189—a Good Start for the Protection of Domestic Workers: An Insider's View." *Progress in Development Studies* 16, 2: 189–202.

Piper, Nicola. 2010. "Temporary Economic Migration and Rights Activism: An Organizational Perspective." *Ethnic and Racial Studies* 33, 1: 108–25.

Sassen, Saskia. 1991. *Global City: New York, London, Tokyo.* Princeton, NJ: Princeton University Press.

Sen, Amartya. 2012. "The Global Status of Human Rights." *American University International Law Review* 27, 1: 1–15.

Smith, Peggie R. 2012. "Work Like Any Other, Work Like No Other: Establishing Decent Work for Domestic Workers." *Employee Rights and Employment Policy Journal* 15, 1: 159–200.

Tomei, Manuela. 2011. "Decent Work for Domestic Workers: Reflections on Recent Approaches to Tackle Informality." *Canadian Journal of Women and the Law* 2, 1: 185–212.

Jennifer N. Fish is a professor and chair of the Department of Women's Studies at Old Dominion University. Her scholarship on domestic labor over the past fifteen years includes *Domestic Workers of the World Unite! A Global Movement for Dignity and Human Rights,* and *Domestic Democracy: At Home in South Africa.* She is a member of the Women in Informal Employment: Globalizing and Organizing (WIEGO) policy institute and a consultant to the ILO.

Moriah Shumpert holds an MA with a certificate in Women's Studies from Old Dominion University. She has worked as an organizer and scholar-activist with the South African Domestic Service and Allied Workers Union and conducted research on the international movement of domestic workers. Her work is influenced by the legacy of feminist anti-racist and anti-capitalist scholar activism and her applied study of labor, migration and social movements.

CHAPTER 11

The Intimate Knows No Boundaries: Global Circuits of Domestic Worker Organizing

Eileen Boris and Megan Undén

It's Beginning...
Won: New York wins first ever Domestic Work Bill of Rights
Won: June 2011 International labor Organization Convention on Decent Work for Domestic Workers
Next: Help Win California ("Meet Today's Help," August 2011)[1]

Released to take advantage of the buzz surrounding the Hollywood movie *The Help,* a controversial story of African American domestics mobilized in 1963 against oppressive conditions in Jackson, Mississippi, the 2011 video *Meet Today's Help* offered a new genealogy of struggle. Through profiles of Caribbean, Latina, and Asian women, this production by the National Domestic Worker Alliance (NDWA) linked efforts to win various state-level Domestic Worker Bill of Rights (DWBOR) legislation with heroic campaigns against Jim Crow, whose structures of exclusion and

E. Boris (✉)
Department of Feminist Studies, University of California Santa Barbara, CA, USA

M. Undén
Department of Sociology, University of California Santa Barbara, CA, USA

© The Author(s) 2017   245
S. Michel, I. Peng (eds.), *Gender, Migration, and the Work of Care,*
DOI 10.1007/978-3-319-55086-2_11

underlying racism had, years earlier, placed household workers outside of New Deal labor standards and social benefits. It reflected the changing face of this workforce, which in many places in the United States consisted of immigrant women of color, who had taken jobs once dominated by African Americans. NDWA generated a feeling of momentum by announcing a progression from one state (New York) to an international accord (ILO Convention 189, Decent Work for Domestic Workers) in order to lobby for legislative passage in the next state (California).

The mention of the ILO in *Meet Today's Help* is only one example of the interaction between the local and the global in the making of social policy in the United States. The domestic workers are not the first women's movement to build momentum for federal legislation by mobilizing on state, national, and global levels. They have followed an often-deployed strategy of activists across social movements to use international conventions and protocols for national and local legislation (Keck and Sikkink 1998). In the early twentieth century, American suffragists connected to a worldwide women's rights movement in their efforts to win voting rights (Cornfield et al. 2001). Similarly, SisterSong, a woman of color reproductive justice organization with a federated organizational model much like the NDWA's, partook of the epistemic community forged at the 1994 UN Conference on Population and Development in Cairo to develop human justice claims for access to abortion, childbirth, and health services for women (Luna and Luker 2013). Trade union women long have sought solidarity abroad by coordinating organizing campaigns and sharing resources and tactics, from the short-lived International Federation of Working Women formed at the same time as the ILO in 1919 to the women's committees of the International Federation of Trade Unions (IFU) (Cobble 2014; Franzway and Fonow 2011).

To push for national reform, to obtain legitimacy as well as model provisions, government officials, worker organizations, and NGO allies have turned to ILO conventions and recommendations—the same instruments that these policy players have sometimes forged by translating their own local and national conditions into various conventions. They create circuits: officials, workers and NGOS develop models at the meso scale of policymaking, bring their experience and platforms to the macro global level and then take the international norm that they helped to generate back to their locales to advance their project, in this case to improve the labor of care and address the challenges of the care work economy, the realm of the micro. Consider this a deliberate process of policy diffusion passed through social movement channels that draws upon and then strengthens an epistemic community, here one consisting of advocates and experts on the conditions of domestic work as well as workers themselves (Haas 1992).

This circulatory process is not new. It occurred with the making of the ILO's Equal Remuneration Convention, 1951 (C100) and its accompanying Recommendation (R90), in which US Women's Bureau director Frieda Miller, who served as a key player in drafting these instruments, incorporated her country's World War II use of job evaluation and then offered the resulting ILO documents as a template to those attempting to pass equal pay bills in US states (Boris and Jensen 2013b). While Miller belonged to a transnational network of labor feminists, she did not represent a grassroots social movement. NGO involvement in shaping the ILO's Home Work Convention (C177) in 1996, led by HomeNet International and community-located home worker campaigners, particularly the Self-Employed Women's Association of Gujarat, India, paved the way for domestic worker participation at the ILO some fifteen years later. Indeed, the domestic workers learned from the experience of the industrial home workers, facilitated by the transfer of knowledge through WIEGO (Women in Informal Employment, Globalizing and Organizing), a Harvard University-based NGO that formed following the Home Work struggle at the ILO (Boris 2017).

Since passage of C189 and its accompanying Recommendation (R201)[2] in 2011, activists across the globe have conducted ratification campaigns as a means to improve national laws and create public awareness of domestic work as "the work that makes all other work possible." Embracing this refrain, their US counterparts attempt to incorporate ILO standards into their own localized efforts rather than engage in a futile effort to obtain national ratification of the convention. Instead, they use it to transform national and state laws, even without legal obligation to do. Their efforts to pass DWBORs at the state level in relation to C189 are the subject of this chapter.

We offer two interventions: First, we consider the involvement of the NDWA, their NGO allies, and US delegates to the International Labor Conference (ILC), the ILO assembly which actually passes measures, in the drafting of the ILO convention and accompanying recommendation. We fully recognize that these were not the only players in making the convention, but we are interested in the relationship between this protean involvement and subsequent deployment of C189. As Secretary of the International Domestic Worker Federation Elizabeth Tang reflected, "Although we know the US government is never interested in ratifying international standards... US activists are heavily supportive of our work" (Bapat 2014, 113).

Second, we highlight how domestic workers in the United States have subsequently utilized the ILO convention in their state campaigns. "We are using the ILO as a tool," an activist from Adhikaar, a Nepalese organizing group in New York, declared (Bapat 2014, 123). It is critical to note the differences between the international (ILO), nation (country) and state (sub-federal or subnational) legislatures as interactive spheres of political power where competing interests shape law, policy and enforcement. We distinguish between an international organization composed of nation-states and transnational networks that operate within its purview, either as worker federations, NGOs, or policy communities. Change often occurs at the international or macro scale through transnational networks. The macro emerges as a space for intervening not only in national (meso) lawmaking but also in the most intimate arena of social life–the (micro) realm of care. Involved is an interactive process: *social* recognition increases visibility, which then aids in expanding *legal* recognition. The actions of the NDWA, moreover, illuminate the possibilities and limits of grassroots empowerment to reconceptualize care work as worthy and, like all other employment, deserving decent standards of labor, along with dignity and social recognition. Its accomplishments suggest the power of using international organizations to support multi-scalar efforts at mobilization and capacity building for social movement interaction at different levels of political institutions and governments.

On a theoretical level, our case study challenges the separation between policy diffusion and social movement analysis. Previous scholarship has focused on the approaches of epistemic communities (Haas 1992) and policy assemblages (McCann and Ward 2013) to explain the global connections necessary for policy diffusion. However, most policy diffusion studies emphasize the ways that elites and government agents replicate policy through rational modeling based on success, informed decision-making, and elite competition for policy innovation (Marsh and Sharman 2009). In contrast, social movement theories explain how an organization with members lacking political standing can use legislative bodies, like the ILC or state assemblies, without reliance on political parties (Staggenborg 2011). But social movements also engage in policy diffusion insofar as they generate epistemic communities through sharing information, values, goals, and strategies (Meyer and Whittier 1994). Political mediation theory (Amenta et al. 2010) also locates policy diffusion and political success as coming from social movement organizations working with elites. Such recent studies challenge previous research which postulated that such hybrid formations of social movements and elites fail in winning policy (Heaney and Rojas 2014). Our case affirms the practice of global policy diffusion, helping to explain the context in which domestic workers lobbied state legislatures in the United States for bills of rights.

The interaction between NDWA activists and the US government and the AFL-CIO during the ILO convention-making process illustrates one way that policy diffusion and social movement action can come together. The linking of the national with the international level of policymaking represents another. This chapter also shows that domestic workers are able to effectively organize and use state legislatures to implement aspects of ILO standards despite the inaction of the US government on ratification or enactment of new national standards.

INTRODUCING THE NDWA

The NDWA is an organization with dedicated staff who draw upon social justice learning and academic communities as well as make strategy and policy in a democratic manner. The knowledge and experiences of the larger membership are central to the creation of demands, platforms, and strategies. Through leadership training, story circles and other forms of participatory education, staff have developed activists. During a period of rising hostility toward unions, rollback of labor standards and attacks on collective bargaining in the United States, this social movement organization has doubled in membership. Formed in Atlanta at the 2007 US Social Forum, a national gathering carrying on the progressive work of the World Social Forum, NDWA federated a number of existing local organizations concentrated in New York and California, most of which reached a specific ethnic and/or geographical community (Boris and Nadasen 2008). The most prominent were the New York City-based Domestic Worker United (DWU), itself a coalition that won the first DWBOR in New York State in 2010, and the San Francisco collective Mujeres Unidas y Activas, which has led efforts to pass various measures in California. As of April 2017, there were 63 local organizations affiliated with the national group (most of which are worker centers) and one chapter that it directly formed in Atlanta, spread across 21 states: California, New York, Massachusetts, Texas, Illinois, Georgia, New Mexico, Colorado, Virginia, Maryland, Washington, Tennessee, Connecticut, Hawaii, New Jersey, Alabama, Arizona, Minnesota, Florida, Wisconsin, and the District of Columbia.[3]

NDWA incorporates overlapping and interactive political spheres into its organizing structure: neighborhood and ethnic grassroots, state-level coalitions, national organizations and global partnerships. It exemplifies a model that has increasingly come to characterize social justice groups: a professional and paid staff at the national, state and international levels that works to empower and develop grassroots leadership and autonomous self-activity in order to serve a specific local constituency and collaborate with other organizations. Tactics include issuing reports, research and policy documents and deploying social media (Facebook, Twitter, e-mail) to frame domestic workers' rights as part of a larger movement of workers excluded from the labor law and sometimes other rights movements (Goldberg and Jackson 2011). It stitches together alliances with other organizations, such as the Paraprofessional Health Institute and the Service Employees International Union, committed to meeting the needs of those requiring care by improving the conditions of care workers, as well as advocacy groups like the National Employment Project, which assists with assembling legal briefs and testimony (Domestic Workers United 2006; Boris and Nadasen 2008).

Convinced that "domestic workers are the heart and soul of millions of families and the invisible infrastructure of this economy" though they are underpaid and devalued (NDWA 2014), the NDWA has facilitated passage of seven DWBORs between 2010 and 2016 and launched two spin-off organizations, We Belong Together and Caring Across the Generations, both of which display its integrative vision: improving domestic worker lives as workers requires family and women-friendly immigration reform and a cross-class care movement. The micro realm is political, so to speak, and justice at home is essential for a just society. Along with forming its only chapter in Atlanta, which has a high concentration of Black household workers, this immigrant-dominant organization has sought to recognize the significance of African Americans to the occupation following Black feminist critiques of *The Help* for obscuring Black agency. In fact, Alicia Garza, an NDWA organizer, was one of the founders of the anti-violence "Black Lives Matter" (NDWA 2015). NDWA has sought to become a truly multi-racial alliance that bases its practice on the feminist theory of intersectionality (Nadasen 2015, 2).

Thus, while the union shop is being eroded by "right-to-work" laws[4] and employers are reclassifying employees as independent contractors amid an explosive new "gig" economy dependent on digital hiring halls, care and household workers – who often are the same individuals – have built what are called "alt-labor" institutions –groups that lack formal collective bargaining recognition but fight for higher wages and better standards, like the organizations of day laborers, taxi drivers, crop pickers, restaurant servers, and domestic workers who formed the United (formerly Excluded) Workers Movement, along with the worker centers supporting them. As others despair over the relevancy of labor law, they are using the law to become visible and obtain long-overdue rights. In doing so, they bridge the intimate, local, state, national, and global.

MAKING CONVENTION 189

As a specialized agency connected to the League of Nations and subsequently the United Nations, the ILO addresses the world of work. It promulgates global labor standards, compiles statistics, conducts research, and provides technical assistance to governments and other organizations, such as how to establish a labor inspectorate or a cooperative. Its instruments have always had an aspirational quality, offering goals and models. Born out of the carnage of World War I, the ILO embodied the views of European social democrats who sought an alternative to the Russian Revolution that would protect workers but also level the playing field of international trade by instituting global labor standards (Rodgers et al. 2009).

Among international agencies, the ILO has a unique tripartite organization, one that calls for formal representation of workers, employers and governments on all committees. Its annual International Labor Conference (ILC), where various conventions and other instruments are voted on, consists of country delegations, each comprising two government, one employer and one worker member. The employer and worker delegates come from major (or "peak") associations, like the US Chamber of Commerce or the AFL-CIO. In addition, there are formal Employers and Workers groups. The International Labor Office, staffed by global civil servants, runs the day-to-day activities of the organization, overseen by the elected Director-General and his assistants. The ILC also elects a Governing Body, which has government, worker, and employer members. The Office can admit civil society organizations – such as international union federations, human rights groups, and international feminist NGOs – to specific meetings of the ILC as observers with limited participation rights (Rodgers et al. 2009).

The ILC regularly passes conventions – treaty-like instruments concerning various aspects of labor and working conditions that are aspirational only, since the ILO lacks enforcement powers. Ratification of a convention by an individual nation-state ("state-party") assumes, however, that its government will bring relevant laws and policies into conformity with the terms of the convention. The United States rarely ratifies ILO conventions. To date it has accepted only fourteen, two of which – "Abolition of Forced Labour," 1957 (C105) ratified in 1991 and "Worse Forms of Child Labour," 1999 (C182) ratified in 1999 – are among the eight most fundamental ones.[5] The United States justifies such behavior by pointing to its federal system, claiming that implementation of labor standards is a prerogative of the states rather than the national government. In fact, Congress has refused to ratify most United Nations-type treaties, including those of the ILO, for fear of ceding sovereignty to any extra-national body (Baldez 2014). In a real shift from the Bush years (2000–2008), President Barack Obama's Department of Labor played a constructive role in ILO deliberations, generally showing a willingness to see what labor standard rules could be changed to address transformations in the world of work. That his first Labor secretary was Hilda Solis, whose mother was a domestic worker, perhaps encouraged greater consideration of that sector.[6] As one of the world's superpowers, US delegates have had considerable say in the shape of ILO instruments, despite their country's refusal to ratify them (Rodgers et al. 2009).

In this era of neoliberal globalization, the Employers bloc has increasingly refused to agree to standards. In 1996, they abstained en masse from the home work convention in an attempt to block it. They fought over every word, sometimes trying to run out the clock in committee so that a measure would not make it to the ILC. Nonetheless, the ILO still seeks international consensus through its conventions and sometimes succeeds, as the domestic worker struggle there exemplifies.

THE ILO PROCESS

Reflecting on the US government's role in developing and passing C189, NDWA director Ai-jen Poo recounted that one of her members felt "a deep sense of pride to be from the United States, for the first time in her life" (Fish field notes 2011). The US delegation usually sided with the workers, even when other industrialized market economy countries (the IMEC [Industrialized Market Economies Countries] group) and the European Union objected to specific items, such as how to calculate working time for payment purposes (ILO 2010). During the two-year (2010–11) process of negotiating the convention, the United States pushed for the rights of migrant workers, health and safety coverage, and the regulation of private employment agencies. Indeed, when its representative first spoke in support of the Convention, those assembled broke into applause (Boris field notes 2010). After the Bush years, it was a turnabout to have the US government delegate defend worker rights. The United States was among those nations, including South Africa and Brazil, with vigorous domestic worker movements that most forcefully supported the convention. Latin American and Caribbean countries were generally in the forefront of domestic worker organizing; Chile and Jamaica, along with the United States and South Africa, included domestic workers as delegates at some point during the deliberations over domestic work (Fish 2017).

US support for a strong convention came through in responses by government and worker organizations to the questionnaire that the ILO Office sent out to member States. As compilations of the world's practices and opinions, these questionnaires served as a preliminary step toward assembling the components of a convention. (Following government, employer, and worker replies, the ILO Office drafts materials for ILC committees, where delegates review and amend versions of conventions and recommendations.) In a departure from previous answers to questionnaires involving low-waged or women workers, like the one on home work (a practice that US unions still wanted to prohibit in the early 1990s), the official US worker response, given by the AFL-CIO, reflected the positions of the *subjects* of the proposed convention (i.e., the domestic workers themselves) and not those of a labor bureaucracy removed from the sector under consideration. This shift occurred because the AFL-CIO jointly submitted its response with the NDWA, which had surveyed its own members and used their knowledge as the basis for the AFL-CIO/ NDWA comments (Undén and Boris 2015).

While US employer organizations ignored the ILO's request, typical of their behavior throughout the process, the worker organizations and the US government (under President Obama) were usually in agreement. However, US workers offered additional, more detailed comments to specific questions. While the government emphasized that standards for domestic workers should be the same as for all workers, the worker replies emphasized specific measures, such as sick leave, maternity leave, and other health and well-being provisions too often absent in the formal economy – which would remain unavailable under the "similar treatment" paradigm offered by the government. While the government wanted outcomes equivalent to those for workers in formal sectors of the economy, it felt that enforcement machinery and procedures might differ for domestic workers, given the location of this sector in private homes (ILO 2010). The AFL-CIO/NDWA called for enforcement that involved organizations of domestic workers and their union partners.

Existing legislation shaped government responses to the question of care work. The US government supported a definition of the term "domestic work" that included housekeeping, child care, and personal care. But it also reiterated the exclusion of casual babysitters, which the Department of Labor (DOL) had determined back in 1976. Its discussion of "home health care" was ambiguous, as the DOL was at that time reviewing the classification of these workers as "elder companions," who fell outside the minimum wage and overtime provisions of the labor law (Boris and Klein 2012). In contrast, the AFL-CIO/NDWA insisted that "part-time, full-time, live-in and live-out workers and workers who provide care for the elderly and sick are included" (ILO 2010, 38, 41).

The joint answers highlighted the perspective of the NDWA. To a question on the contents of the preamble, the AFL-CIO/NDWA replied that it

> should recall that the lack of protection of domestic workers is linked to the historical legacy of slavery, sexism, the undervaluing of work traditionally performed by women and the devaluation of reproductive labour. Domestic work is the work that makes all other work possible.... The intimate nature of the work, taking place inside someone's home, makes it easy to blur what constitutes appropriate employer-employee relations. (ILO 2010, 34)

To a definitional question, it insisted,

While the term "domestic" is still considered by some to have negative connotations, elsewhere it has been re-appropriated and redefined by the workers themselves. Both terms [household worker and domestic worker] should be included... in order to reflect workers' perspectives, experiences and preferences. (ILO 2010, 45)

The workers also specified on-the-job conditions that needed rectifying, like the expectation of continuous availability of live-in workers, sudden termination of employment with subsequent loss of housing, misuse of probation periods, deductions for uniforms, lack of privacy, barriers to cultural or religious expression, abusive employment and recruitment agencies, and in-kind payments. They declared, "The fact that the workplace is a private home means that violence against women is an occupational safety issue" (ILO 2010, 171; Blackett 2012).

As part of a transnational network, the NDWA was aware of the ILO deliberations early on and took advantage of the process to expand its capacity for legislative campaigning. It used the opportunity to strategically analyze existing laws and regulations. In October 2009 the NDWA met with DOL personnel to present specific regulatory reforms, and six months later, before another multi-unit meeting, summarized proposals in four areas where change could occur in keeping with the DOL's own plan for regulation of working conditions The NDWA underscored "the similarities between our regulatory proposals and what you have articulated in your response to the ILO Questionnaire." Proposed were employer responsibility to record hours worked; an "opt-in" system for in-kind payments or wage deductions for food; lodging with a private room with its own lock as a minimal standard; and the availability of "quality/ quantity" of food, including preferred items and facility to cook one's own meal; recognition of standby time as work and not sleeping time; and a domestic worker bureau at the agency as a way to implement draft ILO recommendations on complaint mechanisms, worker capacity building, and worker training.[7]

A new awareness at the AFL-CIO facilitated the access of domestic workers to the DOL and then to the ILO process. Since 2001, the nation's main labor federation had reversed its historic opposition to migrants and come out for immigrant rights. It recognized that the future of the labor movement depended on organizing the growing immigrant workforce (AFL-CIO 2011). Such an effort would require partnerships with alt-labor formations. Whereas in the early 1970s the AFL-CIO had dismissed domestic workers as unorganizable, it now embraced the NDWA – and later the International Domestic Worker Network (IDWN, which became the International Domestic Worker Federation or IDWF in 2013) — that formed out of the movement to gain an ILO convention (Boris and Fish 2014).

The ILO process strengthened ties on the national level. With the goal of enhancing the rights of workers outside of the labor law, the AFL-CIO and NDWA formally signed a partnership agreement in May 2011 to work together on organizing and collective action (AFL-CIO 2011). According to Poo, during the ILO process, "the US labor movement...played an important progressive role in the negotiations, providing a model of the ways in which trade union federations and independent workers movements can work together to improve the lives of working people" (Fish Field Notes, 2011). An example of such a partnership was the appointment of a domestic worker, Juana Flores, co-director of Mujeres Unidas y Activas in San Francisco, as part of the official US trade union delegation. In a joint letter with the NDWA, the AFL-CIO urged trade unions elsewhere "to take up this model of collaboration and partnership: to seat domestic worker representatives as voting delegates at the ILO and to build lasting partnerships to win ratification of the convention and labor standards for domestic workers...." (Fish 2011). In 2010, domestic workers spoke at the ILC and in committees as representatives of international trade union federations and members of observer NGOs. (These included Marcelina Bautista from Mexico and IDWN chair Myrtle Witbooi from South Africa.) The next year, a few national delegations had domestic workers cast votes, notably Shirley Pryce of Jamaica (Fish 2017).

Who sat at the table mattered at both the national and international levels of deliberations. As one US government advisor and substitute delegate from the DOL told ethnographer Jennifer Fish in 2011, "We listened to the NDWA. We listened to Human Rights Watch [a US based international NGO with ILO observer status which allied with domestic workers at the ILO], I mean obviously we have to assess their positions and how they might fit in.... They made some good suggestions, very helpful. We listened all the time to the organizations" (Fish 2011). This process had begun when Ana Avendaño, then assistant to the president of the AFL-CIO for immigrant worker issues, walked NDWA staff through the ILO process and facilitated access to the appropriate offices at the DOL. According to NDWA staff Jill Shenker, Carol Pier, then Associate

Deputy Undersecretary for International Affairs and previously a labor researcher at Human Rights Watch, "got it" (Undén and Boris 2015). Further facilitating NDWA influence in Geneva was the presence of Claire Hobden, a former staffer from DWU, the multiracial New York affiliate of the NDWA that would succeed in passing the first DWBOR in June 2010 after years of concerted campaigning. Hobden had joined the ILO as a specialist in the Bureau for Worker Activities in 2009 and served as notetaker during the deliberations of the committee charged to come up with a convention during the ILC meetings. With the passage of C189, she put together the Research Network on Domestic Worker Rights as a research support for the IDWN.[8]

Hobden kept Shenker informed of developments. Shenker had become the NDWA's international organizing director and focused on building first the IDWN and then the IDWF as its North American coordinator.[9] The ties between Shenker and Hobden were one factor generating informal access for the domestic worker network. This kind of parlaying of personal relations was hardly new; connections between women in the ILO Office and women delegates and NGOs, particularly those from the same nation or organization, often meant that strategies and provisions crossed institutional boundaries, shaping conventions and pronouncements in the process. Marguerite Thibert from France, the first staff person responsible for the employment of women and young workers in the Office, drew upon a wide circle of women correspondents during the interwar years; her successor, Mildred Fairchild from the United States, was in close communication with Frieda Miller, as was Elizabeth Johnson, also from the United States, with US government official Clara Beyer (Boris and Jensen 2013a; Thébaud 2011).

Flores underscored the symbiotic process between NDWA efforts and the ILO convention when she announced, "Our many years of hard work organizing among domestic workers in the United States enabled us to make a significant contribution to this process: The Domestic Worker Bill of Rights – passed by the New York State Legislature in 2010 and now being considered by the California legislature – was one of two pieces of legislation highlighted in the process of developing the convention" (CDWC 2011). The other was the law in Uruguay, which provides for tripartite wage boards; Uruguay became the first nation to ratify C189). During committee deliberations in 2011, the NDWA flashed a video that promoted the New York DWBOR as a model, along with its peer education approach, *The Ambassador's Program*, initiated to inform nannies, elder-care workers, and housekeepers of their new rights. The video announced that domestic workers were no longer forgotten; whether they were documented or not, they deserved the same rights as any other worker: a forty-hour work week, paid sick days and holidays, overtime pay, guaranteed day off, grievance procedures, and protection from discrimination, all included in New York's DWBOR. New York's breakthrough in 2010 had electrified delegates and observers at the ILO (Goldberg 2014).[10] Hobden had already offered the DWU example to the ILO to show "fair labour policies for domestic workers is possible." In 2010 she argued that domestic worker organizations must "make industry-specific demands, but [should] embed them in broad messaging that has the ability to hook the support of a broad section of allies" (Hobden 2010, 31).

In contrast, US employer delegates to the ILO were not receptive to NDWA. The kind of tripartism that had become institutionalized in Geneva was not typical of negotiations between labor and management in the United States; it only became a measure of last resort during certain collective bargaining impasses that led to calling in government mediators. In contrast to their conversations with the DOL prior to departing for Geneva, the NDWA failed to set up a bilateral meeting with US employer advisor John Kloosterman from the San Francisco anti-labor law firm Littler Mendelson. In response to his ignoring requests for consultation, forty people converged onto Kloosterman's offices, including Flores, Shenker, and Guillermina Castellanos from the California Coalition for Domestic Worker Rights and the Women's Collective of the Day Labor Program of La Raza Centro Legal – all of whom were among the US activists traveling to the ILO – and local domestic workers, joined by San Francisco Board of Supervisor David Campos and other elected officials. Campos already had urged Kloosterman to "reflect our city's commitment to safe, healthy, and secure jobs" by affirming "minimum and dignified legal standards," while noting that San Francisco was "sending both worker and employer representatives for the United States," specifically mentioning Flores (Campos to Kloosterman, May 19, 2010). After holding a press conference on the street, protesters moved into the building demanding a meeting and chanting in the lobby when rebuffed. This social-movement tactic of direct action got them nowhere, however. The unionized security guard lost his job over the disruption, raising the question of strategy in the context of ILO negotiations (Undén and Boris 2015).

Overall, employers from around the world played an obstructionist role in the drafting committee, trying to stop the process before any draft convention or recommendation could emerge through amendments and running out the clock. Particularly disrespectful was none other than John Kloosterman, an opponent of action who nonetheless served on the drafting subcommittee. Once at the ILO, he continued to refuse engagement with the other San Franciscans, claiming that the domestic worker observers were "stalking" him and threatening to procure a restraining order against Flores, Shenker and their team (Undén and Boris 2015).

Kloosterman condemned displays of emotion and social movement tactics of chanting and singing. These displays of affect, engaged in by the IDWN observers, certainly disrupted the staid culture of ILC proceedings (Boris and Fish 2014). Kloosterman led the complaints before the ILC, condemning "a lack of decorum... when the Employer Vice-chairperson is hissed at and booed following his comments" and when "there were ovations and sustained applause following some Government and Workers' comments. We also saw a variety of singing and dancing acts in our [committee meeting] room." He condemned pre-Conference "demonstrations aimed at specific Employers' delegates" and articulated what many employers charged–that the deliberation process "broke down" because "it became a four-part discussion" through the presence of NGOs (ILC 2010, 19/41).

The NGO Hand in Hand: The Domestic Employers Network, whose presence in Geneva in 2011 came about with funding from its partner organization, NDWA, stood apart from other employers. Recognizing that "our home is also a workplace," Elizabeth (Betsey) McGee, its representative, called for fair working conditions and mutual respect for the well-being of both employers and workers. The ILO convention could be "a North Star beckoning employers and policy makers to a more just world where care work would be devalued no more," she testified at an NGO-sponsored forum.[11]

INTO THE STATES

After adoption of C189, the question became how to deploy it in the United States. Given the political forces in Washington and local implementation of labor standards, a national ratification campaign was far less likely to yield results than state-level efforts, which also were more likely to mobilize and organize the workforce. NDWA was already campaigning for a DWBOR in California, an effort it hoped would be the first of many state initiatives. Weeks after the ILO victory, Shenker sent a memo to the California Senate Labor Committee on the relevance of C189 to consideration of Assembly Bill (AB) 889, the measure that would establish a state DWBOR. Prefacing her analysis with the authority of the US DOL's advocacy "for a robust ILO Convention," she included URLs for the text of the convention and accompanying recommendation and the US government's opening statement at the ILO, as well as articles addressing components of the California measure. The US statement highlighted Article 10 (1) of the convention on overtime pay, which called for 24 hours of rest per week, while providing greater protection than the California (and general US) reliance on overtime measures to deter "excessive hours." Shenker compared the California bill with ILO dictates on meal and rest breaks, reporting hours of pay, sleep time, the right to cook one's own food, paid vacation days and worker's compensation, to show that California "has the opportunity to provide domestic workers some of the internationally agreed upon minimum standards...and fulfill the call from the Convention to implement the provisions of the convention...."[12] Though the United States was unlikely to ratify, ILO conventions had meaning; Shenker could still invoke the convention to good effect in the states.

By 2011, California was in the midst of a second try to pass a DWBOR. In 2006, then-governor Arnold Schwarzenegger vetoed an initial attempt on the grounds of "overtime costs and the financial burdens and expected additional labor law litigation." Four years later, with this anti-labor Republican still in office, the legislature passed a policy directive finding "that domestic workers are entitled to industry-specific protections and labor standards that eliminate discriminatory provisions in the labor laws and guarantee domestic workers basic workplace rights to ensure that domestic workers are treated with the respect and dignity they so richly deserve." This nonbinding measure recognized the work of the California Domestic Worker Coalition, NDWA, and the IDWN as organizations advancing the rights and dignity of domestic workers at the state, national and international levels of policy making. The "Concurrent Resolution" was specifically modeled on the New York DWBOR (Goldberg 2015). Shenker described the ILO Convention as a "dramatic tool to demonstrate that domestic work is work and should be included under labor protections and social security" to mobilize workers to secure DWBOR as a strategy for empowerment over working conditions and lives (Undén and Boris 2015).

A year later, following the ILO victory, the California coalition, made up of NDWA affiliates and ethnicity-based worker centers, again succeeded with the legislature. But Democratic governor Edmund (Jerry) Brown, Jr. vetoed the bill on fiscal grounds as well as concerns about privacy rights as a barrier to enforcement. He particularly noted a "drafting error" that included In-Home Supportive Service (IHSS) workers, home aides and attendants paid out of state money, which he claimed would cost the state an additional $200 million a year, breaking the budget. The next year, with the IHSS workers specifically excluded and his tax-raising referendum passed by the voters, Brown signed a much watered-down DWBOR, AB 241, which lacked the provisions for food, rest breaks, vacations, and other measures that Shenker had highlighted from the ILO standards. However, it covered many domestic workers still excluded under other state overtime provisions: nannies and personal care attendants who work more than a nine-hour day, providing that such care makes up 80 percent or more of their duties for workweeks of more than 45 hours. Violation of this standard is a misdemeanor, reportable to the California Division of Labor Standards Enforcement. The bill also mandated an advisory committee to study the impact of the law on personal care attendants and their employers (Boris, Jokela and Undén 2015).

But the state continued to follow the exemptions of home care workers established in the 1970s, and the governor refused to release funds that the legislature directed for their overtime pending resolution of legal challenges. Pushing back, the United Domestic Workers of America/American Federation of State, County and Municipal Employees (UDWA/AFSCME) joined with the California Domestic Worker Coalition to lobby for these funds. At their mock trial against the State of California in March 2015, four hundred home care and household workers applauded a surprise visit of leaders from the IDWF, who were on the way to DC to participate in a union training conducted by the AFL-CIO. In such ways, the circuits of domestic worker organizing fed off each other (Boris 2015).

As of fall 2016, seven states had passed DWBORs: New York (2010); Hawaii (2013); California (2013, 2016); Massachusetts (2014); Connecticut (2015) Oregon (2015); and Illinois (2016) (Goldberg 2015; NDWA 2016a; NDWA 2016b). New York provided the model legislation for the states that followed, but these measures vary considerably (Boris, Jokela, and Undén 2015). These states were relatively easy targets since they lacked anti-union right-to-work laws and had legislatures with Democratic majorities and, except for Illinois, governors (NWDA 2016a). While the home care franchise industry sued to hold up implementation of the DOL's 2013 administrative rule to include home aides and personal attendants under federal overtime provisions, it lost on appeal and the Supreme Court refused to consider the case, upholding the rule. The states had to fully abide by the new provisions on home care beginning in June 2016. On the basis of such victories, the IDWF highlighted the success of the NDWA in changing laws, looking at this national example to show how reform can be made (IDWF 2016, 11).

All the DWBORs fall short of the many components of C189 and its accompanying R201 (NELP 2015). Illinois extended existing minimum wage, rest and human rights acts to household workers (NDWA 2016a). Massachusetts passed the most expansive DWBOR, with provisions closest to the ILO, including rights that are similar to those found in collective bargaining agreements that protect workers against exploitation, abuse, and numerous forms of discrimination (race, gender, sexuality, disability, age). This act forbids employers to confiscate passports and other state documents, protects live-in workers from employers' overcharging for room and board and deductions for unwanted services, and requires thirty-day notice, or thirty days of alternative housing or two weeks of severance pay for live-in workers let go without cause. Employers must provide a written contract in the preferred language of the worker; legal rights cover all those working at least sixteen hours a week, though not necessarily with the same employer. The DWBOR offers multiple paths for enforcement, including access to the Massachusetts Commission against Discrimination to fight harassment and discrimination. In campaigning for the law, Massachusetts activists in "Matahari: Eye of the Day," the Dominican Development Center, and the Brazilian Women's Group built upon previous legislation from the 1970s that placed private household workers under its wage and hour, worker compensation, and collective bargaining laws that local activist Melena Case and other members of the African American Women's Service Club of Boston had won. Since their victory in 2014, activists have extended their coalition to include the Boston Center for Independent Living and the New England Jewish Labor Committee (NDWA 2015b).

Connecticut has the weakest protections, since its June 2015 law covers only private households with three or more employees. NDWA sent New York staff and Massachusetts leaders, including Natalicia Tracy from the statewide Brazilian Immigrant Center, to Connecticut for this fight. Its coalition partners, including SEIU and other unions, immigrant rights organizations, legal assistance, church groups, and ethnic associations, led by the Bridgeport Brazilian Immigrant Center, won only a limited measure that covered few workers. But the legislature authorized a task force report to put the state on the path toward considering a broader DWBOR (NDWA 2015a).

In addition to the working conditions of domestic workers, C189 and R201 highlight human trafficking concerns and the exploitation of migrants (Ole 2014). The Massachusetts law clarifies the existing Massachusetts Anti-Trafficking law to cover domestic workers. DWBORs in states with significant immigrant populations, like New York, refer to the vulnerability of this workforce. The NDWA cited the ILO as an authority to argue in its 2015 report, "Beyond Survival: Organizing to End Human Trafficking of Domestic Workers," that "forced migration, spurred by economic necessity, social and cultural discrimination and gender-based violence, puts people at risk for trafficking and exploitation" (NDWA and IPS 2015, 6). In Oregon, an anti-trafficking conference spurred Corvallis state senator Sara Gelser (D) to introduce what became the state's DWBOR in June 2015. While New York, California, Massachusetts, and Illinois represent social movement initiations of legislation, with policy diffusion through the NDWA network, Oregon might be considered a hybrid case of political mediation insofar as political elites pushed a bill, but immigrant rights groups and unions also worked for the measure (Amenta et al. 2010). Hawaii, in contrast, developed its law from the top down, as part of its governor's agenda, without NDWA support–a more traditional form of policy diffusion.

C189 addressed the exclusion of categories of workers from both labor laws and social security (ILO 2010). Except for Massachusetts, the existing DWBORs leave operative the exclusion of domestic workers from collective bargaining, though some laws called for further study (e.g., New York DOL 2010). Personal care attendants, especially those who fall under other state regulations, and workers who are relatives or family members, remain outside all the DWBORs (see Cranford and Chun, this volume). Domestic workers continue to lack equitable social security provisions beyond limited access to state-level workers' compensation and unemployment benefits. But in California, they can take advantage of the state's 2015 law granting paid sick days, which extends to all workers (Goldberg 2015).

CONCLUSION

A vigorous movement over the last decade has produced various DWBORs in an effort to incorporate workers not covered by US labor standards into such regimes. But enforcement remains vexed because it depends on highly vulnerable low-waged workers themselves taking action by initiating complaints without guarantees of speedy redress and with the omnipresent risk of retaliation, unemployment and perhaps deportation. Enforcement mechanisms reflect structures of antagonism for a sector that involves trust and personal contact between nannies, attendants, cleaners, and those they work for. The US movement *preceded* the campaign for C189, and it participated in a cycle whereby local and national groups pushed for the convention which, when finally adopted, served as leverage for those very same local and national groups. So a trajectory moved from the micro and meso to the macro, and then returned to the meso and micro.

Simultaneously, social movement actors travelled between locales within the United States and globally to share models, offer solidarity and provide material and technical support. The push for C189 deepened an emerging transnational network of NGOs, regional and local domestic worker organizations, and trade unions, both national and international (see Fish and Shumpert, this volume). An international labor federation for a woman-dominated occupation run by women is now challenging the devaluation of domestic work by demanding treatment like any other form of labor, thereby interrogating the most intimate and micro-scaled interactions in the struggle for global justice.

Invoking C189, organized domestic workers have expanded US labor laws in spite of several institutional and cultural impediments, including the lack of collective bargaining rights. DWBORs have made the strongest gains in states that are less hostile to unionization. But these laws are still limited, and enforcing labor standards in private homes is nearly impossible. Thus domestic worker organizations seek to educate the general public, including employers, to do the right thing because it is in their interest to have safe and clean homes and good care for their loved ones. Organized domestic workers seek to inform others employed in this sector of their rights, and they support those who speak out or file complaints. Forging circuits of organizing, domestic workers speak up for migrant workers, inscribing the global in the local and both in the national, teaching us that the intimate knows no boundaries.

This chapter affirms that social movement organizations do matter at different political levels – the micro, meso and macro – when it comes to policy diffusion for domestic workers. Domestic workers are able to effectively use state legislatures as fulcrums for public policy incorporating aspects of the ILO convention, even if the United States will not ratify C189 or pass comparable federal legislation. They reveal an interactive connection between local and national social movements and their organizations and global social movements.

Acknowledgements Research for this chapter was made possible through a grant from the UCLA Institute for Research on Labor and Employment.

NOTES

1. https://www.youtube.com/watch?v=-RyEGeZmAn8.
2. http://www.ilo.org/dyn/normlex/en/f?p=NORMLEXPUB:12100:0::
   NO:12100:P12100_INSTRUMENT_ID:2551460:NO and http://www.
   ilo.org/dyn/normlex/en/f?p=NORMLEXPUB:12100:0::NO:12100:
   P12100_INSTRUMENT_ID:2551502:NO.
3. http://www.domesticworkers.org/members, accessed 11/1/16.
4. These prohibit unions from collecting agency fees from non-members who they represented.
5. "Ratifications for the United States," NORMLEX, at http://www.ilo.org/
   dyn/normlex/en/f?p=NORMLEXPUB:11200:0::NO::P11200_
   COUNTRY_ID:102871.
6. These remarks are based on our observation of the Department of Labor during the Obama years.
7. Memo to Pier, 3/13/2010, in authors' possession.
8. Hobden biography at http://www.snis.ch/content/role-fix-740.
9. Shenker biography at http://www.domesticworkers.org/staff/jill-shenker.
10. https://www.youtube.com/watch?v=l0LvvMPK8yA&feature=youtu.be.
11. https://www.youtube.com/watch?v=szJ9N0TzdAg.
12. Shenker to California Senate Labor Committee 7/5/11, in authors' possession.

REFERENCES

AFL. 2011. AFL-CIO, National Domestic Workers' Alliance, National Guestworkers' Alliance Announce Partnership Agreements. Press Release. http://www.aflcio.org/Press-Room/Press-Releases/AFL-CIO-National-Domestic-Workers-Alliance-Nati.

Amenta, Edwin et al. 2010. "The Political Consequences of Social Movements." *Annual Review of Sociology* 36: 287–307.

Bapat, Shelia. 2014. *Part of the Family? Nannies, Housekeepers, Caregivers and the Battle for Domestic Workers' Rights.* Brooklyn: Ig Publishing.

Baldez, Lisa. 2014. *Defying Convention: US Resistance to the UN Treaty on Women's Rights.* New York: Cambridge University Press.

Blackett, Adelle. 2012. "The Decent Work for Domestic Workers Convention and Recommendation, 2011." *American Journal of International Law* 106: 788–794.

Boris, Eileen. 2015. Field notes, Sacramento, California. March 19.

Boris, Eileen. 2017. "SEWA's Feminism." In *Women's Activism and 'Second Wave' Feminism: Transnational Histories*, edited by Barbara Molony and Jennifer Nelson, 79–98. New York: Bloomsbury.

Boris, Eileen and Jennifer Fish. 2014. "'Slaves No More': Making Global Labor Standards for Domestic Workers." *Feminist Studies* 40: 411–443.

Boris, Eileen and Jill Jensen. 2013a. "The ILO: Women's Networks and the Making of the Woman Worker." In *Women and Social Movements International*, edited by Kathryn Kish Sklar and Thomas Dublin: http://wasi.alexanderstreet.com/help/view/the_ilo_womens_networks_and_the_making_of_the_women_worker.

Boris, Eileen and Jill Jensen. 2013b. "The Transnational Forging of Equal Pay." Unpublished paper.

Boris, Eileen, Merita Jokela, and Megan Undén. 2015. "Enforcement Strategies for Empowerment: Models for the California Domestic Worker Bill of Rights." Research and Policy Brief. UCLA-Institute for Research on Labor and Employment, No. 30, May.

Boris, Eileen and Jennifer Klein. 2012. *Caring for America: Home Health Workers in the Shadow of the Welfare State.* New York: Oxford University Press.

Boris, Eileen and Premilla Nadasen. 2008. "Domestic Workers Organize!" *Working USA* 11: 413–437.

Cobble, Dorothy Sue. 2014. "A 'Higher Standard of Life' for the World: U.S. Labor Women's Reform Internationalism and the Legacies of 1919." *Journal of American History* 100: 1059–1063.

Cornfield, Daniel B., Karen E. Campbell and Holly J. McCammon. 2001. *Working in Restructured Workplaces: Challenges and New Directions in the Sociology of Work.* Thousand Oaks, CA: Sage Publications.

Domestic Workers United and Data Center. 2006. *Home is Where the Work Is: Inside New York's Domestic Worker Industry:* http://www.datacenter.org/home-is-where-the-work-is/.

Fish, Jennifer. 2017. *Domestic Workers of the World Unite! A Global Movement for Dignity and Human Rights.* New York: New York University Press.

Fish, Jennifer. 2011. Field Notes, ILO, Geneva.

Franzway, Suzanne and Mary Margaret Fonow. 2011. *Making Feminist Politics: Transnational Alliance Between Women and Labor.* Urbana: University of Illinois Press.

Goldberg, Harmony. 2014. "Our Day Has Finally Come: Domestic Worker Organizing in New York City." *CUNY Academic Works.* http://academic works.cuny.edu/gi_etds/422

Goldberg, Harmony. 2015. "Domestic Worker Organizing in the United States: Reports from the Field." *ILWCH* No.88 (Fall): 150–55.

Goldberg, Harmony and Randy Jackson. 2011. "The Excluded Workers Congress: Reimagining the Right to Organize." *New Labor Forum* 20, 3: 54–59.

Haas, Peter M. 1992. "Introduction: Epistemic Communities and International Policy Coordination." *International Organization* 46, 1: 1–35.

Heaney, Michael T. and Fabio Rojas. 2014. "Hybrid Activism: Social Movement Mobilization in a Multimovement Environment." *American Journal of Sociology* 119: 1047–1103.

Hodben, Claire. 2010. *Winning Fair Labour Standards for Domestic Workers: Lessons Learned from the Campaign for a Domestic Worker Bill of Rights in New York State.* Geneva: ILO.

ILO. 2010. *Decent Work for Domestics.* Report IV (2) Geneva: ILO.

ILC. 2010. *Provisional Record,* 99th Session. Geneva: ILO.

IDWF. 2016. *Annual Report 2015.* http://www.idwfed.org/en/resources/idwf-annual-report-2015-build-organise-organise.

Keck, Margaret E. and Kathryn Sikkink. 1998. *Activists Beyond Borders: Advocacy Networks in International Politics.* Ithaca: Cornell University Press.

Luna, Zakiya and Kristen Luker. 2013. "Reproductive Justice." *Annual Review of Law and Social Science* 9: 327–352.

Marsh, David and J.C. Sharman. 2009. "Policy Diffusion and Policy Transfer." *Policy Studies* 30, 3: 269–288.

McCann, Eugene and Kevin Ward. 2013. "A Multi-Disciplinary Approach to Policy Transfer Research: Geographies, Assemblages, Mobilities and Mutations." *Policy Studies* 34, 1: 2–18.

Meyer, David S. and Nancy Whittier. 1994. "Social Movement Spillover." *Social Problems* 4: 277–298.

Nadasen, Premilla. 2015. *Household Workers Unite! The Untold Story of African American Women Who Built a Movement.* Boston: Beacon Press.

NDWA. 2014. National Assembly program. http://www.domesticworkers.org/assembly2014.

NDWA. 2015. "We Dream in Black" http://www.domesticworkers.org/we-dream-in-black.

NDWA. 2015a. Connecticut Bill of Rights. http://www.domesticworkers.org/connecticut-bill-of-rights.

NDWA. 2015b. Massachusetts: http://www.domesticworkers.org/mass-bill-of-rights.

NDWA. 2016a. Illinois Bill of Rights. http://www.domesticworkers.org/illinois-bill-of-rights

————. 2016b. California Bill of Rights. https://www.domesticworkers.org/ca-bill-of-rights.

NDWA and Institute for Policy Studies (IPS). 2015. *Beyond Survival: Organizing to End Human Trafficking of Domestic Workers.* 2015. http://www.domestic workers.org/reports-analysis.

New York Department of Labor. 2010. *Feasibility of Collective Bargaining for Domestic Workers:* 1-29. https://labor.ny.gov/legal/domestic-workers-bill-of-rights.shtm.

Ole, Martin. 2014. "The ILO's Domestic Workers Convention and Recommendation: A Window of Opportunity for Social Justice." *International Labour Review* 153, 1: 143–172.

Rodgers, Gerry et al. 2009. *The ILO and the Quest for Social Justice, 1919-2009.* Ithaca: Cornell University Press.

Staggenborg, Suzanne. 2011. *Social Movements.* New York: Oxford University Press.

Thébaud, Françoise. 2011. "Réseaux réformateurs et politiques du travail fémi-nine: L'OIT au prisme de la carriére et des engagements de Maurguerite Thibert." In *L'Organisation international du travail: Origine-Développment-Avenir,* edited by Isabelle Lespinet-Moret and Vincent Viet, 27–37. Rennes: University of Rennes Press.

Undén, Meg and Eileen Boris. 2015. Interview Notes with Jill Shenker and Claire Hobden. September 17.

Eileen Boris, Hull Professor of Feminist Studies, University of California, Santa Barbara, is the author, with Jennifer Klein, of *Caring for America: Home Health Workers in the Shadow of the Welfare State* and co-editor with Dorothea Hoehtker and Susan Zimmermann of *Women's ILO: Transnational Networks, Global Labor Standards, and Gender Equity,* forthcoming from Brill. Her current project looks at the construction of the woman worker through global labor standards, using the ILO as her archive.

Megan Undén is a PhD student at the University of California, Santa Barbara in the Department of Sociology with an emphasis in Feminist Studies. Undén's research interests focus on social movements, political sociology, labor, gender, inequalities, intersectionality, and social theory. Her MA and dissertation analyze the successes and mobilization strategies of domestic and care workers in the United States.

CHAPTER 12

Out of Focus: Migrant Women Caregivers as Seen by the ILO and the OECD

Rianne Mahon and Sonya Michel

The rights and needs of migrant women care workers and their families are inherently transnational issues, produced by the departure of women from their home countries and families and their relocation in receiving countries, where they find work as nannies and caregivers for the elderly and persons with disabilities. While women's absence from their families may give rise to one set of problems, their employment in the low-paid, generally unregulated care sector generates another, and both sets may be compounded when women are undocumented migrants. As many other chapters in this book document, states at both ends of the global care chain fail to adequately address these complex issues. Thus, one might look to international organizations to play a role. How and to what extent are they being addressed by the international organizations that together constitute webs of transnational governance?

In this chapter, we focus on two such organizations, the International Labour Organization (ILO) and the Organization for Economic Cooperation and Development (OECD). The ILO, one of the oldest

R. Mahon
Department of Political Science, Wilfrid Laurier University, Canada

S. Michel (✉)
Department of History, University of Maryland, USA

© The Author(s) 2017
S. Michel, I. Peng (eds.), *Gender, Migration, and the Work of Care*,
DOI 10.1007/978-3-319-55086-2_12

members of the UN system, has a somewhat erratic record of concern over the rights of women workers and of migrant workers in general, largely because it has, until quite recently, focused primarily on formal employment, while both migrants and women have been more likely to find work in informal (especially service) sectors. Nevertheless, several of the ILO's conventions have addressed migrant workers' rights – C97 on migration for employment (1949) and C143 regarding the promotion of equal opportunities and treatment of migrant workers (1975) – while a more recent one (C189, 2011) focuses on the right of domestic workers, many of whom are migrant women, to decent work. The OECD, long known as the "rich (capitalist) countries' club" but with its reach now extending to the "emerging" economies of the Global South, has a remit embracing all the relevant fields – migration, development, social policy and gender. Raghuram (2012, 158) notes that the ILO and the OECD are among the few international organizations involved in "policy initiatives on how best to stretch social policy concerning care to take account of the globality of care." We argue, however, that while both organizations have touched on various issues raised by the emergence of global care chains (see, for example, Chapters 5 and 8), neither has addressed them in a comprehensive manner. As a result, neither has proposed multilateral policies that are capable of fully addressing the inequalities to which the global care chains contribute, nor, with their limited powers (both organizations are constituted as *advisory* bodies only), have they been able to implement even the partial measures they have produced.

LOCATING THE ILO AND THE OECD IN THE OVERLAPPING WEBS OF TRANSNATIONAL GOVERNANCE

The issues raised by the emergence of global care chains cut across several fields of transnational governance: migration; development; and social policy (specifically work-family issues). In none of these fields is there a focal institution equivalent to, say, the World Trade Organization governing trade negotiations or the International Monetary Fund (IMF) or Global Financial Board, with their role in overseeing the terms of capital mobility. The ILO and the OECD occupy important positions within the web of networks that constitute each field, but the governance instruments at their disposal – unlike those of the IMF–are largely of the "soft" variety. Even the ILO, which has recourse to conventions that, once ratified, theoretically impose obligations on states, depends on member countries' willingness to ratify them and then bring their own laws into conformity, while the OECD relies on its capacities for surveillance and "meditation" (Mahon and McBride 2008) to coordinate the policies and practices of its member countries. With its tripartite structure, which brings together representatives of governments, employers and workers, the ILO is somewhat permeable by grassroots and "outside-the-box" influences (see Fish and Shumpert, this volume).

With regard to the fields of transnational governance relevant to female migrant care workers, the two organizations have a mixed record. Gender equality, which potentially cuts across all three fields, has been nominally integrated into the mandates of the ILO and the OECD in recent years, but with minimal effect. The ILO has a long, if not untroubled, history of engagement with gender equality (Boris 2014), while the OECD began to address gender issues in the mid-1970s (Mahon 2015). With regard to migration, "[t]here is no global coordination mechanism or commonly agreed framework to guide policy making on migration, meaning the international regulatory framework to protect migrants' rights is fragmented, poorly developed and distinctly marginalised within the UN system" (Jolly and Reeves 2005, 31). The UN organizations built on the interwar years' framework – the ILO and the United Nations High Commission for Refugees – constitute the center of the "thin layer" of multilateral governance of migration. Yet, as Kunz et al. (2011, 8) suggest, "the ILO has issued manifold conventions on labour and migrant rights, yet they have relatively low levels of legal precision and obligation...and are generally undersubscribed by UN member states, in particular migration destination countries."

The ILO has at times collaborated with the International Organization for Migration (IOM), an intergovernmental organization based in Geneva that is not part of the UN system. With its small staff and limited permanent budget, the IOM "has no explicit normative mandate and very little permanent infrastructure. It simply provides services through a network of temporary projects" (Betts 2011, 34) In 2006, in an effort to coordinate more effectively with the various UN agencies concerned with migration, the IOM initiated the Global Migration Group, with the World Bank and the ILO among its original members; in 2014, UN Women joined, going on to chair the 2016 session. The OECD also deals with migration, having inherited the issue from its predecessor, the Organisation for European Economic Cooperation. By its fiftieth anniversary, the OECD could boast that it "remains a privileged observer of migratory movements and policies and a platform for exchange on what works and what does not..." (OECD 2011a, 34). Nevertheless, as neither one of its founders nor a UN agency, it does not belong to the Global Migration Group. Such inclusions and exclusions perpetuate the fragmentation of the field of migration policy.

Throughout the post-World War II period and into the present, the ILO has been active in the field of development, and the OECD, which brought together the countries that accounted for the lion's share of development assistance, also counted as one of the core institutions in this field (Gore 2013). The fields of development and migration began to intersect in the 1990s in response to growing international awareness that migrants were increasingly coming from the Global South. Development assistance was initially understood as a means to stem the flow of migrants (OECD 2011a,11), but a decade later, the UN General Assembly High Level Dialogue on Migration and Development (2006) recognized migration as an important means for promoting development (the so-called "migration-development nexus"). This in turn led to the establishment of the annual Global Forum on Migration and Development. Although states constitute the Forum's core membership, the OECD and the ILO enjoy observer status.

If anything, the field of global social governance is even more fragmented than that of migration (Deacon 2007), though both the ILO and the OECD participate actively in it. From the outset, the ILO included "social protection" as part of its remit but, with the exception of its conventions on maternity leave,[1] until recently "care" did not figure in its concept of social protection. The OECD entered the social policy field in the 1970s, and its Working Party on the Role of Women in the Economy (1974–1999) was the first to deal with issues of care (Mahon 2015)). Upon its demise, the issue was picked up by the Social Policy Division.

The implications of the rise in women's migration and their employment in care work have received scant attention in these international venues. Migrant care work was discussed at the 2011 Forum meetings on "Domestic Care Work at the Interface of Migration and Development," leading to the creation of a checklist that drew on the UN Convention for the Elimination of All Kinds of Discrimination against Women (CEDAW) and the ILO's Convention on Decent Work for Domestic Workers (C189).[2] The 2016–2017 issue of UN Women's flagship publication, *Progress of the World's Women*, will include a chapter on "Human Mobility, Gender and Family Relations." One of the targets of the eighth of the UN's Sustainable Development Goals, announced in 2015, is to protect the labor rights of all workers, including migrant workers and in particular women migrants.

Although the ILO and the OECD were, and remain, well positioned within each of the fields that potentially have an impact on the migrant care workers, their ability and *willingness* to make comprehensive policy has been limited. Moreover, the two organizations approach the issue to different degrees and with somewhat different orientations. The ILO, with its standard-setting role, explicitly embraces a rights-based approach, whereas the OECD formally eschews a "normative" position, even though its work in identifying best practices has a normative function. Although both have embraced the gender equality norm, each translates this according to the way its organizational and cognitive framework is configured. For this reason, it is important to probe the way each organization "sees" its environment(s), as Broome and Seabrooke (2012) have argued.

The ILO

Despite its position as an important actor within the various fields that affect female migrant care workers and the global care chains in which they constitute critical links, the ILO has, until quite recently, paid only intermittent attention to these workers. This section traces how the ILO, acting alone and in concert with some of its UN partners, has grappled with various facets of their situation, focusing on how migration intersects with two of the ILO's main issue areas: employment and working conditions, and work-family balance. It shows that the ILO's treatment of these issues remains siloized, bringing them together only in the past few years and then primarily at the margins of the organization's more general discussions of women in the labor force.

Women as Worker Migrants

In 1939, the ILO became the first international organization to adopt a convention on migration. Revised in 1949 as C97, Migration for Employment, it sought to regularize immigration laws and establish certain rights for migrants and their families, including access to education, health and welfare benefits and protections regarding wages, hours and union membership. The convention was nearly silent on gender. Although it did stipulate that any nation's protective laws regarding women's work should be extended to immigrants, it imagined the migrant worker as male, with dependent family members who had either travelled with him or were awaiting remittances at home. In 1975 the ILO adopted C143

Concerning Migration in Abusive Conditions and the Promotion of Equal Opportunities and Treatment of Migrant Workers, which focused on the informal economy and the "irregular" migrants it tended to attract. Again, women did not receive special attention, though they already made up a sizeable proportion of informal migrant workers.

In terms of employment rights, migrant women caregivers depend in the first instance on the recognition of domestic work *as work*. It was only in 2002 that one of the reports to the International Labour Conference raised the subject of "decent work in the informal economy" (as the sixth item on the agenda). Later that year, the ILO co-authored an important report with WIEGO (Women in Informal Employment: Globalizing and Organizing), *Women and Men in the Informal Economy: A Statistical Picture*, which broke new ground at the ILO and opened the way for the preparatory work for C189, which was finally adopted in 2011, culminating a decades-long struggle for recognition. As Boris and Fish (2014, 415–16) note,

> a convention for domestic workers gained traction because of organizing among national groups and their ability...to form a transnational movement, facilitated by human rights and feminist NGOs and international labor federations. The resulting coalition drew on the ILO's ideological emphases on "fair globalization" and "decent work" to place domestic work on the ILC agenda in 2010. The commitment of key players within the ILO...[also] proved vital to advancing the domestic workers convention.

This account (ibid., 427) highlights the supportive role played by the ILO executive director Juan Somavía (1999–2012) and Manuela Tomei, the director of the Conditions of Work and Employment division, who translated domestic workers' demand for rights into ILO discourse (see also Fish and Shumpert, this volume). Yet the convention has very little to say about migrant workers per se, beyond stipulating in the Preamble that:

> ...domestic work continues to be undervalued and invisible and is mainly carried out by women and girls, *many of whom are migrants* or members of disadvantaged communities and who are particularly vulnerable to discrimination in respect of conditions of employment and of work, and to other abuses of human rights. [ILO Convention 189, 2011; emphasis added. See also ILO R201 (2011).]

The text also referred to other international instruments, such as the International Convention on the Protection of the Rights of All Migrant Workers and Members of Their Families, which pertain to migrant domestic workers. While C189 represented an important symbolic victory, it has to date been ratified by only twenty-four member states[3] and is thus of limited help to the vast majority of migrant care workers. Nonetheless, as Fish and Shumpert (this volume) point out, the very process of introducing and passing the convention did much to strengthen the international domestic workers movement. And, it appears, the convention can have an impact even in countries where it has not been ratified. Thus, in an annex to the Turkey report, a domestic worker recounted that, as a member of the local Domestic Workers Solidarity Union, she had learned from C189 how to draw up a contract that would define her hours, duties, and other aspects of her working conditions (Erdoğdu and Toksöz 2013, 49). Boris and Undén (this volume) also note that although the United States has yet to ratify it, American domestic workers' organizations have used the convention in their state-level campaigns for domestic workers' bills of rights.

Despite the lack of specificity in C189, the ILO has continued to monitor the situation of migrant domestic workers. Thus a 2013 report on care workers in Turkey commissioned by its Conditions of Work and Employment Program described the poor working conditions they faced, cataloging such practices as withholding migrants' passports, which makes them dependent on employers and recruitment agencies; failure to provide workers with formal contracts or clearly defined working hours and duties; low pay and lack of sick pay, paid vacations, health care and social security; lack of concern for workers' health and safety; and general mistreatment, ranging from "despising behavior and attitude" to "harassment and rape beyond swearing and beating" (Erdoğdu and Toksöz 2013, 4). The report also noted that because of domestic workers' isolation and wide dispersal in private homes, unions face great difficulty in trying to organize them.

The ILO has also explained the proliferation of migrant women in care work with reference to both local and global economic and social conditions. In a policy guide entitled *Migrant Workers: Policy Frameworks for Regulated and Formal Migration* (2013), the ILO's Employment and Labour Market Policies Branch devoted several sections to women, contending that when gender discrimination at home pushed them to seek work abroad, they were likely to end up in jobs with poor working conditions and "little or no social protection" – jobs in the service sector that "native workers can afford to shun" (ILO 2013, 2). The report also noted that because these women are often unable to find permanent employment abroad, they tend to become "trapped in a cycle of temporary migration, whereby they must continually re-migrate for work" (ibid., 2–3). Although this document reveals greater sensitivity to the challenges faced by migrant women workers, it generally portrays them as vulnerable and lacking agency. Women migrants appear less well-informed than their male counterparts about their rights, job opportunities and what to expect in destination countries (ibid., 7). Neither this publication nor the above-mentioned report on Turkey reference one another, a reflection of siloization within the ILO. Nor do they acknowledge the substantial wave of multi-leveled activism, from the local to the global, that formed in the wake of C189 (see Chapters 10 and 11 above).

Work-Family Balance

C189 also overlooks the social and emotional consequences of maternal absence for migrants' families, although that issue had surfaced in some of the ILO reports on work-family balance produced during the run-up to the convention. Given the physical separation of families that migration entails, work-family balance means something quite different for those who migrate than for family members who remain at home. Prior to the adoption of C189, the ILO instrument that had the potential for addressing some of the most pressing issues faced by migrant care givers was C156 on Workers with Family Responsibilities (1981). This convention was limited, however, by the fact that it was conceived in *national*, not transnational, terms. Neither the convention nor the accompanying recommendation paid heed to the work-family challenges faced by migrant mothers who were workers, even though their numbers were already increasing around the world.

This blind spot was replicated in many of the country studies in the series subsequently commissioned by the Inclusive Labour Markets, Labour Relations and Working Conditions Branch as a follow up on the implementation of C156 and C183. In the early 2000s, women's international migration for care work jobs was already significant, but it had yet to become a prominent issue within the ILO and thus was absent from that branch's earliest reports. A 2006 study of Thailand was the first to note the increase in women's migration, both rural-urban and international, and with it, the impact on families. The report noted that as women and men began migrating following the Asian economic crisis of the late 1990s, those who were parents often could not bring children along and had to turn to grandparents for care (Kusakabe 2006, xiii). A 2008 report on Trinidad and Tobago reflected on the situation of the children left behind:

> On the one hand, some of them experience supportive relationships within temporary family structures, along with gifts and money from abroad, and promises to join their parent(s).... On the other hand, some experience dissatisfaction and a sense of loss at the separation, especially when parents fail to live up to their promises for reunification.... Yet children within all categories bear marks of abandonment to varying degrees, particularly related to the loss of a mother to a foreign country.... Economic migration, while it might bring some relief to poverty for some, is a persistent trend that fractures family life. (Reddock and Bobb-Smith 2008, 28–9)

Whatever the outcomes of migration for children, nearly all the reports concurred that the impact on elders could be devastating. Although many enjoyed spending more time with grandchildren, having full responsibility for them added to their daily burdens of care and, often, wage-earning. In Thailand, many grandparents, "despite old age and poor health, still have to go out for petty jobs in order to earn a living with their grandchildren. Their important role in the past, as the ones who transmit socio-cultural values to children, is given less importance or is made impossible" (Kusakabe 2006, 34). Moreover, an increasing proportion of grandparents and other elders were finding themselves without care when they needed it because their adult children were far away.

A few years earlier, another ILO unit, the Gender Promotion Program (GPP), had issued *Preventing Discrimination, Exploitation and Abuse of Women Migrant Workers: An Information Guide* (Lim et al. 2003), composed of six booklets. While most of these addressed issues such as immigration regulations and working conditions (especially trafficking), a few focused on the tensions inherent in managing transnational families, pointing out that these tensions were more likely to be associated with women's migration than with men's. A list of the "social costs" of women's migration included the following caution:

> The impact on children without their mothers around can often be adverse, with children getting poor grades or dropping out of school, being drawn into substance abuse, being subject to sexual or physical abuse by other family members, having emotional problems. (Ibid., Booklet 2, 26)

The same booklet cited a 1997 World Health Organization study of the Philippines which "showed that young people with absent parents turn to peers for support. However, this situation results in teen pregnancy, induced abortions, sexually transmitted diseases, AIDS, drug addiction, prostitution, teen marriages and other social problems such as incest and child abuse."[4] Another booklet, "Return and Reintegration," noted:

> Returning mothers often face problems in their relationships with the children they left behind. Many women are dismayed by the lack of closeness with their children upon their return, and have difficulties adjusting to the fact that their children have grown up without them and away from them. While in some cases, children understand the sacrifices that their mothers have made for them, lack of respect by children is an all too common complaint by returning mothers. (Lim et al. 2003, Booklet 5, 16)

While pointing out migrant women workers' important contributions to the economies and societies of receiving countries, including "freeing national women to take up higher status, better paying jobs in the national economy" (Lim et al. 2003, Booklet 4, 37), the GPP assigned responsibility for assisting women with reintegration to the governments of *sending* countries, with the assistance of NGOs and local charities (ibid., 37–57).

In 2009 the ILO reframed the issue of work-family resolution by introducing the theme of "co-responsibility." This theme first appeared in a joint publication with the UN Development Program (UNDP), *Decent Work in Latin America and the Caribbean: Work and Family: Towards New Forms of Reconciliation with Social Co-Responsibility*, which linked work-family reconciliation to a broader conception of responsibility that included the state as well as the family. Unlike most of the ILO's previous publications on women and employment, this one *did* focus on migrant women, devoting an extensive section to their concerns as mothers as well as workers. In elevating giving and receiving care to the status of a right, declaring it to be a national responsibility and linking it to economic progress, the report granted new visibility and status to the unpaid work conventionally assigned to women. At the same time, it regarded "redistributing care responsibilities between men and women, as well as among the family, the State, the market and society as a whole" as "fundamental...for promoting equality in the world of work and reducing poverty" (ILO/UNDP 2009, 9).[5]

With regard to migration from Latin America and the Caribbean, the report noted that it was becoming increasingly feminized, and that women's departure "brings into being endless chains of caring activities handled by mothers, sister and grandmothers who remain in the country of origin. These women fill huge vacuums in the countries to which they move and in their home countries, subsidizing the economy through their work at enormous costs to themselves and their families" (ibid., 41). In the sending countries, few families could afford to hire care workers or domestic servants to replace absent mothers, and even if fathers were present, they did not participate more in care work than they had previously. Families were thus left to fall back on the good will of other relatives, usually female. This practice, however, had its limits:

> [F]irst there are fewer and fewer care-giving grandmothers and aunts, and other support networks of this nature, as a result of the decline of extended families, women's increased labour force participation, migration and the weakening of the social fabric.... Secondly, family networks cannot effectively replace the specialized care required by children and the elderly people. (Ibid., 70)

In other words, while women's migration brought in more money for children's education, elders' health care and other expenses, this often came at tremendous social costs, undermining the very reasons that led to women's decision to migrate in the first place.[6]

This report, one of the first ILO publications to address migrant women and their issues as workers and mothers, made a series of recommendations that took both sets of needs into account. These included:

- Creating sufficient opportunities for decent work for men and women, so that people can earn enough income in their own countries to guarantee their families' financial wellbeing, without having to set out in search of more highly paid jobs, often of inferior quality, elsewhere, which usually require the family to separate (in other words, discouraging employment migration in the first place).
- Facilitating the return of those who migrate, helping family reunification through reintegration and training programs.
- Establishing regulations that make it easier for the families of migrant workers to reunite.

- Guaranteeing that migrant workers have the same labor rights as others, and ensuring they have access to childcare. Developing information campaigns on their rights in this regard.
- Involving the employing sector as co-responsible for obeying the law and making it easier for working parents, for example, in terms of legislation regarding social protection. (ILO/UNDP 2009, 128)

Comprehensive and sensitive to the crucial needs of migrant women workers though these recommendations were, they failed to make their way into key policy discussions, such as those leading up to adoption of the ILO's C189 (for a comprehensive account of those discussions, see Fish and Shumpert, this book).

THE OECD

Like the ILO, the OECD is engaged in the transnational networks that traverse the relevant fields. Its ability to grapple with the complex set of issues posed by global care chains is, however, affected by how its mandate and internal organization structure the way it "sees" its environment. Unlike the ILO, the OECD does not speak the language of rights and obligations, nor can it turn to conventions to pressure its member states to act in particular ways. This is not to suggest that it is "value-free" or that it does not try to influence its members. Rather it uses the language of the "policy sciences" – mainly economics – through which it identifies trends, the common problems to which these give rise, and the range of "appropriate" solutions for its member states. It works to develop these "shared understandings" through "a warren of committees and working groups populated by government officials, staff of the OECD Secretariat, technical experts and sometimes civil society" (Woodward 2009, 7).

For our story, the units of potential interest are: the Migration Division and Working Party 2 (WP2) of the Directorate for Employment, Labour and Social Affairs (DELSA); the Development Advisory Committee (DAC) and the Development Centre,[7] the Social Policy and Health Divisions in DELSA and their associated working parties. In terms of gender, in the past, Working Party 6 (WP6) on the role of women in the economy pushed for the integration of gender into DELSA's work. What is now called GENDERNET[8] performs the same role vis-à-vis the DAC, while the Development Centre's gender and development group prepares the Social Institutions and Gender Index (SIGI), which uses a variety of indicators to rank over one hundred countries, with a focus on gender discrimination.

Migration, Development...and Gender?

Migration has been part of the OECD's remit from the outset. Although it initially focused on intra-European migration, as the old distinction between guest-worker migration and migration to the "settler countries" of North America and the Antipodes became increasingly irrelevant, in the 1980s the latter joined WP2. Even before that, WP2 had begun to talk of the "feminisation of migration" (OECD 2011a, 8), although the women concerned were largely understood as family members accompanying the main (male) migrant. Moreover, under pressure from WP6, during the 1980s WP2 integrated sex-disaggregated statistics into its Continuous Reporting System on Migration, known by its French acronym, SOPEMI. The two working parties also conducted two studies of the experiences of women migrants, both of which focused on barriers to their integration into host economies and societies.

By the 1990s, it was clear that intra-OECD migration was becoming less important than the flow of migrants from the Global South and, following the dissolution of the Soviet Union, from Eastern Europe. Yet no particular note was made of the migration of women from the South to meet care needs in the North, even though scholars had already begun to document the formation of transnational care chains (see, e.g., Hondagneu-Sotelo and Avila 1997). A decade later, WP2's attention began to focus on member countries' growing tendency to court high-skilled migrants while blocking avenues for those considered low-skilled. In line with this trend, a joint European Commission-OECD seminar on migrant women and the labor market in 2005 concentrated on the integration of "skilled migrant women and those involved in enterprise creation," although its concluding panel did take up the issue of migrant women's involvement in formal and informal care provision. The 2009 High Level Forum on Migration cautioned that "because labour needs existed at all skill levels, it was important that the legal channels for the low skilled were not replaced by the hiring of irregular migrants" (OECD 2011a, 14). The 2011 *International Migration Outlook* went further, noting that given the demand for "labour-intensive personal care occupations" arising from population ageing and women's changed roles, blocking avenues for low-skilled workers would simply drive them underground, fueling the market for "irregular" workers (OECD 2011a, 15).

While WP2 thus sees the issues from the standpoint of the labor market and integration problems that migration has generated for its member states, the DAC and the Development Centre are more concerned with the link between migration and development. In the 1990s, DAC saw foreign aid as a means to stem the flow of migrants from the South, but a decade later it was coming to see migration, along with trade and foreign direct investment, as an important tool for development. With this policy shift came an enhanced concern to achieve "policy coherence" through better coordination of aid, trade, and migration policies, but this did not extend to the global care chain. Neither DAC nor GENDERNET has addressed the problems of "families left behind," and while GENDERNET has expanded its horizons beyond aid to include trade policy, it too has ignored the issues raised by the formation of global care chains.

The Development Centre, which appears to have integrated gender into its work, might have been more likely to deal with the difficulties migration poses for women. A search of its major publications, however, shows little evidence of this. For instance *Policy Coherence for Development: Migration and Developing Countries* (Development Centre 2007, 76–77) had but two short paragraphs on "gender and family roles" which note that "daughters are more likely to remit" but that women migrants may be more reluctant to return home, where "they may lose new freedoms acquired in the destination country." Its Gender unit, responsible for production of the SIGI, focuses its attention on discriminatory social institutions, monitoring inter alia discrimination in family codes and bias toward sons. In 2014, it expanded its indicators to include sexual reproduction and health rights, decision-making authority in the family and the issue of unpaid care (OECD 2014, 6).[9] For the first time, OECD countries were also included, thus attempting to break with the silent assumption that "discrimination" is a problem only for developing countries. Despite improvements such as those noted above, however, SIGI still reflects a neo-colonial bias "in the sense that a higher level of discrimination against women is assumed in societies of the Global South" (Liebowitz and Zwingel 2014, 5). In this sense, it sees women of the South in a similar way to the ILO – as victims, not as agents.

Social Policy: Growing Attention to Care (and Gender), But...

In a sense, "care" – at least child care – has been on the OECD's agenda since the 1970s, when WP6 first highlighted the need for public support for child care in the name of equal economic opportunity for (OECD) women (Mahon 2010). In the 1980s, Working Party 1 (WP1, social policy) also began to reflect on growing care needs – for child care to enable lone mothers to work and the care needs arising from population ageing. While its research on the implications of population ageing initially focused on pensions and health care, by the mid-'80s it had also begun to reflect on long-term care needs of an ageing population.[10] In the document "Long Term Care" (MAS/WP1[88]03), it noted that "changing demographic structures in terms of female labour force participation, divorce and declining birth rates all have important consequences for both the financing of acute and chronic care, as well as the available population to assist the elderly with informal and formal personal care." This could mean "labour shortages in the generally low-wage, low-prestige long-term care occupational category" (ibid., 1–2). The study's main concern was not, however, who might fill these positions, nor how to make them more attractive. Rather it focused on the need for better coordination of health and social services and the need for new financing arrangements including incentives to promote informal care.

In the 1990s, WP6 took up the issue of who was providing paid and unpaid elder care. The studies focused, however, exclusively on the gender of the carers (Christopherson1997; Jacobzone 1999; Jenson and Jacobzone 2000), ignoring the increasing recourse to migrants. When WP6 was discontinued in 1998, its work was picked up by WP1 and DELSA's Social Policy Division. In its thematic study, *Babies and Bosses* (2007), however, the focus was on child care as a means to promote work-family reconciliation and even gender equality among the citizenry. No mention was made of the role migrant care workers were playing in making such reconciliation possible – for women in the North. This may be because countries like France, Italy and Spain, where a combination of social policies (cash for care) and migration regimes have led to increasingly reliance on migrant care workers, were not included in the study.[11]

The only OECD report on long-term care that explicitly dealt with the position of migrant caregivers within the system was produced by the Health Division. *Help Wanted? Providing and Paying for Long Term Care* (Colombo et al. 2011) documented the substantial role that migrants are playing in the long-term care sector of a number of countries.[12] It did not hesitate to acknowledge their vulnerable position within the host labor market:

[Migrant care workers] often work with shorter contracts, more irregular hours, broken shifts, for lower pay and in lower classified functions than non-migrant care workers and may have to work with the least favourable care recipients.... Uncertainty about immigration rules and their rights may lead them to adhere more closely to employers' wishes and stay in the job longer than the domestic work force.... They may be subject to verbal abuse or outright refusal to be cared for by the client...but they may also experience such behaviour from colleagues and employees.... Those in round-the-clock live-in arrangements are especially vulnerable to personal and financial exploitation. (Colombo et al. 2011, 175–6)

This report also noted that "the absence of specific reference in labour migration programmes to the labour needs of the long-term care sector is conspicuous" (ibid., 15). While the study did not mention the other end of the care chain, it at least recognized the growing importance of migrant carers and was critical of both the silences in migration policy and the lack of protection afforded them within the host country.

The insights offered by *Help Wanted* were not, however, picked up by the social division/WP1 when the issue of long-term care was (briefly) discussed in the documents for the 2011 social ministers' meeting. In the scant three pages devoted to it in *Paying for the Past, Providing for the Future: Intergenerational Solidarity* (OECD 2011b), no mention was made of migrant caregivers. The social division's work is currently focused on families and children, pensions, income inequality and gender. While the work on families and children, increasingly guided by the concept of "social investment," focuses on what is best for the child, the main document on gender – *Closing the Gender Gap* (OECD 2012) – sketched out a narrower mandate than that afforded WP6, as it focuses exclusively on women's employment, education and entrepreneurship.[13] *Closing the Gender Gap* highlighted the importance of good and affordable child care and more equal sharing of domestic labour between men and women. It also held the promise of breaking the North-South divide by trying to deal with both. Yet, as Razavi (2014, 143) rightly points out, "the report's analysis remains confusingly segmented between 'OECD countries' and 'developing countries,' rather than providing an integrated analysis of the increasingly globalized economies across the traditional 'North-South' divide and pointing to both the commonalities and the differences, as well as the interconnections between them." Thus while the report acknowledges that domestic work constitutes an important, and largely feminized, part of the informal sector in developing countries, it ignores its growing importance in wealthy OECD countries and the fact that many who work in that sector – and who enable the labor force "activation" of women in the Global North – are migrants. For the OECD, then, to some extent the problem is that different units are organized to "see" particular aspects of the transnational care chain – migration, development, child care and elder care – but only these parts, with too little communication across the units. In addition, in the units for "seeing" migration and development, such as DELSA's social policy units/WPs, the OECD is inhibited from devising a coherent approach to the issues raised by the formation of transnational care chains because it has internalized a bifurcated North-South view of the world. For the most part, DELSA focuses on the traditional OECD member countries while DAC and the Development Centre deal with the "other" in the South.

CONCLUSIONS

Scholarly work on global care chains brings into view the various dimensions of the issues generated by the rise in migrant care work. On the demand side, it highlights the inadequacy of elder and child care policies and provisions in the North. Given the labor-intensive nature of care work, in the absence of adequate public support, the only way adult-earner families can afford care support is by finding those who are prepared (or compelled) to work for low wages. The turn to "cash-for-care" policies rather than public service provision only serves to exacerbate the problem. Migration policies also play their part as states focus on trying to attract high-skill workers while making it difficult for those deemed low-skilled (a category that includes care workers) legally to enter destination countries. On the supply side, in addition to the "discriminatory" social institutions tracked by SIGI, poverty, class inequality, and the vicissitudes of the global economy contribute to women's decisions to migrate. In this, again, sending governments, like that of the Philippines, can play a part, hoping to benefit from the resulting inflow of remittances. While remittances have become part of the new conventional wisdom on development, the concept of a global care chain also highlights the impact on the children and elderly left behind: who is meeting their care needs and under what conditions (Badasu and Michel 2015)? Our review of how the ILO and the OECD "see" the world suggests that these organizations have difficulty in bringing both ends of global care chains into focus. Such lags between academic and policy discussions are not unusual, but they do suggest yet another form of siloization which impedes international organizations from "seeing" migrant women's issues in comprehensive fashion.

To be sure, the different parts of the OECD identify pieces of the chain. Thus the Social Policy Division has developed a cogent argument for publicly financed, quality child care and for genuinely shared parental leave, and the Migration Division highlights the problem posed by policies that close off legal avenues for migrants with lower skills, while the Health Division has produced the only report that explores the rise in migrant care work and the adverse conditions such workers often face. The Development Centre's SIGI highlights the discriminatory institutions women may encounter in sending countries but is silent on class or racial inequality. Nevertheless, the OECD has trouble putting the pieces together. In part this is because of the division of labor internalized within the organization. To some extent this is normal, yet the OECD has long stressed the importance of "horizontal" coordination. One such horizontal project involves cross-unit collaboration around gender issues. Yet in the publication where one might have hoped to see the pieces brought together – *Closing the Gender Gap* (2012) –the organization's deeply ingrained bifurcation of North and South came into play. This is perhaps not surprising as the OECD was formed as an organization of rich capitalist countries of the Global North. Although its membership has expanded to include a number of middle-income Latin American countries and it has sought to develop stronger connections to "emerging" economies, it has yet to overcome the old divide in its ways of seeing and understanding the world.

In contrast to the OECD, a few of the studies undertaken by the ILO do bring into focus the care needs of those left behind. The ILO also explicitly champions the rights of migrant workers in general (C97 and C143), and of domestic workers in particular (C189), yet even there, a bias in favor of dealing with the care and service needs of the receiving countries, especially in the North, is evident. Thus, the preamble to C189 highlights "the significant contributions of domestic workers to the global economy, which includes increased paid job opportunities for women and men workers with family responsibilities, greater scope for caring for ageing populations, children and persons with disabilities, and substantial income transfers within and between countries." The implication is that domestic workers (including care workers) are enabling their employers to take up paid job opportunities – while their own employment is somehow insignificant, except insofar as it facilitates, in the case of migrants, remittances to their home countries. Moreover, the personal and social costs to them and their families remain obscured in an employment relationship based on a one-sided calculus of needs.

Thus, despite their differences, both organizations "see" from a position firmly rooted in the North. Until these and other international organizations begin to view this issue in a truly integrated fashion, their ability to aid local and national mobilizations of migrant care workers by advancing principles of balanced transnational governance will remain limited. With UN Women at its helm in 2016-17, the UN's Global Migration Group may be able to start the process.

NOTES

1. The 1952 Convention on Maternity Protection Revised (C103) specified women's right to at least twelve weeks' leave, including cash and medical benefits. The 2000 version (C183) extended the period to fourteen weeks and specified a cash benefit of no less than two-thirds of a mother's previous earnings or the equivalent.
2. CEDAW has been ratified by 187 of the world's 194 countries; among the non-ratifiers are the United States and Iran. The ILO convention, formulated in 2011, came into force in 2013.
3. These do include several migrant-receiving countries – South Africa, Italy, Germany, Switzerland, Ireland, Argentina and Finland (=www. wiego.org/informal-economy/ratification-countries-domestic-workers-convention-c.189).
4. Lim et al. 2003, Booklet 2, 26, quoting Kanlungan Centre Foundation, Inc. *Destination: Middle East, A Handbook for Filipino Women Domestic Workers* (Manila: Kanlungan Centre Foundation Inc., December 1997), 12.
5. Shahra Razavi (personal communication, 2016) has suggested that the introduction of this perspective should be attributed to the fact that this paper was prepared by the ILO's Regional Office in Santiago, Chile. "The regional offices have their own intellectual environment, largely influenced by research and advocacy circles in the region/country where they are based," Razavi wrote. "Given the concern in the LAC [Latin American-Caribbean] region about migrant women workers and also about the care economy, it is not surprising that the ILO office would draw on the many feminist researchers working on these issues to produce such a paper."
6. Of course, child care and family patterns differ markedly from one society to another (Raghuram 2012). In those where child care has been traditionally "outsourced" from nuclear families to other relatives (Badasu and Michel 2015), or where older women (grandmothers) are not typically employed outside the home (Dreby 2010), mothers' migration can be less disruptive.

7. The Development Centre's membership includes countries from the Global South: twenty-one of its current membership of forty-seven countries are "developing or emerging."

8. GENDERNET is the unit that focuses on gender and development for the DAC.

9. The latter is monitored through time-use surveys.

10. For example MAS/WP1(84) 1 on Demographic Trends and the Implications of Ageing Populations and MAS/WP1(88) 03, Long-Term Care identified long-term care as one of three key issues for the upcoming meeting of social policy ministers.

11. The countries included in *Babies and Bosses* were Australia, Austria, Canada, Denmark, Finland, Ireland, Japan, the Netherlands, Portugal, Sweden and the UK. The first report appeared in 2002 and the final synthesis report in 2007.

12. Migrant workers account for 50 percent or more of the long-term care labor force in Austria, France, Italy and Israel (Colombo et al. 2011, 74). They are over-represented in the home-help services of Greece, Portugal, Spain and France and in the institutional care sector in Greece, the Czech Republic, Poland, Austria, Ireland, Switzerland, Finland, the UK, Sweden and Denmark (176).

13. See Mahon (2015) for a discussion of WP6's mandate.

REFERENCES

Badasu, Delali and Sonya Michel. 2015. "On a Collision Course: Millennial Development Goals and Mothers' Migration." In *Migrant Women Workers: Ethical and Political Issues*, edited by Zahra Meghani, 75–100. New York: Routledge, 2015.

Betts, Alexander. 2011. "The Global Governance of Migration and the Role of the Trans-region." In *Multilayered Governance: The Promise of Partnerships*, edited by Rahel Kunz, Sandra Lavenex and Marion Panizzon, 23–45. London: Routledge.

Boris, Eileen. 2014. "Mothers, household managers, and productive workers: The International Labour Organization and Women in Development." *Global Social Policy* 14, 2: 189–208.

Boris, Eileen and Jennifer N. Fish. 2014. "'Slaves No More': Making Global Standards for Domestic Workers." *Feminist Studies* 40: 411–443.

Broome, André and Leonard Seabrooke. 2012. "Seeing like an International Organization." *New Political Economy* 17, 1:1–16.

Christopherson, Susan. 1997. "Child Care and Elderly Care." OECD Labour Market and Social Policy Occasional Paper #27.

Colombo, Francesca et al. 2011. *Help Wanted? Providing and Paying for Long Term Care*. Paris: OECD.

Deacon, Bob. 2007. *Global Social Policy and Governance*. London: Sage.

Development Centre. 2007. *Policy Coherence for Development: Migration and Developing Countries: A Development Centre Perspective*. Paris: OECD.

Dreby, Joanna. 2010. *Divided by Borders: Mexican Migrants and Their Children* Berkeley: University of California Press.

Erdoğdu, Seyhan and Gulay Toksöz. 2013. "The Visible Face of Women's Invisible Labour: Domestic workers in Turkey." Conditions of Work and Employment Series 42. Geneva: ILO.

Gore, Charles. 2013. "The New Development Cooperation Landscape: Actors, Approaches and Architecture." *Journal of International Development* 25, 6: 769–86.

Hondagneu-Sotelo, Pierrette and Ernestine Avila.1997. "'I'm Here But I'm There': The Meanings of Latina Transnational Motherhood." *Gender and Society* 11: 548–71.

ILO. 2013. "6.2 Migrant Workers: Policy Frameworks for Regulated and Formal Migration." In *Promoting Equality and Addressing Discrimination*. Geneva: ILO. http://www.ilo.org/emppolicy/pubs/WCMS_210461/lang–en/index.htm

ILO/UNDP. 2009. *Decent Work in Latin America and the Caribbean: Work and Family: Towards New Forms of Reconciliation with Social Co-Responsibility*. Santiago: International Labour Organization and United Nations Development Programme. http://www.ilo.org/wcmsp5/groups/public/—ed_protect/—protrav/—travail/documents/publication/wcms_travail_pub_55.pdf.

Jacobzone, Stephane. 1999. "Ageing and Care for Frail Elderly Persons: An Overview of International Perspectives." OECD Labour Market and Social Policy Occasional Paper #38.

Jenson, Jane and Stephane Jacobzone. 2000. "Care Allowances for the Frail Elderly and Their Impact on Women Care-Givers." OECD Labour Market and Social Policy Occasional Paper #41.

Jolly, Susie with Hazel Reeves. 2005. *Gender and Migration: Overview Report*. Sussex, UK: BRIDGE/IDS

Kunz, Rahel, Sandra Lavenex and Marion Panizzon. 2011. "Introduction: Governance through Partnerships in International Migration." In *Multilayered Governance: The Promise of Partnerships*, edited by Kunz, Lavenex and Panizzon, 1–20. London: Routledge.

Kusakabe, Kyoko. 2006. "Reconciling Work and Family: Issues and Policies in Thailand." Conditions of Work and Employment Series No. 14. Geneva: ILO.

Liebowitz, Debra and Susanne Zwingel. 2014. "Assessing Global Gender (In) Equality: A CEDAW-Based Approach." Paper presented at the annual meetings of the International Studies Association, Toronto.

Lim, Lin Lean et al. 2003. *Preventing Discrimination, Exploitation and Abuse of Women Migrant Workers: An Information Guide.* Six booklets. Geneva: Gender Promotion Programme, ILO.

Mahon, Rianne. 2010. "Learning, Forgetting, Rediscovering: The OECD's 'New' Family Policy." In *Mechanisms of OECD Governance: International Incentives for National Policy Making?* edited by Kerstin Martens and Anja P. Jakobi, 198–216. New York: Oxford University Press.

Mahon, Rianne. 2015. "Articulating a Feminist Agenda within the OECD: The Working Party on the Role of Women in the Economy." *Social Politics* 22: 585–609.

Mahon, Rianne and Stephen McBride. 2008. "Introduction." In *The OECD and Transnatiomnal Governance,* edited by Mahon and McBride, 3–24. Vancouver: UBC Press.

OECD. 2007. *Babies and Bosses: Reconciling Work and Family Life: A Synthesis of Findings for OECD Countries.* Paris: OECD.

OECD. 2011a. *International Migration Outlook 2011* SOPEMI Paris: OECD.

OECD. 2011b. *Paying for the Past, Providing for the Future: Intergenerational Solidarity* Paris: OECD.

OECD. 2012. *Closing the Gender Gap: Act Now* Paris: OECD.

OECD. 2014. *Social Institutions and Gender Index: 2014 Synthesis Report* Paris: OECD.

Raghuram, Parvati. 2012. "Global Care, Local Configurations: Challenges to the Conceptualization of Care." *Global Networks* 12: 155–174.

Razavi, Shahra. 2014. "The OECD's Closing the Gender Gap Now." *Global Social Policy* 14: 141–144.

Reddock, Rhoda and Yvonne Bobb-Smith. 2008. "Reconciling Work and Family: Issues and Policies in Trinidad and Tobago." Conditions of Work and Employment Series No. 18. Geneva: ILO.

Woodward, Richard. 2009. *The Organisation for Economic Cooperation and Development* (OECD). New York: Routledge.

Rianne Mahon holds a CIGI chair in comparative and global social policy governance at the Balsillie School of International Affairs at Wilfrid Laurier University, Waterloo, Ontario, where she is also a professor of political science. She has published on the place of child care in redesigning welfare regimes at the local, national and global scales, co-edited numerous books, and recently co-authored *Advanced Introduction to Social Policy.* Her current work focuses on the role of international organizations vis-à-vis the growth of transnational care chains.

Sonya Michel is professor emerita of history, American studies and women's and gender studies at the University of Maryland, College Park, and a senior scholar at the Woodrow Wilson International Center for Scholars, Washington, DC. She is a founding editor of the journal *Social Politics: International Studies in Gender, State and Society* and the author/co-author/co-editor of many books and articles on gender and social policy in the United States and comparatively, past and present.

PART V

Going Global?

CHAPTER 13

Care Going Global? Afterword

Shahra Razavi

In 1987, Helga Maria Hernes (1987) coined the expression "reproduction going public." She was referring to the shifts taking place in Scandinavian countries at a time when the public sector in particular was assuming a growing responsibility for financing and delivering care services, especially child care. By this she implied that the division of reproductive work between the family and public institutions had radically altered in the second half of the twentieth century, coinciding with welfare state expansion (Anttonen 2005). The fact that reproduction, and care as a subset of it, is not an exclusively family affair, even though families assume the lion's share, has been a prominent theme in subsequent feminist writings.

Jane Lewis and Mary Daly have analyzed changes in "public-private mixes" of care in the context of welfare state change and restructuring (Daly and Lewis 2000), while the more recent literature on industrializing and developing countries has also tried to overcome the fragmentation in the analysis of care by focusing on shifts in "care diamonds" encompassing different institutions (Razavi 2007; Peng 2012; Ochiai et al. 2012). The development of care policies was, of course, not always uniform across countries, even in seemingly advanced welfare states, nor was it sustained and linear in a de-familializing direction. In the context of economic liberalization in the ex-socialist or state capitalist economies, in particular,

S. Razavi (✉)
Research and Data Section, UN Women, NY, USA

© The Author(s) 2017
S. Michel, I. Peng (eds.), *Gender, Migration, and the Work of Care*,
DOI 10.1007/978-3-319-55086-2_13

295

there has been significant backsliding in public provisioning as state- and enterprise-based services were slashed. In China, for example, the lack of affordable and decent child care services, along with population ageing and massive rural-urban migration, have led to the re-familialization of care, sanctioned by state ideology, with adverse outcomes for women's "occupational choices and time autonomy" (Cook and Dong 2011, 961).

If the mid-twentieth-century narrative was about care "going public," then an epithet for twenty-first-century developments in the sphere of reproduction would be that of "care going global." This is a theme that resonates with the preceding chapters, reflecting as they do the complex triggers, institutional modalities, social formations and broader repercussions of care worker migration as a mode of care transnationalization (Yeates 2011). While centrally concerned with these producer-based forms of transmigration of care workers, to varying degrees, the chapters also draw attention to the ideational, governance and policy dimensions of care transnationalization. Here I would like to point to three overarching themes emerging from the book that resonate with current global policy preoccupations, while lending them greater precision and texture. However, before I do so, a word of caution is in order.

To say that twenty-first-century realities point to "care going global" is not to suggest that care labor migration and its social and familial consequences are historically unprecedented. It is well-known, for example, that the great bulk of immigrants from Ireland to the United States, before, during and after the Irish famine of the 1850s, were young, unmarried and impoverished women and men seeking wage work; large numbers of women in these migrant streams worked in domestic service, much like their counterparts in Europe (Donato and Gabaccia 2015). Being young and unmarried, however, many of these women did not have children themselves, and in this sense were different from many of today's migrants who leave their children behind. Furthermore, contemporary transnational families have significant historical continuities with slave, colonial and settler societies where children were raised by paid and unpaid nonfamilial caregivers because, for a variety of reasons and in a range of circumstances, parents and children could not be physically proximate (Yeates 2011). It is important to recall these continuities as an antidote to the largely "presentist" focus of much of the care migration literature (Yeates 2011), and because of the lasting imprint these preceding patterns of living have left on family and marital structures and care arrangements (Budlender and Lund 2011).

WORLDS APART: INEQUALITY AND CARE

Rising income inequality *within* countries, both developed and developing, over the past two decades has triggered not only a rich array of research by academics (Atkinson 2015) and international organizations (UNRISD 2010), but also resonated with the wider public. This is a welcome development after decades of silence, when inequality was clearly off the agenda, denigrated by neoliberals as smacking of a "politics of envy." At the same time, while there are controversies about whether global inequality has increased or decreased, what is clear is that there is no convergence between the world's richer countries and poorer countries; in fact, since 1960 the gap in GDP per capita of the world's dominant power, the United States, and several developing regions has roughly tripled in size (Hickel 2016).

In broad-brush terms, this is the context within which increasing, almost endless, flows of people are moving across countries and regions. While some of this movement is occurring between countries and regions that are at fairly comparable levels of economic development, much of it is between countries that offer divergent levels of prosperity and opportunity, between South and North to be sure (from Mexico to the US, the Philippines to Canada, or the Pacific Islands to Australia, as illustrated in several chapters in this book), but also South-South movements within developing regions, from their "periphery" to "core," for example, from Nicaragua to Costa Rica, from the Philippines and Indonesia to Singapore and Taiwan, or from Mozambique and Malawi to South Africa.

To use the supply-and-demand metaphor, much of the literature on gendered migration and care has focused on the latter, taking post-industrial developed countries as its point of reference. Increasing demand for care services, whether by institutions or families, is associated with a range of factors, including population ageing, rising rates of female labor force participation, shifts in welfare state provisioning toward more cash allowances and vouchers allowing households to hire care, as well as rigidities in gender roles and the pervasive tendency among heterosexual couples to continue to "do gender." The textured analyses in this book attest to the relevance of some of these themes not only to the United States, Canada and Australia, but also to the industrializing countries of East Asia, such as South Korea, Taiwan and China.

Much less attention, however, has been paid to the forces propelling women to migrate through regional and global care chains – the "supply" factors. The forces behind these population movements are more complex than simple income inequalities would suggest, encompassing living standards in a much broader sense of the term, including the search for livelihood options where local economies are stagnant or devastated by development-led population displacement, education and health services in tatters, and physical and social insecurity pervasive across large swathes of developing countries. It is important to remind ourselves that women also migrate in response to oppressive social norms and violent relationships, as well as to militarization and more generalized conflicts that also affect men. At the same time, the literature also contests the simplistic bureaucratic view of "family migration" as a dependent and largely feminized flow related to the social realm, as opposed to labor migration that derives from economic imperatives and is dominated by men (Kofman 2015). Women may migrate as members of families, but this does not preclude their active search for paid work in destination countries. Placing women's migration under the "family" rubric obscures their agency as economic actors. As research from Asia suggests, the boundaries between marriage as a migration strategy and migration as a marriage strategy are often blurred (Jones and Shen 2008).

Inequality, however, is not just about income or social class. As we see in many of the chapters in this book, gender inequalities intersect with multiple other hierarchies, including those of race, ethnicity and migrant status, to shape care markets and care relationships more broadly. In these care relationships, we see the "intersectionality" that has been so important to feminist theorizing and praxis, with racialized and migrant groups of women clustered at the bottom of the social hierarchy.

One of the themes that emerges powerfully from the textured analyses in several chapters in this book is the pervasive devaluation of care, whether it is paid or unpaid. Care emerges as gendered, racialized and disdained, in the words of Liu Hong (this book), "as menial work for lowly migrants" – a description that rings true across time and place. There are also distinct hierarchies within care work, placing child care above elder care, on the pretext that the former entails "human capital investment" but the latter mainly "custodial" services, while both are placed above the employment experiences of poor women and women of color "who do the back-room work of social reproduction" (Duffy 2005, 79) – cleaning, cooking and washing – which do not include the relational and "nurturance" aspects of care.

Even when care work is taken into the public sector and protected by public-sector unions, as it is in countries like Japan, though the conditions of work are much better than they are in under-regulated markets, it is not enough to dispel the lowly status of care workers, especially if they are immigrants (Peng this book).

CARE POLICY AND GOVERNANCE: CONTEXT (STILL) MATTERS

The fact that care transnationalization is about the "processes of heightened connectivity revolving around consciousness, identities, ideas, relations and practices of care which link people, institutions and places across state borders" (Yeates 2011, 1113) means that the global public fora and cross-border spheres of governance through which claims are directed and care policies are formulated should also be considered. Several contributions to the book reflect on these transnational governance fora (especially the ILO and OECD as critical nodes) as well as on claims-making by a variety of non-state actors (be they trade unions, domestic workers organization or migrants rights groups) as well Member States. National-level debates and policy agendas around care are often influenced by the discourses, ideas and policy blueprints that are championed by international organizations, which may diverge in the policy advice they offer (Mahon 2010). However, there is also a sense in which processes of neoliberal globalization are giving greater credence to the market-friendly blueprints propagated by the international financial institutions and the OECD, as opposed to the more rights-based alternatives favored by UN agencies which may not have the same financial and policy leverage as the former. Why do market alternatives command such attraction, especially to (seemingly cash-strapped) governments?

Good-quality care, whether it is paid or unpaid, is very labor-intensive and therefore said to be afflicted with a "cost disease" (Donath 2000, drawing on William Baumol's analysis of the service sector more generally [see Baumol and Bowen 1965]). The attempt to raise the productivity of care work by increasing the numbers of people cared for at any one time quickly runs into the risk of reducing the quality of the output (that is, care). In other words, there is a definite limit to the number of infants and small children or frail elderly and handicapped adults that one person can care for. "Going beyond this limit results in neglected children, not productivity improvements" (Donath 2000, 118). How the problem of high labor content and relatively constant productivity in care services is dealt with varies depending on where care takes place.

For-profit care services frequently attempt to keep wages down (or to increase the hours of work for the same wage) by using "docile" labor provided by socially marginalized employees, making racialized and migrant groups particularly attractive targets for recruitment. In the public care sector the problem of low productivity and related cost increases are often interpreted as signs of inefficiency, "rather than as the consequences of an inherent characteristic of care [work]" (Himmelweit 2005, 7). This contributes to political pressures for the commercialization and privatization of public services and efforts to make the public sector behave more like profit-making entities, by raising user charges, "rationalizing" staff time, and/or out-sourcing care to for-profit and not-for-profit sectors in what are widely referred to as "public-private partnerships."

Given the inherent labor-intensive nature of care, without some form of public provision (either direct or through some type of subsidy paid either to providers or via vouchers or allowances to service users), those needing care services most (frail elderly persons, low-income families with children or people with disabilities), are likely to be the ones least likely to be able to afford care. Thus it is not difficult to see why governments show a proclivity for the employment of socially marginalized groups, including migrants, either by encouraging it through targeted admission of migrant care workers (such as Canada's Live-In Caregiver program; see Boyd, this book) and/or low individualized payments and vouchers, or by turning a blind eye to their employment as informal or undocumented labor (especially in the case of migrants), in what Michel and Peng (2012) call a "demand and denial" approach.

This strategy is, however, not without its own complications: resistance from trade unions and/or migrant rights organizations to adverse working conditions and worker abuse, public resistance to immigration, and in some cases, "path dependencies" due to policy legacies of institutional provision. As several chapters in this book attest, policy exceptions do persist (see Peng on Japan and South Korea, above), and there is also considerable resistance to the wholesale commercialization of care at the local, national and global levels as different forms of claims-making by care workers and care users demand greater accountability from public authorities and "push the government" (Cranford and Chun, this book) to improve services and the conditions of work. In fact, both care workers and users "share a common interest in maintaining quality of care and should try to develop stronger coalitions to prevent market forces from lowering it" (Folbre 2006, 2). Yet despite these commonalities, the emergence of such coalitions remains the exception rather than the rule.

MIGRATION: THE GREAT EQUALIZER?

One of the critiques of late-twentieth-century economic liberalization is that it has been inconsistent in the way its principles have been applied in practice: while the cross-border movement of finance and goods has been liberalized, unprecedented barriers have been put in place with regard to the movement of people/labor. In recent years, as the "migration-development nexus"—the proposition that migration has an important impact on development in countries of origin and destination alike—has attracted renewed interest from policy actors, particular emphasis has been placed on the fact that the remittances received by developing countries far outstrip what they obtain through overseas development cooperation, or foreign aid. Implicit in these narratives is the idea that migration to more well-off countries represents a major means of improving family circumstances and welfare provisioning, while remittances offer one of the most reliable means by which poor countries can generate foreign currency. It is not surprising that many governments explicitly sponsor or tacitly condone the export of female labor and as a result "harvest a share of migrant remittances for general purposes" (Yeates 2011, 1119).

The problem with this narrative is that it obscures the ways in which the migration of labor, especially of female labor in the care sector, is a response to uneven development *and* does little to address its root causes, while reconfiguring rather than resolving the power and status hierarchies involved. Nowhere are these dynamics better illustrated than in global nursing care chains. Countries at the top of the chain are fed by those lower down the ranks: for example, the United States draws nurses from Canada; Canada draws nurses from England to make up for its losses to the United States; England draws from South Africa to fill its vacancies; South Africa draws on Swaziland. Countries at the bottom end of the nursing chain may supply international markets but not replenish their stocks by importing health workers from other countries and consequently experience chronic nursing shortages (Yeates 2011, 1120)—in other words, a care drain.

This painful irony has become evident in the context of the HIV/AIDS pandemic, where severely underfunded African health systems continue to lose their nurses and doctors. These nursing flows are constantly attracting new recruits, even though many nurses who migrate may be subject to de-skilling because they have trouble meeting professional qualifications in destination countries and end up in occupations with requirements that are lower than their training (Boyd, this book). The decision to migrate may be a "choice" for many women (and men), but it is hardly a meaningful one when it is made within highly constrained circumstances.

The appropriate response to the kind of "brain drains" and "care drains" afflicting many developing countries is not to impose restrictions on people's right to migrate or choose where they want to live and have their families. The response, rather, must include the key elements highlighted by the ILO/UNDP (cited in Mahon and Michel, this book):

- creating sufficient opportunities for decent work so that people can have a decent livelihood for themselves and their families without having to move
- making it easier for families of migrant workers to reunite
- guaranteeing that migrant workers have the same rights as other workers, and
- facilitating the return of those who migrate and helping their families reunite with them.

In short, there is a need for a different model of development, one that prioritizes local economic and social development, livelihood generation, the right to an adequate standard of living, labor rights, migrant rights and the right to family reunification. This is very different from the current scenario facing millions of women for whom the decision to migrate in order to be able to work and sustain themselves and their families is a highly constrained one. For many of these women the ability to enjoy the fundamental right to family life has to be traded off against the right to an adequate standard of living – harsh "choices" that defy the spirit of the feminist notion of "choice."

REFERENCES

Anttonen, Anneli. 2005. "Empowering Social Policy: The Role of Social Care Services in Modern Welfare States." In *Social Policy and Economic Development in the Nordic Countries*, edited by Olli Kangas and Joakim Palme, 88–117. New York and Abingdon: Routledge/UNRISD.

Atkinson, Anthony B. 2015. *Inequality: What Can Be Done?* Cambridge, MA and London: Harvard University Press.

Baumol, William J. and W.G. Bowen. 1965. "On the Performing Arts: The Anatomy of their Economic Problems." *American Economic Review* 50: 495–502.

Budlender, Debbie and Frances Lund. 2011. "South Africa: A Legacy of Family Disruption." *Development and Change* 42: 925–946.

Cook, Sarah and Xiao-yuan Dong. 2011. "Harsh Choices: Chinese Women's Paid Work and Unpaid Care Responsibilities under Economic Reform." *Development and Change* 42: 947–965.

Daly, Mary and Jane Lewis. 2000. "The Concept of Social Care and the Analysis of Contemporary Welfare States." *British Journal of Sociology* 51: 261–298.

Donath, Susan. 2000. "The Other Economy: A Suggestion for a Distinctively Feminist Economics." *Feminist Economics* 6: 115–23.

Donato, Katharine M. and Donna Gabaccia. 2015. *Gender and International Migration.* New York: Russell Sage Foundation.

Duffy, Mignon. 2005. "Reproducing Labour Inequalities: Challenges for Feminists Conceptualizing Care at the Intersections of Gender, Race, and Class." *Gender & Society* 19 (1): 66–82.

Folbre, Nancy. 2006. "Demanding Quality: Worker/Consumer Coalitions and "High Road" Strategies in the Care Sector." *Politics and Society* 34, 1: 11–31.

Hernes, Helga-Maria. 1987. *Welfare States and Woman Power: Essays in State Feminism.* Oslo: Norwegian University Press.

Hickel, Jason. 2016. "Global Inequality May Be Much Worse than We Think." *The Guardian,* 8 April.

Himmelweit, Susan. 2005. *Can We Afford (Not) to Care: Prospects and Policy.* GeNet Working Paper No.11. Gender Equality Network. Cambridge, UK: Economic and Social Research Council.

Jones, Gavin and Hsiu-hua Shen. 2008. "International Marriage in East and Southeast Asia: Trends and Research Emphases." *Citizenship Studies* 12, 1: 9–25.

Kofman, Eleonore. 2015. "Family Migration as an Economic Matter." Paper presented at conference on Migration as a Family Matter. Perspectives from Inside and Outside the Law. 30–31 March, VU Amsterdam.

Mahon, Rianne. 2010. "After Neoliberalism? The OECD, the World Bank and the Child." *Global Social Policy* 10, 2: 172–192.

Michel, Sonya and Ito Peng. 2012. "All in the Family? Migrants, Nationhood, and Care Regimes in Asia and North America." *Journal of European Social Policy* 22: 406–18.

Ochiai, Emiko, Aya Abe, Takafumi Uzuhashi, Yuko Tamiya and Masato Shikata. 2012. "The Struggle against Familialism: Reconfiguring the care diamond in Japan." In *Global Variations in the Political and Social Economy of Care: Worlds Apart,* edited by Shahra Razavi and Silke Staab, 61–79. New York and Abingdon: Routledge/UNRISD.

Peng, Ito. 2012. "The Boss, the Worker, his Wife and no Babies: South Korean Political and Social Economy of Care in a Context of Institutional Rigidities." In *Global Variations in the Political and Social Economy of Care: Worlds Apart*, edited by Shahra Razavi and Silke Staab, 80–100. New York and Abingdon: Routledge/UNRISD.

Razavi, Shahra. 2007. *The Political and Social Economy of Care in a Development Context:* Conceptual Issues, Research Questions *and Policy Options.* GD Programme Paper No. 3, Geneva: UNRISD.

UNRISD. 2010. *Combating Poverty and Inequality.* Geneva: UNRISD.

Yeates, Nicola. 2011. "Going Global: The Transnationalization of Care." *Development and Change* 42: 1109–1130.

Shahra Razavi is the chief of the Research & Data Section at UN Women, where she is research director of UN Women's flagship report, *Progress of the World's Women*. She specializes in the gender dimensions of development, with a particular focus on work, social policy and care. Her recent publications include *Seen, Heard and Counted: Rethinking Care in a Development Context; Underpaid and Overworked: A Cross-National Perspective on Care Workers* (with Silke Staab); and *The Gendered Impacts of Liberalization: Towards 'Embedded Liberalism'?*

INDEX

© The Author(s) 2017   305
S. Michel, I. Peng (eds.), *Gender, Migration, and the Work of Care*,
DOI 10.1007/978-3-319-55086-2

Female labor force participation, 23,
118, 145, 152, 156, 167, 297
Fenna, Alan, 145
Fernandez-Kelly, Maria Patricia, 93
Filial piety, 30, 44, 51, 55, 116, 136,
137, 197–198
Filipina care workers in Canada, 120,
130, 170–172, 177, 205,
226, 230
Fish, Jennifer, 18, 27, 33, 217–243,
253, 256, 259, 264, 274, 280
Fisher, Berenice, 44, 61
"Five guarantees," 71
See also "Three nos"
Floating people, 4
Flores, Juana, 256, 257–258, 259
Folbre, Nancy, 84, 301
Fonow, Mary Margaret, 246
Forbes Martin, Susan, 93
Foreign domestic worker
(FDW), 115–139
Filipina, 120, 128, 130
Indonesian, 120, 121, 128
Foreign Domestic Worker
Movement (FDWM), 168,
169, 170–171
Foreign Live-in-Caregiver Program
(Taiwan), 195
Franzway, Suzanne, 246
Fraser, Nancy, 31
Fresnoza-Flot, Asuncion, 94
Fudge, Judy, 10
Fujisawa, Rie, 82

G
Gabaccia, Donna, 296
Gallin, Dan, 234
Geneva, 12, 218, 220, 223, 225, 236,
257, 258, 259, 271
Giles, John, 74
Glenn, Evelyn, 25, 41, 43, 44, 61

Global governance (or transnational
governance), 16, 18, 26,
228–229, 231, 269–271, 272,
287, 296, 299
Global health care strategy, 33
Global justice, 31, 31, 34, 264
Global North, 10, 11, 23, 24, 31, 43,
281, 285–286, 297
Global South, 9, 11, 23, 24, 43, 184,
281, 285–286, 297
Goldberg, Harmony, 260, 261, 263
Goodwin, Sue, 150
Gore, Charles, 272
Gorodzeisky, Anastasia, 173
Government Organized NGOs
(GONGOs), 134, 135
Greenville, Jarad, 145
Griffin, Anne, 84
Groves, Julian, 137
Gu, Danan, 73, 76
Guevarra, Anna, 24, 26, 173
Guo, Man, 74
Gurney, Sam, 233

H
Haas, Peter M., 247, 248
Hamann, Edmund, 94
Hanley, Jill, 178
Heaney, Michael, 249
Heath, Joanna, 151
Herd, Richard, 73
Hernes, Helga Maria, 295
Heron, Alex, 155
Heymann, Jody, 95
Hickel, Jason, 297
Himmelweit, Susan, 300
Hirsch, Jennifer, 94
Hobden, Claire, 257, 258
Hochschild, Arlie, 10, 83, 84, 94, 96,
108, 172
Hodge, Jarrah, 174

CPSIA information can be obtained
at www.ICGtesting.com
Printed in the USA
LVOW13*1942171017

552759LV00010B/27/P